Consumption and Wealth in Luke's Travel Narrative

Biblical Interpretation Series

VOLUME 88

Consumption and Wealth in Luke's Travel Narrative

By

James A. Metzger

BRILL

LEIDEN • BOSTON
2007

This book is printed on acid-free paper.

Library of Congress Cataloging-in-Publication Data

A C.I.P. record for this book is available from the Library of Congress

ISSN 0928-0731
ISBN 978 90 04 16261 7

PRINTED IN THE NETHERLANDS

In Memoriam
W. James Metzger, Jr. (1945–2000)

CONTENTS

Acknowledgements ix

Chapter One Introduction 1
A. Wealth and Possessions in the Gospel of Luke: A History of Interpretation 1
1. Salvation without Renunciation 3
2. Be Generous! 6
B. Reconsidering Luke's Discourse on Wealth and Possessions 13
1. The Nature of Parabolic Discourse in Luke 15
2. Jesus' Announcement in Nazareth as Programmatic for Reading the Parables 25
3. Delineating the Methodological Approach: Reader-Response Criticism, Narrative Criticism/Narratology, and Intertextuality 31
4. Delineating the Reader-Position 56
5. Procedure 60

Chapter Two Challenging Overconsumption 63
A. The Parable of the Wealthy Landowner (12:16–21) 63
1. Exploring the Pre-text: Impressions of Jesus' Teaching on Wealth and Possessions in 9:51–12:12 63
2. Reading the Parable: 12:16–21 69
3. Summary 83
B. The Parable of the Father and his Two Sons (15:11–32) 84
1. Impressions of Jesus' Teaching on Wealth and Possessions in 12:22–15:10 84
2. Reading the Parable: 15:11–32 86
3. Summary 106

Chapter Three Criticizing Wealth 109
A. The Parable of the Unjust Steward (Luke 16:1–13) 109
1. Reading the Parable: 16:1–13 109
2. Summary 130

B. The Parable of the Rich Man and Lazarus (16:19–31) 132
1. Exploring the Pre-Text: 16:14–18 132
2. Reading the Parable: 16:19–31 134
3. Summary 135

Chapter Four Eliminating Wealth 159
A. Jesus' Encounter with the Rich Ruler 160
1. Exploring the Pre-text: 17:1–18:17 160
2. Reading Jesus' Encounter with the Ruler: 18:18–23 160
3. Exploring the Post-text: 18:24–30 167
4. Summary 169
B. Jesus' Encounter with Zacchaeus 170
1. Exploring the Pre-text: 18:31–43 170
2. Reading Jesus' Encounter with Zacchaeus: 19:1–10 171
3. Summary 180

Chapter Five Conclusion 183
A. Retracing our Steps: A Brief Synopsis of the Journey 184
B. Implications 189
C. A Rejoinder 193

Bibliography 201

Index 213

ACKNOWLEDGEMENTS

Although writing a dissertation may often feel like a solitary endeavor, many have made this journey possible. I am especially appreciative of four years of financial assistance from the United Church of Christ. The "Make a Difference! Doctoral Studies Award" (2002–2006) provided resources each fall to help cover student fees, living expenses, and books for comprehensive exams and dissertation research. I also wish to thank Dean James Hudnut-Beumler, Dean Alice Hunt, and Vanderbilt University Divinity School for generously offering me three consecutive years of employment as an instructor of Koine Greek, a position that I enjoyed immensely.

I am very grateful for guidance provided by members of my Dissertation Committee, who, particularly during the earliest phases of the project, encouraged me to think about the broader implications of my research and assisted me in sharpening the thesis. I am especially indebted to my advisor Professor Fernando F. Segovia, who has been both a mentor and friend to me over the past several years. His enthusiasm for the project, insightful comments and constructive criticisms throughout all of its phases, and words of encouragement were invaluable. He has taught me so much—both inside and outside the classroom. I also wish to thank Professor Elena Olazagasti-Segovia; in addition to offering support along the way, her willingness one frigid, windy afternoon in January outside Wesley Parking Garage to share her own experiences of writing the dissertation gave me much-needed inspiration at a critical moment. Three people in particular have devoted talent, time, and labor to preparing the manuscript in its present form, and I would like to thank them as well: Ivo Romein, for coordinating all aspects of the editorial process; Caroline van Erp, for generating the proofs and proofreading; and Dan Connolly for creating the index (on very short notice, I might add!).

Finally, I could not have completed this book without Esther's love, patience, and faith in my abilities, Luke's irrepressible energy, joy, and wonder, as well as the unfailing support of my mother, Carol. It is to them that I owe my greatest debt.

CHAPTER ONE

INTRODUCTION

A. Wealth and Possessions in the Gospel of Luke: A History of Interpretation

Introduction

Though Jesus and John have more to say about wealth and possessions in the Gospel of Luke than in any of the other Gospels, readers have had a very difficult time constructing a consistent viewpoint or set of instructions. As Luke Timothy Johnson has said, "Luke consistently speaks about possessions... [but] does not speak about possessions consistently."[1] On the one hand, Jesus asks more of his disciples in Luke than he does in Matthew or Mark. For instance, Jesus asks those who wish to be his closest traveling companions to leave behind not only their former occupations but *everything* (πάντα; Luke 5:11,28).[2] Furthermore, only in Luke does Jesus specify that in "saying good-bye to everything" (ἀποτάσσεται πᾶσιν; 14:33) his disciples must also "hate" (μισεῖ) their spouses (14:26). Even when Jesus addresses a wealthy man outside of his inner circle, he asks him to sell "everything—as much as you have" (πάντα ὅσα ἔχεις; 18:22). Neither Matthew nor Mark presents this demand with such (overstated) clarity.[3] However, juxtaposed alongside these radical calls to complete divestiture are sayings that appear to require only generous almsgiving (6:30; 19:1–10) or faithful adherence to traditional Augustan ideals (3:10–14).[4] John the Baptist, for instance, in his opening address asks crowds to share their resources with

---

[1] *The Literary Function of Possessions in Luke-Acts* (SBL Dissertation Series 39; Missoula, MT: Scholars Press, 1977), 13.

[2] Cf. Matt 4:20, 22; Mark 1:18, 20.

[3] Thus, John Gillman, from a redaction critical perspective, writes: "Luke not only preserves most of the material about renouncing wealth from his sources, Mark and Q, but in many instances also *accentuates* it" (italics mine; *Possessions and the Life of Faith: A Reading of Luke-Acts* [Collegeville, MN: The Liturgical Press, 1991], 15).

[4] See, e.g., Paul Walasky's discussion on John's ethical counsel in 3:10–14 (*"And So We Came to Rome": The Political Perspective of St. Luke* [New York: Cambridge University Press, 1983], 30–31).

those in need, tax collectors to collect only what has been prescribed for them, and soldiers to refrain from extortion and be satisfied with their wages (3:10–14). No one is asked to leave behind property, family members, or occupations. Zacchaeus's vow to give away only *half* of his possessions and provide fourfold restitution to anyone he may have defrauded is often viewed as a paradigm *par excellence* for would-be followers of Jesus (19:1–10).[5] Of course, if Jesus does accept Zacchaeus's promise to relinquish only half of his possessions, then he has relaxed the rigorous demand presented to the rich ruler only moments earlier (18:22). Thus, in surveying the Gospel's teaching on wealth and possessions, one finds diverse perspectives and traditions that often seem in tension, even contradictory.

Not surprisingly, much of the literature on wealth and possessions in Luke focuses on accounting for or even resolving the tension between the two traditions of renunciation and almsgiving. Generally, the literature attests to two consensuses: 1) addressed at least in part to wealthy Christians, the Gospel extends the possibility of salvation to them, but without requiring the divestiture of all property and possessions;[6] and 2) wealthy readers are encouraged to engage in some form of almsgiving, which, if practiced with regularity, will secure a place for them in the kingdom of God. In effect, readers are not to look to Jesus or the disciples in search of a discipleship model; rather, John's advice to crowds, tax collectors, and soldiers in 3:10–14 and Zacchaeus's vow in 19:8 are taken to be paradigmatic and to provide the surest counsel for readers whose socio-economic status is similar to the Gospel's narratee, the "most excellent" (κράτιστε) Theophilus (1:3). Of course, each of the above consensuses is found with several variations, and the problem of accounting for or reconciling the two traditions of divestiture and almsgiving has been approached from diverse methodological perspectives. Below, I will delineate a few representative variations within each

[5] See, e.g., Walter Pilgrim, *Good News to the Poor* (Minneapolis: Augsburg, 1981), 129–31; Luise Schottroff and Wolfgang Stegemann, *Jesus and the Hope of the Poor* (trans. Matthew J. O'Connell; Maryknoll, N.Y.: Orbis, 1986), 117.

[6] Cf. John Donahue's analysis of the literature on wealth and possessions in Luke ("Two Decades of Research on the Rich and Poor in Luke-Acts," in *Justice and the Holy: Essays in Honor of Walter Harrelson* [ed. Douglas A. Knight and Peter J. Paris (Atlanta: Scholars Press, 1989)], 129–44). This first consensus incorporates two emerging but separate consensuses that he identified in 1989 (143).

of these consensuses and indicate which methods have thus far been employed in grappling with this problem.[7]

1. *Salvation without Renunciation*

Luise Schottroff and Wolfgang Stegemann have offered one of the most influential proposals in recent decades for resolving the tension between dispossession and almsgiving.[8] They argue that the Gospel's earliest readers would have associated its portrait of Jesus and his disciples with wandering Cynic philosophers,[9] who also embraced an itinerant (or semi-itinerant) lifestyle and carried very little with them on their journeys.[10] According to Pseudo-Lucian, however, Cynicus himself never demanded that others imitate his asceticism but hoped that he and his followers might offer, by means of their alternative existence, "a penetrating criticism of wealth and the luxury of the rich."[11] The life of the wandering Cynic philosopher therefore served as "a living criticism of a culture that takes its tone from the rich with their wasteful luxury."[12] Likewise, the dispossession traditions in the Gospel associated with Jesus and his earliest traveling companions are not to be emulated but to function "as a critique and warning for the rich" in Luke's own time.[13] Ultimately, Luke, while "an exceptionally keen critic of the rich," hopes that they too "will see the salvation of God" (3:6) and has therefore preserved these early traditions in order to "motivate them to a conversion that is in keeping with the social message of Jesus."[14] In effect, divesture as a requirement for following Jesus is assigned to an ideal, bygone era but still serves to motivate a change of heart among

[7] Others have done an excellent job of briefly summarizing influential books and articles on the theme of wealth and possession in Luke. See especially Donahue, "Two Decades of Research on the Rich and Poor in Luke-Acts," 129–44; Robert Karris, "Poor and Rich: The Lukan *Sitz-im-Leben*," in *Perspectives on Luke-Acts* (ed. Charles H. Talbert; Perspectives in Religious Studies; Edinburgh: T. & T. Clark, 1978), 112–125; Thomas Phillips, *Reading Issues of Wealth and Poverty in Luke-Acts* (Studies in the Bible and Early Christianity 48; Lewiston, N.Y.; Edwin Mellen Press, 2001), 5–43. I have chosen to proceed in this fashion so as not merely to reduplicate their efforts here.

[8] *Jesus and the Hope of the Poor*, 67–120.

[9] Ibid., 85.

[10] Compare Jesus' prescriptions for the disciples before they embark on their missionary journeys (9:3; 10:4).

[11] *Jesus and the Hope of the Poor*, 85.

[12] Ibid., 86.

[13] Ibid.

[14] Ibid., 91, 117.

Luke's authorial audience.[15] Others have embraced their resolution. Walter Pilgrim, for instance, also argues that Luke's portrait of Jesus and the earliest disciples does not provide a rigid model for readers to follow but is "intended for the wealthier Christians of his day, who are...sharply challenged with the need to wrestle more seriously with their own use of possessions."[16] More recently, Thomas E. Phillips, at the conclusion of his sequential reading of the wealth and poverty traditions in Luke-Acts, reiterates that renunciation was "limited to persons who were involved in those specific missions at that specific time" and therefore "not incumbent upon all persons," although the traditions might still challenge readers to "practice generosity and to spurn greed."[17]

Hans Joachim Degenhardt and Walter Schmithals argue that Luke extends salvation to wealthy Christians as well, but they do so without confining the dispossession traditions to a bygone era. In fact, for both, divesture remains a very real possibility for certain members of the Christian community in Luke's own time. Degenhardt suggests that only ecclesiastical leaders and itinerant preachers were asked to emulate the disciples' rigorous mode of life. All others may remain with their families and in their current occupations provided they give generously to those in need.[18] Schmithals proposes that the divestiture traditions *may* apply to any member of the Christian community during times of extreme hardship or persecution. Followers of Jesus need not give up all of their belongings during periods of relative tranquility, but given the uncertain, volatile political climate in Roman-occupied Judea during the first century, Christians must always be prepared to forgo them.[19] Although Degenhardt's thesis has been abandoned,[20]

---

15 Schottroff's and Stegemann's proposal builds upon Hans Conzelmann's division of Lukan salvation history into three stages: 1) the time of Israel; 2) the time of Jesus; and 3) the time of the church. Divestiture belongs to the time of Jesus, which was superseded shortly thereafter by the time of the Christian church. There is continuity between the two eras, to be sure, but the church faces a different set of challenges and is not bound by the rigorous manner of life embraced by Jesus and his disciples.

16 *Good News to the Poor*, 102. Cf. Gillman's position (*Possessions and the Life of Faith*, 73).

17 *Reading Issues of Wealth and Poverty in Luke-Acts*, 180–82.

18 *Lukas Evangelist der Armen: Besitz und Besitzverzicht in den lukanischen Schriften* (Stuttgart: Katholisches Bibelwerk, 1965), especially 36–41, 215–22.

19 "Lukas—Evangelist der Armen," *Theologia Viatorum* XII (1973–1974): 153–67.

20 Degenhardt's two-tier ethic is built upon a rigid distinction between οἱ μαθηταί and ὁ λαός in the Lucan writings that has long since collapsed. μαθητής, for instance, can describe persons other than Jesus' closest companions (e.g., 6:17).

Schmithal's proposal has endured, though not without modification. For example, Robert Karris argues that while the divestiture model is by no means a norm to be embraced by all, members of Luke's community must nevertheless "be ready to renounce their possessions" if persecution should arise or if "they stand in the way of their fidelity to Jesus Christ."[21] For David Peter Seccombe, while the divestiture traditions serve primarily to remind readers that discipleship "has *no* limits," in the event of a crisis these passages may very well become applicable for Christians who are forced to give up everything.[22] Under normal conditions Christians need not literally abandon all they have, but because "the extreme situation of the last journey to Jerusalem" could conceivably become a reality again for certain communities, they must always be prepared to follow in the footsteps of Jesus and his earliest companions by divesting entirely.[23]

Still others have emphasized how unexpected is Luke's interest in the salvation of the rich in view of the Gospel's privileging of the poor (4:18–19) and strongly negative characterization of the wealthy in its early chapters (1:53; 6:24–25).[24] According to John Gillman, for instance, in the infancy narrative it is the "little people," or those "without power, wealth, or influence," who "enjoy God's special favor."[25] God's visitation among persons "of humble origin" and promise of showing special favor to them (1:48)[26] contrasts sharply with the judgment already rendered against the "proud... powerful... [and] rich" (1:51–53).[27] J. O. York has argued that the Gospel, by means of a "repetitive form" he calls "bi-polar reversal," conditions its readers to expect the downfall of the influential, powerful, and wealthy coupled with a positive reversal for any who are "without honor, status, wealth, or religious appearance."[28]

---

[21] "Poor and Rich: The Lukan *Sitz-im-Leben*," 121–23.

[22] *Possessions and the Poor in Luke-Acts*, 115–17.

[23] Ibid.

[24] See Thomas D'Sa, "The Salvation of the Rich in the Gospel of Luke," *Vidyajyoti* 52 (1988), 179–80; George W. E. Nickelsburg, "Revisiting the Rich and the Poor in 1 Enoch 92–105 and the Gospel According to Luke," *SBL Seminar Papers* 37 (1998), 595–99; Gillman, *Possessions and the Life of Faith*, 38–41, 81; J. O. York, *The Last Shall Be First: The Rhetoric of Reversal in Luke* (JSNTSS 46; Sheffield: Sheffield Academic Press, 1991), 92–93, 160–61, 182–84.

[25] Gillman, *Possessions and the Life of Faith*, 38–41.

[26] Ibid., 38.

[27] See, e.g., the string of verbs in the aorist tense in these verses: διεσκόρπισεν... καθεῖλεν... ἐξαπέστειλεν.

[28] *The Last Shall Be First*, 92–93, 160.

For readers who share York's perspective on the presence of this repetitive form of bi-polar reversal, it may be all the more surprising when Zacchaeus, a "wealthy" and powerful "chief tax collector" (19:1–2), becomes a recipient of God's salvation (19:9). Luke's extension of the possibility of salvation to the rich may indeed come as a surprise, but the Gospel's interest in their conversion is unmistakable.[29]

One general consensus, then, is that Luke is interested in the conversion of the rich and offers them salvation but does not ask them to divest entirely as Jesus and his disciples did. The renunciation traditions are therefore not to serve as a discipleship model for readers. Where, then, in the Gospel are readers to look for guidance? What must possessors like Theophilus do so that they too might participate in God's kingdom? To these questions we now turn.

2. *Be Generous!*

For those who conclude that readers are not asked to divest themselves of property and possessions, Luke's almsgiving traditions naturally assume center-stage. Therefore, John's counsel to crowds, tax collectors, and soldiers in 3:10–14 and Zacchaeus's vow in 19:8 will become paradigmatic, exemplary texts, and passages that portray a complete break with one's past and possessions will recede into the background. However, a range of viewpoints with respect to two issues in particular may be found: 1) the kind of almsgiving Luke recommends; and 2) the rationale for giving alms. Each of these issues will be addressed below.

a. *Almsgiving: Nature and Purpose*

Generally, two types of almsgiving may be identified in the literature on wealth and possessions in Luke. Most common is a type that is largely in continuity with already existing forms of almsgiving attested in both the Jewish and Greco-Roman traditions. Less common is a type that is viewed as discontinuous with existing forms of almsgiving and has the potential to challenge or subvert the social order.

Exponents of the first type would include Douglas Oakman, Thomas Phillips, and Walter Pilgrim. Oakman argues that Luke has engaged

[29] D'Sa goes so far as to say that, among all four Gospels, Luke *alone* shows that salvation is possible for the wealthy ("The Salvation of the Rich in the Gospel of Luke," 178).

in a "discriminating use of the radical Jesus tradition" to urge creditors and landlords in his authorial audience to show generosity toward non-elites in the community.[30] But elites are neither asked to abandon their large estates nor participate in reforming society at large. Luke therefore advocates "a rather innocuous sharing-ethic"[31] that embraces only non-elites within the Christian community and has very little (if any) impact on Roman society or culture at large. In effect, "[n]o dramatic social reconstruction ... is to be expected or is necessary."[32] Social stratification and the hierarchical benefaction system of the Greco-Roman world are taken for granted and will remain unchallenged. The Gospel therefore offers readers an understanding of almsgiving that is neither new nor potentially subversive; it is fully consistent with practices already in place. As Oakman says, "Lazaruses may expect to become part of the estate, but not be rid of the estates altogether."[33] T. Phillips and W. Pilgrim both view John's advice in 3:10–14 to crowds, tax collectors, and soldiers as a central component of the Lukan perspective on wealth and possessions. Phillips, for instance, when reflecting on his sequential reading of wealth and poverty in the Gospel, concludes that the ethical norms proposed by John—"practice generosity and ... spurn greed"—"provide the basic themes around which a consistent reading of the third gospel may be developed."[34] Though it is possible that Zacchaeus's vow in 19:8 may serve as a model for some readers, the issue of how much one must give is ultimately "left unresolved"[35] and therefore up to each individual, as both conscience and circumstance dictate. Pilgrim, in *Good News to the Poor*, concludes his chapter on "The Right Use of Possessions" with a discussion of John's counsel in 3:10–14 since, for him, it provides a helpful synopsis of Luke's overall perspective on how readers should make use of their money and property.[36] Of course, John's advice requires no structural changes: tax collectors and soldiers are not asked to leave their occupations or push for reform but simply to abide by the law. Indeed, as Paul W. Walasky has argued, John's response to queries from crowds, tax collectors, and

[30] "The Countryside in Luke-Acts," in *The Social World of Luke-Acts: Models for Interpretation* (ed. Jerome Neyrey; Peabody, M.A.: Hendrickson, 1991), 176–78.
[31] Ibid., 177.
[32] Ibid.
[33] Ibid., 176.
[34] *Reading Issues of Wealth and Poverty in Luke-Acts*, 180–81.
[35] Ibid., 181.
[36] *Good News to the Poor*, 143–46.

soldiers in 3:10–14—share, collect only what has been prescribed, be satisfied with your salaries, and refrain from extortion—does reflect then-current Augustan ideals, which were designed to preserve or further ensure the existing social order by promoting order and peace.[37] Each of these authors, then, portrays Luke's perspective on almsgiving in such a way as to place it in continuity with already existing forms of giving that in large part do not disrupt the social order.

Proponents of a discontinuous form of almsgiving that does have the potential to call the social order into question would include Halvor Moxnes, Kyoung-Jin Kim, and John Gillman. All three argue that Luke presents readers with a model of generous, even limitless almsgiving that subverted the patronage system, a central feature of ancient Roman society that worked to sustain the power and privileges of the elite.[38] By giving freely without expecting a return of any kind (whether in the form of public honor or monetary compensation), possessors redistribute money in the interest of the common good and seek to make *friends* instead of clients. Luke's vision, Moxnes argues, is ultimately "based on the solidarity of the village community"[39] and may have an impact not only upon the inner dynamics of Christian communities but upon society at large. Moxnes thus argues for a subversive type of almsgiving that Oakman believes should be ascribed only to Jesus himself and not to Luke's superficial and "discriminating use of the radical Jesus tradition."

b. *Rationale for Engaging in Almsgiving*

Again, two major trajectories in the literature on wealth and possessions may be discerned. Some foreground Jesus' concern for the poor and downtrodden and therefore view almsgiving primarily as a means for

---

[37] *"And So We Came to Rome": The Political Perspective of St. Luke*, 30–31. When commenting on John's advice in 3:10–14, Schottroff and Stegemann also argue that the "primary thing" the Gospel asks of its readers "is that they abandon any illegal behavior," which would add nothing to Augustan ideals (*Jesus and the Hope of the Poor*, 116). However, they do go on to suggest that Zacchaeus's vow in 19:8 to relinquish half of his belongings "becomes a standard that gives guidance to the rich" (Ibid., 117), which would imply that John's advice, while still remaining a "primary" requirement, is just a starting point on the path to authentic discipleship.

[38] Halvor Moxnes, *The Economy of the Kingdom: Social Conflict and Economic Relations in Luke's Gospel* (Philadelphia: Fortress Press, 1988), 157, 165; Kyoung-Jin Kim, *Stewardship and Almsgiving in Luke's Theology* (JSNTSS 155; Sheffield: Sheffield Academic Press, 1998), 282–83, 287; Gillman, *Possessions and the Life of Faith*, 114.

[39] Moxnes, *The Economy of the Kingdom*, 159.

resolving social inequalities, redistributing money and other resources, or (more generally) meeting the immediate needs of any who suffer from deprivation or want. Others place the spiritual health or eternal destiny of possessors in the foreground and thus see almsgiving as a means to securing a place in God's kingdom by amassing heavenly capital. These two trajectories are not mutually exclusive but a matter of emphasis. One can, for instance, foreground concern for the poor and downtrodden as a primary motivation for almsgiving and still hold that there is personal benefit for possessors who engage in this practice regularly.

Richard Cassidy, Walter Pilgrim, and John Gillman all prioritize concern for the poor over the spiritual health or eternal destiny of possessors. For these authors, Jesus' inaugural address in 4:18–19 at the synagogue in Nazareth serves as a programmatic text that establishes the basis or primary motivation for Jesus' and his disciples' subsequent teaching and healing ministry.[40] Jesus' announcement in Nazareth introduces a central Lukan theme—"good news for the poor" (4:18)—in light of which the remainder of the narrative, including the almsgiving traditions, is to be read. Almsgiving is ultimately performed for the benefit of "the poor... the captives... the blind... [and] the oppressed" (4:18–19). Concern for the possessor, however, is not necessarily excluded for any of these authors; rather, it is not prioritized. For instance, although Pilgrim does take 4:16–30 as both "the programmatic text" and "interpretive key to Luke's understanding of Jesus' ministry,"[41] the majority of passages he examines toward the end of his book in Chapters 5 and 6 ("The Dangers of Wealth" and "The Right Use of Possessions") offer possessors like Theophilus concrete guidance so that they might resist the allure of wealth and thereby find favor with God.[42] Nevertheless, for all three, Jesus' teaching, including his instructions on giving alms, is offered first and foremost to improve the conditions of the poor.

---

[40] Richard Cassidy, *Jesus, Politics, and Society: A Study of Luke's Gospel* (Maryknoll, N.Y.: Orbis Books, 1978), 20–24; Pilgrim, *Good News to the Poor*, 64–66; Gillman, *Possessions and the Life of Faith*, 45–48. Justo Gonzalez also argues that Jesus' and the disciples' ministry is based on a desire to improve the conditions of the poor but focuses his attention on the *koinonia* traditions in Acts 2 and 4: "No matter how much Luke's Gospel has made of renunciation, what is described in Acts is a community where people relinquish their possessions, not for the sake of renunciation, but for the sake of those in need" (*Faith and Wealth: A History of Early Christian Ideas on the Origin, Significance, and Use of Money* [San Francisco: Harper & Row, 1990], 82).

[41] *Good News to the Poor*, 64, 66.

[42] Ibid., 103–46.

T. E. Schmidt and D. P. Seccombe, on the other hand, focus largely on the benefit received by possessors in giving alms. Schmidt, who finds "little evidence of sympathy for the poor as such" in Luke (or, for that matter, in any of the synoptic Gospels), argues that "the evil of wealth consists not primarily in lack of care for the poor but in independence from God."[43] The primary purpose of either divesting or giving alms is to inculcate "*Gottvertrauen*," an attitude of trust in and dependence upon God.[44] Seccombe agrees that Luke shows very little concern for the literally (or materially) poor. According to Seccombe, in fact, when readers encounter the term "poor" in Luke, they are to think not of disadvantaged persons existing at the margins of society but of all "Israel in her great need of salvation,"[45] including Israel's wealthy elite. Jesus is therefore as interested in saving Israel's elite, who are too often seduced away from God by the allure of mammon, as he is in saving Israel's poor. In order to redirect the gaze of the rich away from the material things of this age and toward the promised kingdom, he asks them to give alms. The poor, of course, do benefit from their almsgiving, but the focus remains on the benefit accrued by possessors. This is especially clear in Seccombe's interpretation of Jesus' encounter with a rich ruler on the way to Jerusalem (18:18–25). When Jesus asks him to "sell... and distribute to the poor" (v.22), he does so primarily with the intention of disclosing to the rich man how his "love for the things of this world is greater than his desire for the Kingdom."[46] For Seccombe, the literal poor are *not* in view: possessors are asked to give alms primarily because material things "exercise too great a power over men, binding them to this age and preventing them from embracing the promised Kingdom."[47]

Summary

Two general consensuses, then, may be identified in the literature on wealth and possessions in Luke, each with several variations. First, the

[43] *Hostility to Wealth in the Synoptic Gospels* (JSNTSS 15; Sheffield: Sheffield Academic Press, 1987), 136, 161.
[44] Ibid.
[45] *Possessions and the Poor in Luke-Acts*, 19. Seccombe bases his conclusion in part upon "a traditional characterization of Israel" in the Hebrew Bible, where Israel is called poor on account of "its suffering and humiliation at the hands of the nations and... its own disordered life" (Ibid., 94).
[46] Ibid., 127.
[47] Ibid., 195.

Gospel extends the possibility of salvation to wealthy readers but without requiring them to divest and embrace the itinerant, ascetic lifestyle of Jesus and his closest companions. Second, although wealthy readers are not expected to renounce everything, they are encouraged to be generous with their material resources and give alms. Luke's almsgiving traditions, moreover, are generally conceived in one of two ways. Some argue that they merely replicate already exiting forms of beneficence and offer little (if any) challenge to the social order while others hold that they stand in tension with and therefore offer an implicit critique of the most common redistributive practices. Finally, while some commentators suggest that the primary rationale for giving alms is to improve the conditions of the poor, others emphasize how such a practice might benefit possessors, whether in this life or in the life to come.

Methodological Approaches Employed for Reading Wealth and Possessions in Luke

The vast majority of studies on wealth and possessions in Luke may be situated broadly within the historical-critical paradigm. That is, most proceed from the vantage point of an (objective) reader-construct and employ empirical methods in search of how an author or editor intended a work to be received by its first hearers/readers. Some, such as L. Schottroff's and W. Stegemann's *Jesus and the Hope of the Poor*[48] and R. Karris's "Poor and Rich: The Lukan *Sitz-im-Leben*,"[49] are historical in orientation and use the wealth and possessions traditions in Luke to help identify the Gospel's Sitz im Leben. Others, however, such as W. Pilgrim's *Good News to the Poor*[50] and J. Gillman's *Possessions and the Life of Faith*,[51] are literary in orientation and seek to describe, with the help of redaction criticism, Luke's unique perspective on this theme. Moreover, these studies may draw heavily on one method in particular or employ a variety of methods. For instance, H. Moxnes in *The Economy of the Kingdom* draws largely upon social-scientific criticism while J. Gillman in *Possessions and the Life of Faith* employs a multifaceted approach that is "sociohistorical-redactional, cultural-anthropological, and literary symbolic."[52] Finally, while a few proceed sequentially through the

[48] 68–69.
[49] 112, 124.
[50] 13.
[51] 15, 35, 112.
[52] 35.

Gospel, analyzing stories and sayings related to wealth and possessions in the order in which they are presented,[53] many pull relevant passages out of narrative context and group them according to sub-themes. R. Cassidy,[54] P. Seccombe,[55] and W. Pilgrim[56] all proceed in this fashion. Pilgrim, for instance, classifies wealth and possessions traditions in *Good News to the Poor* under the following headings: "The Call to Total Surrender of One's Possessions"; "The Dangers of Wealth"; and "The Right Use of Possessions." Seccombe offers a similar classification in *Possessions and the Poor in Luke-Acts*: "Renunciation and Discipleship"; "Possessions and the Christian Life"; and "Fellowship and the Church." All of these studies, however, do fit broadly within a historical-critical framework given their use of a universal reader-construct and interest in describing how Luke's wealth and possessions traditions were intended to be received by the Gospel's original hearers/readers.

Two studies may be situated within the literary-critical paradigm. L. T. Johnson, in *The Literary Function of Possessions in Luke-Acts*, first identifies what he believes to be the dominant literary pattern in Luke-Acts (acceptance and rejection) and then shows how the motif of possessions functions symbolically to help illuminate this pattern. Characters who accept Jesus and his message demonstrate their receptiveness by divesting or giving alms and those who reject him disclose their resistance by refusing to part with their possessions. Thus, how people handle their possessions exteriorizes an inner disposition of acceptance or rejection.[57] T. Phillips, in *Reading Issues of Wealth and Poverty in Luke-Acts*, draws upon Wolfgang Iser's phenomenology of reading, particularly his notion of "consistency-building," to offer a sequential analysis of Luke's wealth and poverty traditions. Although Phillips is committed to creating a consistent, coherent interpretation of these diverse and often conflicting traditions, he does attend to "the alien associations which inevitably haunt (and perhaps temporarily thwart) the reader's consistency-building efforts."[58] However, by the time one reaches his concluding reflection on how these traditions have taken shape, the "alien associations" have long disappeared. For Phillips, John's advice in 3:10–14 serves as a sufficient

---

[53] See, e.g., Gillman, *Possessions and the Life of Faith.*
[54] *Jesus, Politics, and Society: A Study of Luke's Gospel.*
[55] *Possessions and the Poor in Luke-Acts.*
[56] *Good News to the Poor.*
[57] 121–31, 220–21.
[58] 80.

synopsis of the whole: "The reader concludes that the ethical norms introduced by John the Baptist provide the basic themes around which a consistent reading of the third gospel may be developed. The Baptist exhorted his listeners to practice generosity and to spurn greed."[59] An overemphasis on consistency-building as a goal of the reading process ultimately cancels textual indeterminacy and ambiguity.

While studies on Luke's wealth and possessions traditions have been approached from a variety of methodological perspectives, most fall broadly within the historical-critical paradigm. Some, for instance, use the wealth and possessions traditions to help identify a Sitz im Leben for the Gospel while others pull relevant sayings and pericopae out of narrative context and analyze them according to sub-themes such as the dangers of wealth or the proper use of possessions. A few, however, proceed from within a literary-critical paradigm and focus on how the Gospel's narrative mechanics guide readers' responses.

B. Reconsidering Luke's Discourse on Wealth and Possessions

Looking Ahead

Sayings and stories related to the theme of wealth and possessions may be found in nearly every chapter of the Gospel. Because this theme is so prevalent, I have chosen to focus on four parables in Luke's "Travel Narrative" (12:13–21; 15:11–32; 16:1–13; 16:19–31), the locus of most of Jesus' instruction on this topic. These parables have been selected not only because they constitute part of Luke's discourse on wealth and possessions but because they share similar characters (wealthy men), settings (residences of the elite), and a common motif (overconsumption). They are further related by a progression among protagonists from merely considering a life of overconsumption to long-standing, deeply ingrained practice: in 12:16–21, a rich landowner contemplates spending all of his "good things" (vv.18–19) on himself; in 15:11–32, a father's younger son liquidates his inheritance and 'scatters' it (v.13) in a distant land; in 16:1–13, readers infer that a steward recently 'scattered' possessions in view of accusations brought against him (v.1); and in 16:19–31, Jesus introduces a wealthy man who long ago embraced an extravagant lifestyle marked by conspicuous, habitual overconsumption

[59] Ibid., 180–81.

(16:19–31).[60] I will argue that Jesus criticizes overconsumption in each of the four parables but only gradually advances a critique of wealth, which climaxes in the final parable (16:19–31). While many have consigned Luke to advocating a benign form of almsgiving that has little impact on the social order, a reader engaged with these parables from Luke's Travel Narrative may hear a call to do much more than distribute surplus funds. They may, in fact, inspire broad social reform and/or radical lifestyle changes.[61]

All four parables will be examined according to the order in which they occur in the Gospel, and special attention will be given to their cumulative effect upon the reader. Reader-response criticism will therefore serve as the primary method for the analysis. However, narratological and narrative critical studies will be consulted in order to provide conceptual tools and terminology for describing how the text is being processed and structured, and intertextuality will furnish a theoretical foundation for formulating intertextual relations.[62] The study, moreover, will proceed against the backdrop of Jesus' inaugural address at the synagogue in Nazareth (4:18–19), a programmatic announcement specifying that the overarching purpose of his ministry is to improve conditions for the poor (and not to convert the rich or train disciples in *Gottvertrauen*). Finally, while the analysis of the four parables will be the centerpiece of this study, a brief discussion of Jesus' subsequent encounters with two wealthy men, an anonymous Jewish ruler (18:18–25) and a "chief tax collector" named Zacchaeus (19:1–10), while still "on the way" to Jerusalem will follow. The purpose of this section is to explore whether or not the construction of Jesus' teaching on consumption and wealth as presented in the four parables may be substantiated in the remainder of the Travel Narrative (17:1–19:27).

---

[60] This observation is based upon a preliminary, cursory reading of the four parables. Although the in-depth analyses in succeeding chapters may alter these initial impressions, the observed progression does, at this point, offer added impetus for exploring these parables as a group.

[61] In keeping with the primary method selected for the analysis (reader-response criticism), at this point the thesis is stated only in the broadest possible terms so as to allow for gradual structuration and "progressive discovery" (See Robert Brawley, *Centering on God: Method and Message in Luke-Acts* [Literary Currents in Biblical Interpretation; Louisville: Westminster/John Knox Press, 1990], esp. Chapter 9). A full synopsis of the journey and its implications will be presented in Chapter 5.

[62] The methodological approach, then, may be situated broadly within the literary-critical paradigm.

Before turning to the parables themselves, it will be necessary to: 1) explore the nature of Luke's parabolic discourse; 2) identify in what way Jesus' inaugural address in Nazareth will function programmatically for a reading of the four parables; 3) describe the composite reader-oriented approach; 4) delineate the reader-position to be employed; and 5) explain how the study will proceed.[63]

1. *The Nature of Parabolic Discourse in Luke*

Luke's own parables of Jesus[64] have been called the most vivid and memorable in the canon because they present us with realistic and often conflicted characters of questionable moral fiber and display an unusual attention to detail[65] in a genre elsewhere known for its economy of description and stock characters, settings, and motifs. For instance, we find in the foolish farmer (12:16–20), the prodigal son (15:11–32), the unjust (or dishonest) steward (16:1–8), and the unjust judge (18:2–5) "realistic portraits of ordinary people caught being themselves, quick sketches of authentic, though troubled individuals, grasping for help or advantage in life's crucial moments."[66] The Lukan Jesus, by means of interior monologue, adds depth and dimension to these characters (who, in Matthew and Mark, are otherwise relatively flat, one-dimensional plot functionaries) by exposing their "frantic thoughts and calculations" and often questionable motivations.[67] Moreover, Luke's parables, it has been argued, are less often interpreted allegorically by the parabler

[63] Two of the studies mentioned above also examine Luke's wealth and possessions traditions sequentially: John Gillman's *Possessions and the Life of Faith* and Thomas Phillips's *Reading Issues of Wealth and Poverty in Luke-Acts.* Gillman, however, does not account for the active, creative role a reader plays in shaping meaning, and Phillips ultimately overwrites the diverse traditions in Luke by permitting John's exhortation in 3:10–14 to crowds, tax collectors, and soldiers to account for the entirety of the Gospel's instruction on wealth and possessions (180–81). This study will employ a reader-oriented approach that: 1) employs a flesh-and-blood reader who, in dialogue with the text, produces meaning and; 2) is attentive to the tension between the two dominant traditions of divestiture and almsgiving.

[64] I.e., those traditionally designated as "L" parables.

[65] J. Drury, *The Parables in the Gospels: History and Allegory* (London: SPCK, 1985), 111, 115.

[66] Phillip Sellew, "Interior Monologue as a Narrative Device in the Parables of Luke," *JBL* 111 (1992), 253. Admittedly, though, these characters are hardly "ordinary," and they certainly are not "little," as Sellew describes them (Ibid.). In fact, the farmer, the prodigal son, and the judge may have been among Judea's elite, and one could plausibly locate the steward in the retainer class.

[67] Ibid.

and narrator than they are in Matthew and Mark.[68] For example, one finds several "example stories" (*Beispielerzählungen*) in Luke that do not point beyond themselves to external events or scenarios but illustrate for readers in a rather straightforward way how one ought to behave (or not behave) as a follower of Jesus.[69] With such stories, the difficulty of first identifying a metaphorical "network or structure of possibilities" and then discerning which elements of this network deserve emphasis vanishes.[70] In brief, not only do several of Luke's parables of Jesus eschew the problematic metaphorical dimension altogether, but human beings and their everyday issues and ethical dilemmas generally command center-stage.

It is, perhaps, for these reasons that many believe Luke's parables are also among the most accessible. J. Drury, for instance, writes: "The L parables tell themselves. We need no key; there is no code to break. People act so intelligibly that a modest knowledge of human character is all we need to grasp them."[71] But Drury's remarks would stand at the far end of a continuum encompassing many who find Luke's parables more accessible than those of Matthew or Mark.[72] More common are readings that maintain the distinction between insiders and outsiders

[68] See, e.g., Drury, *The Parables in the Gospels*, 111, 116.

[69] I am not arguing that the four example stories in Luke (10:30–35; 12:16–20; 16:19–31; 18:9–13) are straightforward, only that such an argument has been made. See Jeffery T. Tucker's challenge to this popular classification (*Example Stories: Perspectives on Four Parables in the Gospel of Luke* [JSNTSS 162; Sheffield: Sheffield Academic Press, 1998]).

[70] See Bernard Brandon Scott's brief discussion on metaphor in *Hear Then the Parable: A Commentary on the Parables of Jesus* (Philadelphia: Fortress Press, 1989), especially 50–51.

[71] *The Parables in the Gospels*, 116.

[72] Though Frank Stagg ("Luke's Theological Use of Parables," *Review and Expositor* 94 [1994]: 215–29) first argues that in Luke 8:9–10, 16–18 and 10:21–22 he finds an unresolvable tension between a theology of divine determination whereby many are denied access to the secrets of the parables and a theology of human responsibility that posits our ability to comprehend their meaning (221), in his subsequent analysis of select Lukan parables he rather quickly locates their "point" and so seems to stand with Drury: Luke's parables tell themselves. According to Stagg, for instance, the Parable of the Two Debtors (7:36–50) is "not a riddle or allegory, understandable only to the initiated... [but] an analogy understandable to anyone with ears willing to hear"; the Parable of the Rich Fool (12:16–21) is "straightforward... [and] readily understandable"; and the Parable of the Widow and the Judge (18:1–8) has a very precise "point" (222, 224, 227). François Bovon leans in this direction when he says that Luke "retains the saying of Jesus about the μυστήρια of God only out of faithfulness to tradition" (*A Commentary on the Gospel of Luke 1:1–9:50* [trans. Christine M. Thomas; Hermeneia; Minneapolis: Fortress Press, 2002], 312). In other words, according to Bovon one cannot assume that Jesus' statement in 8:9–10 accurately reflects the theological viewpoint

(see Luke 8:9–10) that is so central in Mark (4:10–12) and Matthew (13:10–17) but argue that the line that separates the two groups is not drawn as sharply.[73] Charles Hedrick, for instance, argues that while Jesus' parables in Luke contain "secrets about the kingdom of God that must be explained to the disciples (8:9–10a, 11) and concealed from outsiders (8:10b)," the Gospel is generally "optimistic about the potential ability of the outsider to understand."[74] For Luke T. Johnson, while a distinction between outsiders and insiders is indeed present, the "motif of secrecy is only *vestigial* in Luke" (italics mine).[75] E. Cuvillier has argued that Luke's parables were fired primarily in the kiln of the Aristotelean rhetorical tradition (rather than the Jewish apocalyptic tradition) and so are designed to clarify rather than conceal divinely revealed mysteries from the unworthy or uninitiated.[76] For Cullivier, however, the parables provide guidance on the way to salvation *only* for committed followers of Jesus; for those without faith, they remain enigmatic and refuse to speak. For many, then, the distinction between insiders and outsiders in not as prominent in Luke as it is in Matthew and Mark, and there is hope that many—even outsiders—will be able to comprehend Jesus' parables and therefore receive mysteries of the kingdom. But, can we really be "optimist about the potential ability of the outsider to understand"? Do Luke's parables, as Cuvillier argues, stand broadly within the Greco-Roman rhetorical tradition and so function—at least for followers of Jesus—to further clarify or illuminate? Are Luke's parables really more accessible than those of Matthew or Mark?

---

of the writer, who may have believed that Jesus' parables were once broadcast widely with the hope that as many as possible would understand.

[73] See Charles Hedrick, *Many Things in Parables: Jesus and his Modern Critics* (Louisville: Westminster John Knox Press, 2004), 32.

[74] *Parables as Poetic Fictions: The Creative Voice of Jesus* (Peabody: Hendrickson Publishers, 1994), 20. Hedrick further comments: "Luke 8:18 stresses that one should take care 'how' one 'hears,' a statement suggesting that one may be able to understand if one listens carefully" (Ibid.).

[75] *The Gospel of Luke* (Sacra Pagina 3; Collegeville, MN: The Liturgical Press, 1991), 132.

[76] "*Parabole* dans la Tradition Synoptique," *ETR* 66 (1991), 42–44. For further discussion on the function of παραβολή in the rhetorical tradition, see Burton L. Mack and Vernon K. Robbins, *Patterns of Persuasion in the Gospels* (Sonoma, CA: Polebridge Press, 1989), 146–48; Madeleine I. Boucher, *The Parables* (New Testament Message 7; Wilmington, DE; Michael Glazier, 1981), especially 34–39; Jean Zumstein, "Jésus et les Paraboles," in *Les Paraboles Évangéliques: Perspectives Nouvelles* (Lectio Divina 135; Paris: Cerf, 1989), especially 94–97.

In Luke 8:4–8, Jesus tells his first narrative parable. Though he has already offered a few proverbs or aphorisms that would broadly qualify as parabolic discourse (e.g., 4:23; 5:36; 6:13), the Parable of the Sower is the first with a clearly discernable beginning, middle, and (open-) end.[77] While it may not bear the weight of a "master parable" that guides readers into deciphering much of what has already taken place in the narrative and foreshadows what is yet to come,[78] it is nevertheless followed by a short statement on the function of parabolic discourse in general (8:9–10) and provides readers with an initial (and perhaps paradigmatic) response of incomprehension (see v.9). Thus, those who proceed through the narrative sequentially would probably begin forming their first impressions of the nature and function of Jesus' parabolic discourse here. It is the first of many narrative parables that Jesus will tell, and he does pause to address the purpose of the parables directly (vv.9–10) before offering an interpretation (vv.11–15).[79]

The Parable of the Sower (8:4–8), spoken in the presence of the twelve, several women who were providing material resources for Jesus and his disciples, and a large crowd (8:1–3), is punctuated with a resounding call to all in earshot: "Let anyone with ears to hear listen!" (v.8). At this point, readers may assume that Jesus' parable will serve as a helpful aid for further understanding the nature of his ministry and the kingdom that he was sent to proclaim (4:43; 8:1).[80] But the phrase

---

[77] The term "narrative parable" is drawn from John Dominic Crossan's three-fold classification: aphoristic parables, extended parables, and narrative parables. While extended parables "are but the predictable unfolding of what is implicit in aphoristic parables," narrative parables, in addition to possessing a beginning, middle, and end with at least a rudimentary plot, present the reader with some "minimal amount of surprise or unpredictability" ("Parable," *ABD* V, 149).

[78] Mary Ann Tolbert argues that the Parable of the Sower has precisely this function in the Gospel of Mark (*Sowing the Gospel: Mark's World in Literary-Historical Perspective* [Minneapolis: Fortress Press, 1989], 122–28); cf. John Paul Heil, "Reader-Response and the Narrative Context of the Parables about Growing Seed in Mark 4:1–34," *CBQ* 54 (1992): 271–86.

[79] Some have argued that, unlike the corresponding episodes in Matthew and Mark, Jesus in 8:9–10 is really only speaking about "this parable" (αὕτη ἡ παραβολή; vv.9, 11) and not about parables in general (see Herman Hendrickx, *The Third Gospel for the Third World Volume Two-B: Ministry in Galilee (Luke 7:1–9:50)* [Collegeville, MN: The Liturgical Press, 1998], 127; Bovon, *Luke* 1, 311.). However, Jesus uses the plural form of the word in v.10 (παραβολαῖς), which suggests that his observation on the consequence of having spoken a parable ("seeing they may not see and hearing they may not understand") applies not only to the Parable of the Sower but to parabolic discourse in general.

[80] See Stagg, "Luke's Theological Use of Parables," 217.

"ears to hear" (ὦτα ἀκούειν) is ambiguous: Is Jesus issuing an open call to all with ears (i.e., to everyone) in hope that as many as possible will grasp the story's meaning, or he is only addressing those endowed with a special set of "ears to hear" in a certain way (i.e., to move behind the story in search of a hidden, esoteric meaning)? We must suspend judgment until further information comes to light.

The disciples are completely mystified by the story (v.9), and readers may reasonably infer that the crowds are as well. After all, if even his closest traveling companions cannot understand, what are the chances that strangers will? The story, then, has thus far not been a success and has failed to bring further good news about God's kingdom (see 8:1). So, the disciples press him: "What can this parable mean" (v.9)? Jesus responds: "To you it has been given (δέδοται) to know the mysteries about the kingdom of God, but for the others [it has been given for them to know these mysteries] in parables, so that[81] seeing they may not see and hearing they may not understand" (v.10).[82] Jesus' use of the perfect tense (δέδοται) is surprising since the disciples still do not understand the story and the "mysteries" remain beyond their grasp. In fact, at this point they are no different from "the others" since, though they have seen and heard, neither do they comprehend. For now, it appears that both the disciples and the others "must be content with the coded language of the parables."[83]

By v.10, readers have thus been presented not only with the parabler's own authoritative observation on how parabolic discourse will generally be received[84] but a response that may prove paradigmatic: the disciples, initially perplexed by Jesus' strange story about a sower and his seed, are forced to confront the parabler in search of an explanation. It appears that disciples will have no advantage over "the others" unless the parabler himself intervenes to explain the meaning of his

[81] ἵνα may signify either a purpose clause or a result clause (see Joseph A. Fitzmyer, *The Gospel According to Luke I–IX* [Anchor Bible 28; Garden City, NY: Doubleday, 1981], 708–9; Bovon, *Luke* 1, 312). If the ἵνα marks a purpose clause, we find "a hint of divine predestination" that, frankly, is "troubling" (Ringe, *Luke*, 114). However, if we read it as introducing a result clause, Jesus' statement merely conveys a "tragic realization" (Hendrickx, *The Third Gospel for the Third World*, 130).

[82] Just prior to this episode, the narrator tells us that Jesus was "bringing good news about the kingdom of God" (8:1), but now he suddenly and somewhat surprisingly refers to "*secrets* about the kingdom of God" (8:10).

[83] Johnson, *The Gospel of Luke*, 132.

[84] In the Gospel of Luke, Jesus is a fully reliable character whose pronouncements and observations are to be trusted.

stories. Throughout the remainder of the Gospel, Jesus will, to be sure, occasionally offer an interpretation for his disciples, as he does in vv.11–15.[85] But many parables are left un-interpreted either by the parabler himself or by the narrator. We shall soon see what this might mean for readers.

In vv.11–15, Jesus provides an allegorical interpretation of the parable for the disciples, which should provide clarification and so privy them to the kingdom's mysteries. However, the narrator at no point informs us that the disciples have understood, and the disciples themselves provide no indication of having grasped Jesus' reading of the story. But Jesus assumes they have, for he asks them to broadcast what they have learned to others. With their newfound insight, they are to illumine the way of "the others" who are entering the kingdom (v.17).[86] In fact, says Jesus, they will be the ones through whom all things hidden will be disclosed (v.18). But they must pay attention to how (πῶς) they hear the parables, for there is much at stake: those who are able to comprehend will understand even more, but those whose minds and hearts (see v.15) fail them will lose everything (v.18). As one commentator has observed, "everything is hanging in the balance."[87]

If the disciples are to count themselves among "those who have" (ὅς...ἔχῃ) and so be given even more (v.18), they must, "having [first] heard the word with a noble and good heart, hold it tight (κατέχουσιν) and bear fruit in steadfast endurance" (v.15). Oddly, comprehension, the primary obstacle faced by "the others" (8:10), is nowhere explicitly made part of the equation: "hear the word...hold [it] tight...bear fruit." If understanding is to occur at all, it apparently takes place as one "holds tight" the word—perhaps as one listens, reflects, mulls the story over, and tests one's reading in conversation with other members of the community. Even for Jesus' disciples, then, comprehension is not a foregone conclusion, although they can "hold tight" the word and *labor* toward illumination. In the absence of an explanation from the parabler

[85] Sometimes, too, our fully reliable and omniscient Lukan narrator will offer a brief interpretive comment for readers, but the characters in the story do not have access to these remarks.

[86] See S. Ringe on vv.16–18: "By implication, we learn that the disciples who have received the plain explanation of what others know only in parables are given the task of 'enlightening' the others" (*Luke*, 115). Cf. Fitzmyer's comment: "The gift granted to the disciples to know the secrets of the kingdom is destined by God to a wide and public broadcasting" (*The Gospel According to Luke I–IX*, 718).

[87] Hendrickx, *The Third Gospel for the Third World*, 149.

himself, disciples must exert effort in interpreting the parables—and without any guarantee of success. The stakes are high indeed: not only do the disciples themselves face losing everything if they refuse the challenge of "holding tight" the word, but if they fail to understand, "the others" miss out on the "mysteries of the kingdom" too.[88]

Having briefly explored Jesus' first narrative parable (8:4–8) and his subsequent explanation on the function of parabolic discourse in general (8:9–10), let us revisit our initial questions: Are Luke's parables of Jesus really more accessible than those of Matthew or Mark? Can we really be more optimistic about our ability as readers to comprehend? For believers, do they all function, as E. Cuvillier has argued, to offer further clarity or illumination? Based on a reading of 8:4–18, I have tried to show that in the absence of an explanation by the parabler himself disciples have no advantage whatsoever over "the others" and so face the same threat of incomprehension (μὴ συνιῶσιν; v.10). Moreover, even after Jesus offers an allegorical reading of the Parable of the Sower (vv.11–15), neither the narrator nor the disciples provide any indication that his interpretation has been understood. If Jesus' closest companions must approach him for an explanation of his parables and even afterward fail to provide a clear indication that they have grasped or benefited from his reading, how confident can readers be that the parables will be a sure and steady guide into the "mysteries of the kingdom"?

In Luke, it seems, the burden for interpreting Jesus' parables will rest largely on readers. Like disciples and "the others," in the absence of hermeneutical guidance, readers too must accept the challenge of "holding tight" (κατέχουσιν) the word and laboring toward illumination, without any guarantee of success. Even when an interpretation is offered (as in vv.11–15), one cannot be assured that comprehension will follow. It may be assumed that the disciples, by virtue of their new vocation as "learners," listened attentively to Jesus' interpretative remarks. Readers too may wish to listen carefully to Jesus' comments when they are offered, but, as with the disciples (who do not provide a

[88] Jesus will soon define his true "mother and brothers" as "those who hear the word of God and do it" (8:21). Missing again from the equation is the element of comprehension, but if disciples are to move from 'hearing' to 'doing,' comprehension in some form must be assumed. Disciples (and readers) who wish to be numbered among Jesus' "mother and brothers" have here further motivation to pay careful attention to how the parables are heard and to "hold [them] tight."

clear indication of comprehension), confusion still remains a possibility, and we may very well find ourselves among those who have seen but not really seen and heard but not understood (8:10). But for the narratee and for any who wish to move from simply "hearing the word" to "doing it" and so count themselves among Jesus' true "mother and brothers" (8:21), the parables must be interpreted—even if what results is utter bewilderment.

Among the four parables to be examined in this study, two receive no explicit interpretive remarks by the narrator or the parabler (15:11–32; 16:19–31), one is introduced briefly by the parabler and appended with a concluding application[89] (12:15–21), and another receives relatively extensive commentary only by the parabler (16:1–13). Therefore, with 15:11–32 and 16:19–31, the burden rests entirely on readers to make sense of what lies in front of them: they will receive no explicit help from the parabler or the narrator. Jesus does offer some guidance in 12:15–21 (albeit very brief) and supply further commentary for the disciples in 16:1–13, but there is no indication that Jesus' remarks in 12:15, 21 and 16:8b–13 were of benefit to those who heard them. His comments may have fallen on deaf ears.

There is little evidence that Luke's parables will be easier to access than those in Matthew or Mark. Interpreting Lukan parables is a profoundly reader-oriented enterprise that will require hard work and creativity. This book, in large part, represents but one attempt at "holding tight" (κατέχουσιν) four of these parables in search of greater understanding.

Toward an Approach to Reading Parables in Luke

For many, Jesus' parables are helpful guides on the path to greater understanding that function to clarify religious truths.[90] For this reader, however, Jesus' parables often elude, frustrate, tease, and intrigue. They overflow with possibility; gaps and ellipses abound; they are replete with moments of "undecidability";[91] attempts to pin them down fail. Their

[89] The final remark in v.21 may be attributed either to Jesus or to the narrator. This ambiguity will be addressed in Chapter 2.

[90] In the modern era, this widespread interpretative trend is traceable to Adolph Jülicher's work on parables (*Die Gleichnisreden Jesus* [Darmstadt: Wissenschaftliche Buchgesellschaft, 1969]).

[91] See Paul de Man, "The Resistance to Theory," in *Readers and Reading* (ed. Andrew Bennett; Longman Critical Readers; New York: Longman, 1995), 201. For de Man,

interpretive frames and settings may offer guidance but never exhaust their polyvalence. Thus, based on prior encounters with Jesus' parables generally, it is expected that these four parables in Luke's Travel Narrative too will often "disperse themselves" and "resist efforts to grasp their 'essence.'"[92] I therefore begin this study by foregrounding a "surplus of meaning" or an "unreadable otherness"[93] that will alternately frustrate and draw the reader yet further into the parables' strange worlds, where, like "travelers... [we] move across lands belonging to someone else, like nomads poaching their way across fields they did not write, despoiling the wealth of Egypt to enjoy it themselves."[94] As readers of narratives so terse and so elusive, we have no choice but to 'poach' and 'despoil,' to glean where we have not sown, to write and rewrite the parables for ourselves and so wrest an interpretation—if we can. Faced with a "surplus of meaning," the reader's task is then to limit their meaning-potential and impose some form of order, aware that any such ordering hovers over a "seething-flux" that threatens to unsettle interpretive repose.[95]

The Gospel's author may have hoped that the parables would, in Aristotelean fashion, help illustrate and clarify, but s/he has assumed enormous risk by inserting a mode of oral discourse that depends upon a lively, ongoing, dialogical interchange between parabler and audience for effective communication to take place. According to Werner Kelber, parables more so than other genres do not comply well with "linguistic contextualization" in a written medium: gone are the "[g]estures and facial expressions, pitch and tone of voice, economic and political experiences" that are necessary for an oral form to generate effective, meaningful communication.[96] Readers may therefore be encouraged to imagine or construct these missing elements and participate in reviving

some words or phrases present readers with several choices, none of which are obvious or self-evident based on grammar or context. During these moments of undecidability, "the reader has to break off his understanding at the very moment when he is most directly engaged and summoned by the text" (201).

[92] Patrocinio P. Schweickart and Elizabeth A. Flynn, "Introduction," in *Reading Sites: Social Difference and Reader-Response* (ed. Patrocinio P. Schweickart and Elizabeth A. Flynn; New York: MLA, 2004), 17.

[93] Ibid.

[94] Michel de Certeau, "Reading as Poaching," in *Readers and Reading*, 159.

[95] Stephen Moore, *Literary Criticism and the Gospels: The Theoretical Challenge* (New Haven: Yale University Press, 1989), 136.

[96] *The Oral and Written Gospel: The Hermeneutics of Speaking and Writing in the Synoptic Tradition, Mark, Paul, and Q* (Philadelphia: Fortress Press, 1983), 109, 112.

some of the parables' dialogicity. Moreover, John Dominic Crossan has observed that Jesus' parables may in fact "be no more than plot summaries of stories that might have taken hours to tell."[97] If this is indeed so, then it is no wonder that readers today find so many ellipses, vacancies, and fissures in his parables and are almost overwhelmed at times by indeterminacy and interpretive possibility. Parables, in short, are *scriptible* narratives that cannot merely be read but must be written or produced.

In this study, while close attention will be given to the narrative setting of each parable and interpretive remarks provided by the narrator or the parabler,[98] the parables will be considered apart from their frames as well.[99] The strange, new world introduced by Jesus, the embedded narrator, may take the reader off-guard and momentarily disassociate or distance her from the larger narrative within which the parable is set.[100] A parable presents readers with a brand new setting, cast of characters, and series of events that ask for a hearing in their own right. As V. George Shillington has observed, "[o]nce inside the parable plot, the participant is caught in the narrative interplay,"[101] immersed in the parable's own story-world, and temporarily displaced from the larger tale of which it is a part. Eventually, however, either the narrator or Jesus himself will call the reader back and ask her to place her experience of the parable in conversation with the Gospel's larger discourse. Will subsequent nimshalim confirm her experience of the parable and help solidify a germinating interpretation, or will the parabler's remarks undermine initial reflections and send her in an unexpected direction? The narrator's or parabler's reading (if offered) need not override or

---

[97] "Parable," in *ABD* V, 149.

[98] For studies that treat Jesus' parables within their narrative contexts, see, e.g., Drury, *The Parables in the Gospels: History and Allegory*; John Donahue, *The Gospel in Parable: Metaphor, Narrative, and Theology in the Synoptic Gospels* (Philadelphia: Fortress Press, 1988); D. Noel, *Parables in Context: Developing a Narrative-Critical Approach to Parables in Luke* (Ph.D. diss., Southern Baptist Theological Seminary, 1986); A. M. Okorie, "The Function of the Parables in the Narrative of Luke," *Revista Biblica* 60 (1998): 183–93.

[99] Analyzing parables apart from their narrative contexts and the interpretive frames provided by the evangelists has been the dominant trend in contemporary parable research.

[100] See Herman Hendrickx, *The Parables of Jesus* (rev. ed.; Studies in the Synoptic Gospels; San Francisco: Harper & Row, 1986), 10.

[101] "Introduction," in *Jesus and His Parables* (ed. V. G. Shillington; Edinburgh: T. & T. Clark, 1997), 18.

cancel the reader's own experience of the parable, but in this study it will be heard and engaged.[102]

2. *Jesus' Announcement in Nazareth as Programmatic for Reading the Parables*

All four parables will be read in light of Jesus' inaugural address at the synagogue in Nazareth, which outlines the nature and purpose of his ministry (4:16–21). Scholars are nearly unanimous in treating Jesus' reading of Isa 61:1–2 and 58:6 and subsequent sermon in v.21 as in some way "programmatic" for understanding the Gospel since it is located at the very beginning of Jesus' public ministry and introduces key themes and motifs that recur throughout the narrative.[103] The whole episode in Nazareth (4:16–30), in fact, has been understood as a sketch of the Gospel's plot in miniature.[104] But debate continues over the identity of the beneficiaries of this "good news" and the precise nature of the program to which Jesus refers in vv.18–19. For instance, Who are "the poor"? Are readers to assume that the term is primarily economic in orientation? Might it function more generally as "a cipher

[102] Marisa Bortolussi and Peter Dixon have observed that most real readers tend to treat the narrator not as an authoritative voice that cannot be challenged but "as a conversation partner" (*Psychonarratology: Foundations for the Empirical Study of Literary Response* [New York: Cambridge University Press, 2003], 72, 84). An attempt here will be made to construct and engage the narrator's interpretive remarks, but they need not be taken as the only possible reading of a given parable. Contrast, for instance, Brad Young, who argues that "the function of the parable is dependent upon the storyteller himself... [and] the context of the parable often determines the message being conveyed" (*Jesus and His Jewish Parables: Rediscovering the Roots of Jesus' Teaching* [New York: Paulist Press, 1989], 105). Cf. Craig Blomberg's similar emphasis upon the importance of the evangelists' nimshalim in guiding readers into an appropriate interpretation ("The Parables of Jesus: Current Trends and Needs in Research," in *Studying the Historical Jesus: Evaluation of the State of Current Research* [ed. Bruce Chilton and Craig A. Evans; New York: E. J. Brill, 1994], 235).

[103] See Jeffery Staley, "'With the Power of the Spirit': Plotting the Program and Parallels of Luke 4:14–37," *SBL 1993 Seminar Papers*, 291.

[104] See Ringe, *Luke*, 71. Jesus' proclamation of healing to the infirm and liberation to captives (vv.18–19) quickly becomes a reality, even before the end of Chapter 4 (vv.31–44): the resistance he faces from the townspeople (vv.28–29) continues to intensify until his adversaries eventually include high ranking religious authorities and Roman governmental personnel; the threat of death in v.29 will eventually give way to a brutal, public execution (23:26–49); Jesus' narrow escape in v.30 by "passing through their midst" will be reenacted later on a much larger scale first with his resurrection from the dead and then with his "exit" (ἔξοδον; 9:31) from the earthly sphere altogether. Cf. Fitzmyer, *The Gospel According to Luke I–IX*, 529; Staley, "'With the Power of the Spirit': Plotting the Program and Parallels of Luke 4:14–37," 287.

for those of low status"[105] or possibly even describe the Jewish people as a whole[106] (as it does in Isa 61)? Do "the poor" include "the captives," "the blind," and "the oppressed," or is each group to be treated separately? Finally, are readers to expect *literal* release from captivity or debt, restoration of physical sight, and relief for the oppressed, or have we, with the citation from Isa 61 and 58, been presented with veiled references to forgiveness of sin[107] and spiritual enlightenment?[108]

Following Jesus' baptism (3:21–22) and temptation (4:1–13), the narrator informs us that Jesus returned to Galilee "in the power of the Spirit" and "began teaching" in synagogues to receptive audiences who were initially impressed by his words (4:14–15). The episode in Nazareth will offer readers one example of the kind of teaching in which he was engaged. Following a brief aside highlighting Jesus' regular attendance at Sabbath synagogue services, the narrator describes in great detail Jesus' reception and opening of an Isaiah scroll. The slowed pace focuses the reader's attention on Jesus' every move:[109] he stands; he receives the scroll; he unrolls it; he locates Isa 61:1–2 and 58:6; he rolls it back up; he hands it to the synagogue attendant; he sits down.[110] The centerpiece of the event, however, is the citation from Isaiah,[111] by which Jesus, now anointed with the Spirit (see 3:21–22), identifies himself as a herald appointed by God to bring good news to the poor and usher in a new era characterized by release, recovery

[105] Joel Green, *The Gospel of Luke* (NICNT; Grand Rapids: Eerdmans, 1997), 211.

[106] Seccombe, *Possessions and the Poor in Luke-Acts*, especially 19, 94–96.

[107] ἄφεσις (v.18) is used elsewhere in the Gospel to refer to forgiveness of sin (see 1:77; 11:4; *BDAG*, 155).

[108] ἀναβλέπω (v.18), although it can mean either acquiring the ability to see for the first time or recovering one's sight, has been used figuratively by some writers to refer to spiritual illumination (see especially John 9:11, 15, 18; *BDAG*, 59).

[109] J. Siker, "'First to the Gentiles': A Literary Analysis of Luke 4:16–30," *JBL* 111 (1992), 77–79.

[110] Oddly, at no point does the narrator tell us that Jesus actually read from the scroll, even though almost every other conceivable physical movement is noted (see Jean-Noël Aletti, "Jésus a Nazareth [Lc 4, 16–30]: Prophétie, Écriture et Typologie," in *À Cause de L'Évangile: Études sur les Synoptiques et les Actes offertes au P Jacques Dupont, OSB* [Paris: Éditions de Cerf, 1985], 435). However, given the narrator's previous remark that Jesus intends to read (I read ἀνέστη ἀναγνῶναι in v.16 as an infinitive of purpose) and Jesus' subsequent interpretation in v.21 ("This scripture has been fulfilled in your ears"), which would make little sense had he not actually read from the scroll, most readers will likely assume that Jesus did read aloud from Isa 61:1–2 and 58:6 (passages that once offered consolation and hope to Jewish exiles returning from Babylon).

[111] J. Siker ("'First to the Gentiles': A Literary Analysis of Luke 4:16–30") argues that one can locate Jesus' speech in vv.18–19 at the center of a chiasm (77).

of sight, and newfound freedom.[112] Because in vv.18–19 Jesus is citing Hebrew poetry, so often composed in parallel, complimentary stanzas where the second serves to reinforce or further clarify the first,[113] it is reasonable to view "the poor" (πτωχοῖς) as the *primary* designation for the intended recipients, whose make-up is then further delineated by the list that follows: "the captives"; "the blind"; "the oppressed." In effect, Jesus' initial statement—"He has anointed me to bring good news to the poor"—may be understood as a thesis that is subsequently expanded by a second statement—"He has sent me to preach release to the captives and recovery of sight to the blind, to set free the oppressed, and to preach a favorable year from the Lord"—which not only adds further dimension to the inclusive category of πτωχοί but informs readers of the ways in which this good news will be manifested.[114]

As all eyes gaze intently upon this son of Joseph and former resident of Nazareth, he sits down to offer the sermon,[115] which, quite unexpectedly, consists of a single sentence: "This scripture has been fulfilled in your ears" (v.21).[116] Since Jesus' comments on Isa 61 and 58 have been offered in the synagogue at Nazareth, readers may anticipate that (at least) those present for the Sabbath service have been designated recipients of the promised "release... recovery of sight... [and]

---

[112] While readers may immediately identify Jesus as the herald of Isa 61 in light of his recent baptism and the narrator's claim that, following the temptation in the wilderness, Jesus returned to the Galilee "in the power of the Spirit" (4:14), the townspeople, while likely intrigued and even encouraged by the possibility that such a person is close at hand, may have no idea that *Jesus* has just announced his prophetic role in inaugurating a new era. In fact, Jesus' sermon in v.21, while it may have caused a great deal of excitement, may also have left many utterly perplexed: "Of whom, exactly, is Joseph's son speaking? Is this 'anointed one' among us? Can we expect his arrival at some point in the near future?"

[113] Poetic verse in parallel structure is rhetorically effective especially in oral/aural cultures where texts are generally read aloud in public forums rather than in solitude. Because hearers often do not have a chance to return to and mull over prior passages, verse in parallel structure can help readers better comprehend what is being read by enabling them to stay with an idea, theme, concept, or image for a longer period of time.

[114] See, for instance, Hendrickx, *The Third Gospel for the Third World Volume Two-A: Ministry in Galilee (Luke 3:1–6:49)* (Collegeville, MN: The Liturgical Press, 1997), 129.

[115] Bovon notes that the synagogue sermon "was to be delivered sitting down" (*Luke* 1, 154).

[116] May we assume that Jesus offered a sermon of standard length but that we have been provided only with a brief summary? Cf. J. D. Crossan's speculative but insightful remark regarding Jesus' parables, which are often frustratingly yet tantalizingly terse: "[His parables] may well be no more than plot summaries of stories which might have taken hours to tell" ("Parable," in *ABD* V, 149).

freedom" (v.18). From what we know today about the small, rural hamlet of Nazareth,[117] the vast majority of the townspeople were likely peasant farmers engaged in the notoriously precarious occupation of subsistence agriculture and so could conceivably be classified among "the poor." Curiously, however, they will not be beneficiaries of Jesus' good news.[118] The people react in a hostile way to Jesus' words[119] and attempt to throw him off a nearby precipice. Readers must revise conjectures that favored the townspeople of Nazareth as recipients and continue their search.

Of special importance is the co-text[120] that follows in vv.31–44, where we receive our first glimpse of the beneficiaries of this "favorable

---

[117] See J. D. Crossan and Jonathan L. Reed, *Excavating Jesus: Beneath the Stones, Behind the Texts* (San Fransisco: HarperSanFransisco, 2001), especially 15–36.

[118] Aletti believes this pericope is essentially typological and functions to show readers that Jesus, because he is rejected by his own people, is to be counted among Israel's "true" prophets. Just as Elijah and Elisha (considered "true" prophets) were rejected by their own people (vv.25–27), so must Jesus be rejected by his people in order to confirm his status as an authentic spokesperson for God ("Jésus a Nazareth [Lc 4, 16–30]: Prophétie, Écriture et Typologie," 440–42). Thus, while the people of Nazareth may plausibly be numbered among "the poor" of Galilee, they will not receive the good news since "true" prophets—as a kind of rule of thumb for readers working with the LXX as their primary literary intertext—must be rejected by their own people (v.24).

[119] There is some discussion over whether the townspeople respond negatively to Jesus from the outset or whether Jesus brings the synagogue attendees' hostility on himself with a defensive posture and unprovoked retort: "Perhaps you will quote me this proverb, 'Doctor, heal yourself'!" (v.23) Part of the problem concerns the narrator's highly ambiguous statement in v.22, which is normally rendered: "And all spoke well of him and were amazed at the gracious words that were proceeding from his mouth." Such a translation which would fit well with the praise Jesus had already received by many throughout the countryside (see 4:15). However, one can render the statement so that Jesus receives a hostile response immediately after finishing his sermon: "And all spoke badly of him (where αὐτῷ would be a dative of disadvantage) and were astonished at the words about [God's] grace (where τῆς χάριτος would be an objective genitive rather than a descriptive genitive) that were proceeding from his mouth" (Michael Prior ["The Liberation Theology of the Lucan Jesus," *Liber Annuus* 49 [1999], 88] is one of the few who opts for this translation). Since one of the Gospel's objectives is to enhance Jesus' ethos (and not diminish it by portraying him as a cantankerous, paranoid herald), I much prefer viewing the narrator's remark in v.22 as a negative response, even if it is impossible to identify precisely why the townspeople react in this way to "good news." Prior has suggested that Jesus deliberately omits nationalistic and ethnocentric portions of Isaiah 61 and so incurs the people's wrath ("The Liberation Theology of the Lucan Jesus," 89). Jesus may also have deviated from a prescribed *haphtarah* reading first by truncating it and then by blending two passages (Isa 61:1–2 and 58:6), thereby incurring the audience's disapproval.

[120] For an excellent discussion of "co-text," see Joel Green, "Discourse Analysis and New Testament Interpretation," in *Hearing the New Testament: Strategies for Interpretation* (ed. Joel Green; Grand Rapids: Eerdmans, 1995), 183–84.

year" (v.19) and the nature of Jesus' program. Shortly after entering Capernaum, Jesus heals a man with an "unclean demon" (vv.31–37). This episode is followed by a brief account of the healing of Simon's mother-in-law (vv.38–39) and a diegetic summary that highlights Jesus' many exorcisms and his healing of the "various kinds of diseases" that plagued so many in the region (vv.40–41). Then, accosted by crowds who were seeking to prevent him from departing, Jesus announces that he "must bring good news (εὐαγγελίσασθαί με δεῖ) about the kingdom of God to other cities" (v.43), a statement reminiscent of his inaugural speech in vv.18–19 ("He anointed me to bring good news... [ἔχρισέν με εὐαγγελίσασθαι]").[121] This *inclusio* confirms for readers that they have just witnessed what "bringing good news to the poor" (v.18) will look like: it will involve teaching (ἐδίδασκεν; v.15) and preaching (κηρύξαι; v.18), to be sure, but also freeing people from demons and curing their illnesses (vv.31–44). Readers have just been introduced to the kind of people for whom the good news is intended (the sick and demon-possessed) and witnessed the sort of program Jesus plans to carry out in the remainder of the narrative (a ministry of healing and release).

Thus, from a literary perspective, one may argue that it is the sick and demon-possessed in vv.31–44 who, at least in part, constitute "the poor." Does this suggest that marginality or dishonorable status often associated with physical and mental illness should figure most prominently in defining οἱ πτωχοί and so overshadow the economic aspect of the term? Indeed, many commentators have opted for a more inclusive definition of πτωχοί that, while certainly "not devoid of economic significance,"[122] would include all those of low status or rank who had been relegated to the periphery of society.[123] However, given the kind of people Jesus meets in vv.31–44, I see no reason why readers at this point may not foreground as primary the economic valence of πτωχοί. While the narrator does not explicitly designate these people as "poor," the sick and demon-possessed, because of their physical or mental condition, were often unable to find occupations or participate in institutions that might allow for regular income. In fact, they were likely dependent

[121] Aletti, "Jésus a Nazareth (Lc 4, 16–30): Prophétie, Écriture et Typologie," 439. See also Ringe, "Luke 4:16–44—A Portrait of Jesus as Herald of God's Jubliee," 73–84.

[122] Green, *The Gospel of Luke*, 211.

[123] Ibid.; Johnson, *The Gospel of Luke*, 79. The general tendency among many commentators is exemplified by Bovon's remark: "Luke hardly understands the various categories of people in a merely literal sense..." (*Luke* 1, 154).

upon others for many of their basic needs, which would place them in a very precarious position economically. Moreover, in NT literature (especially in the Gospels), πτωχοί most often refers to the *literally* poor, those who are "economically disadvantaged... [and] dependent upon others for support."[124] And, since, as Herman Hendrickx has argued, "the rest of the Gospel depicts the poor as the literally poor," there is little reason to overshadow (or, as some have done, even displace) the economic implications of the term here. The "poor" of 4:18, who take center-stage in vv.31–44 as the sick and demon-possessed whom Jesus heals and sets free, are likely those "who are economically on the rocks."[125] This is not to say that one may not work with a more inclusive definition of "the poor" (i.e, those of low status and existing at the margins of society), but we need not eclipse the term's economic valence either.

What, then, appears to be Jesus' program for "the poor"? Many have observed that Jesus' citing of passages from Isa 61 and 58 recalls jubilary language and themes from Lev 25 and Deut 15:1–11,[126] but not all agree on whether Jesus is simply evoking utopian legislation from Israel's past as a way of foreshadowing in a very general way the kinds of deeds and reforms that will characterize his ministry or institute a literal year of jubilee when debts are forgiven, slaves are manumitted, and people are permitted to return to their family lands. J. H. Yoder, in his book *The Politics of Jesus*, has argued that Jesus did indeed advocate a one-time implementation of a jubliee year,[127] but the majority of scholars generally agree that, while the citation may recall jubilary themes, a literal prescription does not seem to fit the narrative context. In the ensuing chapters, Jesus does not work to enact jubilary legislation as presented in Deuteronomy or Leviticus. More likely, the citations from Isaiah constitute a "symbol or vision of the new age":[128] Jesus' preaching of the kingdom and his ministry of healing and release will reflect the same core values and vision assumed by Deuteronomic and Levitical jubliary legislation, which sought to even the playing field by repairing unequal relationships, redistributing resources that rightfully

[124] *BDAG*, 896.

[125] *The Third Gospel for the Third World Volume Two-A*, 122, 131.

[126] See, e.g., R. B. Sloan's book, *The Favourable Year of the Lord: A Study of Jubilary Theology in the Gospel of Luke* (Austin, TX: Schola Press, 1977).

[127] (2d ed.; Grand Rapids: Eedrmans, 1994).

[128] Hendrickx, *The Third Gospel for the Third World Volume Two-A*, 128.

belong to all, and offering a fresh start to those who had lost property and even their freedom. At this point in Luke's narrative, the reader cannot know precisely what Jesus' ministry will look like or how it will unfold, but by evoking jubilary language and themes and then offering readers a glimpse in vv.31–44 of what is to come, it seems clear that Jesus' mission will be geared first to improving the conditions of "the poor"[129] and not toward converting the wealthy[130] or training possessors in *Gottvertrauen.*[131]

3. *Delineating the Methodological Approach: Reader-Response Criticism, Narrative Criticism/Narratology, and Intertextuality*

a. *Reader-Response Criticism*

Reader-Response Criticism in Biblical Studies: Characteristics and Criticisms

Within the field of Biblical Studies, reader-oriented approaches have been theorized and applied in a variety of ways. Practitioners of reader-response criticism in particular, however, seem unified in their common aim of accounting for the role and/or experience of the reader as s/he moves sequentially through a text.[132] As one might expect, this shared objective receives a range of emphases: some focus on the search for meaning while others concentrate upon the twists and turns of the reading experience itself; some privy cognition and treat passages as riddles or puzzles that must be solved while others prioritize emotional impact; some view the text as a sure and steady guide that in large part determines how readers will react while others key in on indeterminacies or gaps and so leave room for a wide array of responses. In general, though, biblical critics have been rather

---

[129] This text has thus played an important role for many liberation theologians. See, e.g., M. Prior's comment: "The Lucan Nazareth text is an obvious one for developing a liberation theology. At the heart of contemporary liberation theologies is the urge to improve the lot of the poor and the oppressed" ("The Liberation Theology of the Lucan Jesus," 91).

[130] See, e.g., Seccombe, *Possessions and the Poor in Luke-Acts*, 195.

[131] See Schmidt, *Hostility to Wealth in the Synoptic Gospels*, 136, 161.

[132] See, e.g., James Resseguie, "Reader-Response Criticism and the Synoptic Gospels," *Journal of the American Academy of Religion* 52 (1984), 307; Edgar McKnight, "Reader-Response Criticism," in *Biblical Criticisms and Their Application: To Each its Own Meaning* (ed. Steven L. McKenzie and Stephen R. Haynes; Louisville: Westminster John Knox Press, 1999), 230.

conservative in their appropriation and application of this approach. For instance, they have drawn heavily on the work of text-centered theorists such as Wolfgang Iser and (early) Stanley Fish to the exclusion of subjectivist theorists like Norman Holland and David Bleich and employed universal reader constructs such as implied, ideal, or informed readers rather than real readers. In short, while a range of emphases within biblical reader-response criticism may be found, it seems that "New Testament critics who have grappled with the issue of reading have tended to stay close to shore."[133] Confirmation may be found in a brief survey of introductory articles and select studies[134] on reader-response criticism in Biblical Studies.

Several excellent introductory articles on reader-response criticism have appeared over the last two decades. Articles authored by Edgar McKnight,[135] Robert Fowler,[136] James Resseguie,[137] and Kevin Vanhoozer[138] are especially helpful for including sections on theory and demonstrations of how the critical approach might be applied, in each case to passages from the Synoptic Gospels.

Drawing primarily upon the work of Iser, Edgar McKnight traces the cognitive and emotional responses of an implied reader, pausing frequently to identify major themes and assess the "overall meaning" of short narrative units.[139] McKnight's ultimate goal, it appears, is to "make sense."[140] While, like Fish, McKnight does engage in "a slow-motion

---

[133] Moore, *Literary Criticism and the Gospels*, 73.

[134] Given the focus of this book, I will look primarily at studies on the Gospel of Luke. Reader-response analyses have focused in large part on the Synoptic Gospels, though not exclusively so. For instance, studies have appeared on the Pauline letters (Brendan J. Byrne, *Reckoning with Romans: A Contemporary Reading of Paul's Gospel* [Good News Studies 18; Wilmington, DE: Michael Glazier, 1986]) and on the Catholic Epistles as well (Randall C. Weber, *Reader-Response Analysis of the Epistle of James* [San Francisco: International Scholars Publications, 1996]). Even a few introductory textbooks to the New Testament now make use of reader-response criticism in some form (See, e.g., Russel Pregeant, *Engaging the New Testament: An Interdisciplinary Approach* [Minneapolis: Fortress Press, 1997]).

[135] "Reader-Response Criticism": 230–52.

[136] "Reader-Response Criticism: Figuring Mark's Reader," in *Mark & Method: New Approaches in Biblical Studies* (ed. Janice Capel Anderson and Stephen D. Moore; Minneapolis: Fortress Press, 1992): 50–83.

[137] "Reader-Response Criticism and the Synoptic Gospels": 307–24.

[138] "The Reader in New Testament Interpretation," in *Hearing the New Testament: Strategies for Interpretation* (ed. Joel B. Green; Grand Rapids: Eerdmans, 1995): 301–28.

[139] "Reader-Response Criticism," 243, 246.

[140] Ibid., 245. See also his introductory comments, where he defines reader-response in terms of the reader's role in creating "meaning and significance" (230).

process of reading,"[141] priority is not given to the actual experience of the reader for its own sake but to discerning a "meaning." However, unlike those working in a New Critical mode (where the text is treated as autonomous and therefore analyzed apart from its historical and social milieu), McKnight argues for a reader-oriented approach that does not preclude sound historical and sociological work.[142] In fact, according to McKnight, even the historical author and his or her intention may remain a legitimate research avenue, although for reader-response critics it becomes "penultimate."[143]

Following Fish, Robert Fowler proceeds sequentially and slows down the reading process, focusing not on hurrying toward the end or formulating a "point" but on the "intriguing journey."[144] He pays careful attention to how readers identify and fill gaps, form expectations and subsequently confirm or revise them in light of new information, reconstruct verbal and dramatic/situational irony, and respond to statements or episodes that "seem to say something but then take it back."[145] While Fowler does not work with a real reader, he does acknowledge that readers' responses may be plotted along a continuum from assent to resistance. One may, for instance, try to set aside biases, predispositions, and commitments in order to (at least temporarily) accept and learn from the work's evaluative point of view, or one may consistently resist oppressive rhetoric throughout. Ultimately, for Fowler, reader-response criticism "helps readers read with greater awareness and self-consciousness...which can lead us to take greater personal responsibility for our reading and our response."[146]

James Resseguie draws both upon Fish's moment-by-moment, clause-by-clause, word-by-word reading program and upon Iser's notions of defamiliarization, theme and horizon, consistency-building, anticipation and retrospection, and textual gaps (which one must fill in order to create a coherent work). Following Iser, meaning for Resseguie represents "the text's intention," and though several realizations of the text are possible, "they are always implied and circumscribed by the text."[147]

---

[141] Ibid., 244.
[142] Ibid., 240.
[143] Ibid., 248.
[144] "Reader-Response Criticism: Figuring Mark's Reader," 56–57.
[145] Ibid., 70. The phrase in quotation marks refers to Stanley Fish's "self-consuming artifact."
[146] Ibid., 81.
[147] "Reader-Response Criticism and the Synoptic Gospels," 322.

Finally, Kevin Vanhoozer, before laying out his own position on reader-response criticism, briefly surveys and classifies approaches currently used in Biblical Studies. There are, he argues, both "conservative" and "radical" reader-response practitioners in the field: while conservative critics make use of a reader inscribed in or implied by the text and emphasize the importance of "textual constraints" that restrict the reader's activity to simply "receiving... [and] surrendering oneself to the text," radical critics privilege the reader's role in *producing* meaning and so make "the reader into a writer."[148] For radical critics, meaning is not a textual property but, as Fish later argued, "a function of the community to which he or she belongs."[149] Vanhoozer locates himself among those conservative critics whose primary obligation, he believes, is to guard the text's unique voice and "communicative aim," which is to be received "on its own terms" and "according to its nature and intention."[150]

Many biblical critics have drawn upon reader-response criticism in some form, and it would be impossible here to account for even a majority of its applications. Instead, I will introduce only three studies, all of which are in some way related to the subject matter of this book: John Darr's *On Character Building: The Reader and the Rhetoric of Characterization in Luke-Acts*;[151] Robert Brawley's *Centering on God: Method and Message in Luke-Acts*;[152] and John Paul Heil's "Reader-Response and the Narrative Context of the Parables about Growing Seed in Mark 4:1–34."[153]
John Darr, who hopes to "re-enact how Luke-Acts was first read,"[154] works with a highly informed first-time reader and "culturally literate member of the late first-century Mediterranean world."[155] S/he, for instance, is "at home in popular Greco-Roman literature," possesses "an intimate knowledge of the Jewish scriptures in Greek," understands "the cultural scripts and norms" of the Mediterranean world, and is

[148] "The Reader in New Testament Interpretation," 309–11.
[149] Ibid., 311.
[150] Ibid., 316–18, 325.
[151] (Literary Currents in Biblical Interpretation; Louisville: Westminster/John Knox Press, 1992).
[152] (Literary Currents in Biblical Interpretation; Louisville: Westminster/John Knox Press, 1990).
[153] *CBQ* 54 (1992): 271–86.
[154] *On Character Building*, 36.
[155] Ibid., 27.

broadly familiar with "basic historical, political, geographical, and ethnic facts about the Roman Empire, and about how that empire functions both militarily and politically."[156] Darr does acknowledge that his reader is to some degree a reflection of his own predispositions and cultural horizon,[157] but it is also implied by the text. It is therefore a "hybrid reader," "part ancient" and "part modern."[158] Darr's reading process is closely modeled on Iser's: in search of a coherent "work," he moves sequentially through the text by filling gaps and trying to "'fit everything together.'"[159] A stable text constrains the reading process and allows only for a "range of critically acceptable interpretations."[160] In fact, for Darr, there appears to be very little room for co-creation on the reader's part since s/he is so often "bombarded with an array of rhetorical weaponry" and "positioned and maneuvered—indeed, shaped—by the rhetoric of the text."[161] The reader, in the end, does not seem to play much of a role at all: s/he simply follows rhetorical cues carefully laid out in advance by the author.

While Robert Brawley draws upon a number of methods in his analysis of Luke-Acts (e.g., structuralism and narratology), he turns to Iser for his notions of "progressive discovery" and the "unformulated text." "Progressive discovery" is the process by which an interpreter moves through the text sequentially in search of how themes develop and characters gradually take shape.[162] The "unformulated text" is all that "is presumed but left unsaid"[163] but must nevertheless be filled in so as to move from the written text to a fully coherent work. Ideally, information for filling these textual vacancies is to be drawn from

---

[156] Ibid., 27–28.

[157] Ibid., 25. Darr, for instance, elsewhere writes: "Readers to whom critics refer are heuristic constructs that inevitably mirror the persons who construe them" (170).

[158] Ibid., 26.

[159] Ibid., 30–31.

[160] Ibid., 20.

[161] Ibid., 53, 59. Cf. similar comments in his article "'Watch How you Listen' (Luke 8.18),'" in *The New Literary Criticism and the New Testament* (ed. Elizabeth S. Malbon and Edgar V. McKnight; JSSNTSS 109; Sheffield; Sheffield Academic Press, 1994), especially 87, 95, 98. Darr here emphasizes how Luke's rhetoric has been designed to constrain or "control" readers' responses.

[162] See especially the brief illustrative section in Chapter 9 of *Centering on God* where he amasses "a set of interpretive notes following a stream of consciousness" based on a reading of the Parable of the Good Samaritan (214).

[163] Ibid., 159.

historical data, cultural codes, and literary conventions and parallels from the first century Mediterranean world.[164]

J. P. Heil traces the responses of an implied reader to the parables in Mark 4. Following (early) Fish, he is particularly interested in "what the text does to and how it *affects* the imagined reader that it presupposes, that is, what the text causes its 'implied reader' to experience in order to create the meaning latent in the text and thus to bring its act of communication to completion."[165] For Heil, then, not only is "meaning" embedded in a stable text, but its rhetoric has been designed to affect readers in a very precise way. The reader, in short, is maneuvered by the text and simply responds on cue to its rhetoric.

While far from comprehensive, I hope that the foregoing survey of introductory articles and select studies based on the Synoptic Gospels has helped generate a tenable sketch of reader-response criticism in Biblical Studies. Generally, biblical reader-response critics have preferred universal and ancient reader constructs to real readers and emphasized a text's rhetorical power to maneuver its reader into a prescribed, pre-structured response. By working to "fit everything together" and "make sense," the ultimate goal is to eliminate gaps or vacancies in the text in order to fashion a fully coherent and unified work. Meaning is largely pre-structured in a stable text, and the interpreter's job is to uncover one of its many possible realizations.

This relatively uniform and conservative application of the method has elicited criticism from within the discipline, most notably from Stephen Moore.[166] While Moore believes reader-response criticism has much to offer as "the best analogue available to the modern exegete of the psychodynamics of the oral-aural encounter that would have constituted the original noetic horizon in which the Gospels were written and received,"[167] he laments its tendency to eschew subjectivism in favor of textual constraints, overemphasize the cognitive to the neglect of the emotional, and eliminate ambiguity or polyvalence as quickly

---

[164] Ibid. See especially Chapter 7. This is the functional equivalent of Wolfgang Iser's "repertoire" or Roland Barthes's "cultural codes."

[165] "Reader-Response and the Narrative Context of the Parables about Growing Seed in Mark 4:1–34," 272.

[166] *Literary Criticism and the Gospels*, especially Chapters 6 and 7.

[167] Moore also includes among the method's advantages its treatment of the textual encounter as "as a dynamic event rather than as static object" and its ability to make "the implicit features of our critical reading explicit by narrativizing our standard moves" (106).

as it arises in search of coherence and consistency.[168] Furthermore, he argues, biblical critics have generally downplayed or even ignored aspects of Iser's and Fish's work that grant priority to real readers in fashioning meaning. Many, for instance, have "seized on the undifferentiated, prescriptive side of Iser's implied reader—its textually defined, manipulated side—and relegated its individualistic, actual reader side to the margins."[169] Moreover, when biblical critics refer to Fish's work, they tend to concentrate on his earlier, formalist criticism and overlook more recent essays, where texts "have no status whatsoever independent of interpretive acts"[170] and "formal features" are ascribed solely to interpreters. In Fish's later work, full interpretive authority is thus awarded to individuals—now writers and not readers—situated within reading communities, each with their own sets of assumptions and hermeneutical strategies.[171] In short, argues Moore, with its focus on tracing the pre-structured responses of implied, informed, or ideal readers, "reader-response criticism in gospel studies is largely an extension of narrative criticism."[172]

Reader-response criticism has its fair share of critics outside the discipline of Biblical Studies as well. Some are willing to admit that the reader-response movement offered a significant step forward over formalist modes of criticism by shifting ultimate responsibility for the production of meaning away from the so-called "formal features" of texts to readers,[173] but many others felt that it fell far short of actually doing so. Interpretive authority was not, in fact, transferred from texts to readers, since the readers to whom most critics referred were merely idealized

[168] See especially 77, 81, 83–84, 92, 106, 110.

[169] Ibid., 102.

[170] Ibid., 117.

[171] The beginning of Fish's shift "from a method of reading in which the reader is constrained by objective features in the text to a theory of reading in which the reader is constrained only by his or her situation in a community with shared interpretive premises" (Ibid., 112) may be found in his now famous 1976 essay entitled "Interpreting the *Variorum*" (Reprinted in *Reader-Response Criticism: From Formalism to Post-Structuralism* [ed. Jane P. Tompkins; Baltimore: Johns Hopkins, 1980]: 164–84).

[172] Ibid., 73.

[173] Vincent B. Leitch, *American Literary Criticism from the Thirties to the Eighties* (New York: Columbia University Press, 1988), 231. Cf. Jane P. Tompkins, "An Introduction to Reader-Response Criticism" and "The Reader in History: The Changing Shape of Literary Response," in *Reader-Response Criticism: From Formalism to Post-Structuralism*, xxv, 225. Todd F. Davis and Kenneth Womack call reader-response criticism "one of the principal driving forces behind the advent of the cultural studies movement" (*Formalist Criticism and Reader-Response Theory* [New York: Palgrave, 2002], 155).

constructs implied by or inscribed within texts. Readers, they argued, should not be abstracted from texts but considered in relation to their various social and political locations and ideological commitments.[174] In addition to working with depoliticized, universal reader constructs, the reader-response movement also tended to dehistoricize literary texts by detaching them from their contexts of production.[175] The effect of reading texts apart from their social and material matrices was to make them into aesthetic objects of consumption "'available for privatized leisure use.'"[176] Others, particularly deconstructionists, have criticized reader-response criticism for treating reading as a "'means toward an end'—the end of a 'hermeneutically successful reading'"—where everything is supposed to fit together and make sense.[177] Still others have keyed in on what many see as a "liberal humanist ideology" at work, particularly in Iser's reception theory. According to Terry Eagleton, Iser believes that "we should be flexible and open-minded, prepared to put our beliefs into question and allow them to be transformed."[178] Readers, therefore, with strong ideological commitments may be inadequate to the task of reading since they are "less likely to be open to the transformative power of literary works."[179] Indeed, it appears that Iser, who does view reading as a means for intellectual and personal growth, did not consider the possibility that certain writings are infused with an oppressive rhetoric that, from an ethical perspective, ought to be resisted from the outset.[180]

---

[174] Andrew Bennett, "Introduction," in *Readers and Reading*, 4.

[175] I have loosely paraphrased Mary Louise Pratt's remarks in "Interpretive Strategies/Strategic Interpretations: On Anglo-American Reader-Response Criticism" (1982) as quoted by Leitch (*American Literary Criticism*, 229).

[176] Ibid.

[177] Bennett, "Introduction," in *Readers and Reading*, 4, 11. The single quotation marks demarcate phrases in Paul de Man's "Introduction" (Hans Robert Jauss, *Toward an Aesthetic of Reception* [trans. Timothy Bahti; Brighton: Harvester Press, 1982], ix). Terry Eagleton criticizes Iser for seeking to gradually eliminate gaps and inconsistencies in order to construct a coherent, unified, consistent work. Eagleton writes: "Textual indeterminacies just spur us on to the act of abolishing them, replacing them with a stable meaning. They must, in Iser's revealingly authoritarian term, be 'normalized'—tamed and subdued to some firm structure of sense" (*Literary Theory: An Introduction* [2d ed.; Minneapolis: University of Minnesota Press, 1996], 71).

[178] Eagleton, *Literary Theory*, 69.

[179] Ibid.

[180] Such is Judith Fetterly's approach (*The Resisting Reader: A Feminist Approach to American Fiction* [Bloomington: Indiana University Press, 1978]), who argues that a feminist reader of the American novel ought to "'become a resisting rather than an assenting reader

In light of these criticisms, reader-response as a discipline has matured considerably. While the later work of Fish, Bleich, and Holland began to acknowledge the role social and political forces play on today's situated and ideologically committed readers,[181] only recently have reader-response analyses explored what this "epistemological revolution... to repoliticize literature and literary criticism"[182] might look like. For instance, a recent volume edited by Patrocinio P. Schweickart and Elizabeth A. Flynn[183] examines reading "as a cultural practice in a variety of contexts" and therefore "from the point of view of actual readers in concrete situations."[184] Kenneth M. Roemer, in *Utopian Audiences: How Readers Locate Nowhere*,[185] explores how "actual readers" have responded to E. Bellamy's *Looking Backward*, bearing in mind that "meaning creation is constrained, guided, and encouraged by powerful cultural, historical, and personal situations and forces" such as "gender roles," "literacy rates," "interpretive communities," and "almost infinite varieties of individual psychologies."[186] Within Biblical Studies, one may point to the recent volume edited by Ingrid R. Kitzberger, *The Personal Voice in Biblical Interpretation*,[187] which "testifies to the irruption of the 'I' within the critical task and to the insertion of a personal point of view."[188] Although Kitzberger refers to this collection of essays as "autobiographical" or "personal voice criticism," it clearly reflects

---

and, by this refusal to assent, to begin the process of exorcizing the male mind that has been implanted in us'" (xxii; Quoted in Leitch, *American Literary Criticism*, 227).

[181] Leitch writes: "In its later stages reader-response criticism often broke through its earlier limiting personalism and narcissism, catching glimpses of the impersonal sociological and cultural forces that conditioned the self and its activities" (*American Literary Criticism*, 236). Specific examples include Fish's notion of interpretive communities and strategies, Holland's acknowledgement that "'culture enables and limits the individual,'" and Bleich's admission that knowledge "'finds itself, at least in part, under the authority of communal and societal motives'" (*The I* [149] and *Subjective Criticism* [265], respectively; Quoted in Leitch, *American Literary Criticism*, 236).

[182] Tompkins, "An Introduction to Reader-Response Criticism," in *Reader-Response Criticism: From Formalism to Post-Structuralism*, xxv.

[183] *Reading Sites: Social Difference and Reader-Response.*

[184] Schweickhart and Flynn, "Introduction," in *Reading Sites*, 10.

[185] (Boston: University of Massachusetts Press, 2003).

[186] See 4–6. Because Roemer will "place much more emphasis on representations of actual historical and modern readers" than did American reader-response critics of the late 1970s and early 1980s, he draws upon "relatively large samples of living readers who come from different backgrounds—different enough to reflect some of the cultural, historical, and personal variables that constrain, guide, and encourage readers to accept, reject, ignore, or transform textual invitations" (6).

[187] (New York: Routledge, 1999).

[188] 2.

reader-response criticism's concern to account for the role a reader—one whose socio-historical context is here taken into account—plays in producing meaning. Kitzberger identifies four assumptions that all of the articles in this volume share: 1) texts are not autonomous or self-sufficient but open; 2) "*all critical readings are actually based on ordinary readings*"; 3) texts are by nature polyvalent and will therefore elicit multiple readings; and 4) the "*ethical dimension of all interpretations*" is of central importance (rather than, for instance, whether a given interpretation "correctly" reflects how first century Mediterranean persons might have heard a given passage). In light of how Kitzberger has characterized these essays, it is clear that the criticisms leveled at reader-response critics from within literary, philosophical, and cultural studies have begun to be acknowledged and engaged.

Reader-Response Criticism as Appropriated for this Study Below, I will offer a brief description of how reader-response criticism will be appropriated and employed in this study. Special attention will be given to two questions: 1) Which elements from the work of biblical reader-response critics and from the reading programs[189] of Stanley Fish and Wolfgang Iser will be retained?; and 2) In light of the foregoing criticisms of reader-response criticism advanced from within Biblical Studies and from without, what modifications to the method will be made? I will first describe the approach in very general terms and then identify which aspects of Fish's and Iser's programs in particular will be retained and which will be modified or omitted.

Broadly speaking, the reading will proceed sequentially and cumulatively. First, each word or phrase will be processed in sequence and in accord with the temporal flow of the reading process and therefore attentive to the specific ordering of each event in relation to the Gospel's plot.[190] Second, judgments, expectations, and attitudes generated

[189] To be more precise, while Fish does refer to his version of reader-response criticism as a "method" ("Literature in the Reader: Affective Stylistics," in *Reader-Response Criticism: From Formalism to Post-Structuralism*, 74), Iser's is better described as a phenomenology of reading.

[190] This procedure, Moore argues, "is the best analogue available to the modern exegete of the psychodynamics of the oral-aural encounter that would have constituted the original noetic horizon in which the Gospels were written and received," that is, before the emergence of the lectionary tradition, which parceled the Gospels into discreet reading units isolated from their larger narrative contexts (*Literary Criticism and the Gospels*, 92).

during the reading process will determine how forthcoming sections of the Gospel will be heard and experienced. Conversely, new experiences and information will shape how past units have been received.[191] Third, I will pause occasionally to assess how larger rhetorical units are taking shape and what overall impact they may have.[192] All three of these features are part of reader-response criticism as traditionally conceived. In light of recent criticisms, however, this study will employ a situated, committed flesh-and-blood reader, account for the literary, social, and material matrices of the world to which the text refers,[193] and proceed with the awareness that all narrative elements or features so identified have been imposed on the text from without and do not inhere within the text itself.

Aspects of Stanley Fish's Reading Method Relevant for this Study I have found Fish's program (presented succinctly in "Literature in the Reader: Affective Stylistics" and "Interpreting the *Variorum*") to be particularly helpful as "a language sensitizing device," which slows down the reading experience so as to raise to awareness events that may not elicit attention in "normal time," and so will retain several of its foci for this study.[194] Fish broadly defines his method as a moment-by-moment, word-by-word "*analysis of the developing responses of the reader in relation to the words as they succeed one another in time.*"[195] Of central importance, however, is his assertion that the *experience* of reading should remain the focus of description and analysis. Instead of focusing on a text's so-called "formal features," "the reader's activities are at the center of attention,

[191] To employ Iser's language, as each theme is engaged, the horizon—a repository of decisions, revisions, expectations, and attitudes at a certain point during the reading experience—will be reconstituted. This horizon, always in flux, becomes the foundation from which the next theme is encountered. See, e.g., Resseguie's concise summary in "Reader-Response Criticism and the Synoptic Gospels," 319–20. Cf. Iser's own remark: "The basic idea of theme and horizon can be strikingly illuminated by poems, where the reading of the second stanza occurs against the background or horizon of the first and is conditioned by it" (*Prospecting: From Reader-Response to Literary Anthropology* [Baltimore: The Johns Hopkins University Press, 1989], 54).

[192] McKnight engages in a similar task ("Reader-Response Criticism," 240–47), though he prioritizes establishing "the overall meaning" (243) of narrative units and 'making sense' (245). I have deliberately left this third aspect of the process a bit vague so as to allow for other factors to assume center stage, e.g., emotional effect.

[193] I am interested not in the hypothetical social location of the author(s) and his or her community but in the world about which the story speaks.

[194] "Literature in the Reader: Affective Sylistics," in *Reader-Response Criticism: From Formalism to Post-Structuralism,* 74, 98.

[195] Ibid., 73.

where they are regarded, not as leading to meaning, but as *having* meaning."[196] While, like Fish and Iser, I take for granted that many readers seek to "make sense," if such "sense" does not emerge, one is still left with the experience of, for instance, having worked through a particular problem, empathized with certain characters, or been introduced to new ethical possibilities through a protagonist's actions. Meaning-making need not be what drives the reading process.[197] The interpreter, while certainly not abandoning the quest for meaning, rather places in the foreground the question, "[W]hat does this word, phrase, sentence, paragraph... *do*?"[198] Asking "[W]hat does this sentence mean?"[199] is by no means ruled out entirely but considered secondary. Included in the description and analysis will be "the making and revising of judgments, the rendering and regretting of judgments, the coming to and abandoning of conclusions, the giving and withdrawing of approval, the specifying of causes, the asking of questions, the supplying of answers, and the solving of puzzles."[200] In short, emphasis will remain on describing not formal features but "a moving field of concerns, at once wholly present (not waiting for meaning, but constituting meaning) and continually in the act of reconstituting itself."[201]

A few elements of Fish's earlier work will not be appropriated, however. For instance, in "Literature in the Reader: Affective Stylistics," Fish argues that one's approach to the hermeneutical task should be "rigorous and disinterested" and that all that is "personal and idiosyncratic" should deliberately be suppressed in the interest of recording the responses of a reader-construct he calls an "informed reader." The responses of this "informed reader" represent how most real readers who seek to acquaint themselves with issues of genre, literary conventions, etc. will experience the text.[202] Fish later dispensed with "the assumption that there *is* a sense that... is embedded or encoded in the

[196] "Interpreting the *Variorum*," in *Reader-Response Criticism: From Formalism to Post-Structuralism*, 172.

[197] Contrast McKnight, "Reader-Response Criticism," where the search for "meaning and significance" assumes center-stage (230).

[198] "Literature in the Reader: Affective Stylistics," in *Reader-Response Criticism: From Formalism to Post-Structuralism*, 73.

[199] Ibid., 72.

[200] "Interpreting the *Variorum*," in *Reader-Response Criticism: From Formalism to Post-Structuralism*, 172.

[201] Ibid.

[202] "Literature in the Reader: Affective Stylistics," in *Reader-Response Criticism: From Formalism to Post-Structuralism*, 73, 86–87.

text"[203] and placed ultimate authority in the hands of a situated and interested interpreter, who approaches the text with specific strategies "'not for reading...but for writing texts.'"[204] Interpreters acquire these strategies from the communities to which they belong. So, like the later Fish, I here view all so-called "formal features" as "a function of the interpretive model one brings to bear," "constituted by an interpretive act."[205] No longer embedded in the text and simply awaiting recovery, such "features" are produced by readers.

Aspects of Wolfgang Iser's Phenomenology of Reading Relevant for this Study

While Iser does not engage in the kind of moment-by-moment close-reading characteristic of Fish's program, he does conceive of reading as a dynamic event that proceeds sequentially and cumulatively. Moreover, like Fish, Iser emphasizes a text's many "unexpected twists and turns,"[206] how characters take shape and storylines gradually unfold,[207] and how expectations fare when the reader is presented with a new episode or scene—whether, for instance, one's preliminary judgments are confirmed or shattered and subsequently revised.[208] Iser's description of what actually transpires when we read, in fact, is not unlike that proposed by Fish: "We look forward, we look back, we decide, we change our decisions, we form expectations, we are shocked by their nonfulfillment, we question, we muse, we accept, we reject; this is the dynamic process of recreation."[209] The above emphases from Iser's approach will be retained for this study.

Additionally, though with some modification, I will make use of Iser's notions of textual vacancies or gaps, consistency-building, and *Konkretisation*.

According to Iser, gaps and indeterminacies, which in large part appear to be pre-structured in texts and so part of their original design,

---

[203] "Interpreting the *Variorum*," in *Reader-Response Criticism: From Formalism to Post-Structuralism*, 172.

[204] Davis and Womack, *Formalist Criticism and Reader-Response Theory*, 84.

[205] "Interpreting the *Variorum*," in *Reader-Response Criticism: From Formalism to Post-Structuralism*, 176–77.

[206] "The Reading Process: A Phenomenological Approach," in *Reader-Response Criticism: From Formalism to Post-Structuralism*, 55.

[207] This is what R. L. Brawley calls "progressive discovery."

[208] Iser classifies this second aspect under "anticipation and retrospection" ("The Reading Process: A Phenomenological Approach," in *Reader-Response Criticism: From Formalism to Post-Structuralism*, 55, 61).

[209] Ibid., 62.

invite the reader to fill in the "unwritten" portions of texts.[210] The process of filling gaps or resolving indeterminacies, which for Iser necessarily involves "our own preconceptions," is "always accompanied by 'alien associations'" that threaten to unsettle or even undermine the emerging, coherent work.[211] Iser has been unfairly charged by some with seeking to eliminate ambiguity and close up gaps as soon as they arise. I would argue, however, he is simply acknowledging that readers, when presented with gaps and indeterminacies, must at some point make a choice in order to move forward. Never is ambiguity completed eliminated, for these lingering "associations" do remain and remind the interpreter that his or her reading is only just an "illusion." For Iser, in fact, all reading is "a process of trial and error" that involves the "building and breaking of *illusions*" (italics mine).[212] This study will incorporate one significant change to Iser's understanding of gaps and indeterminacies: they will be viewed as constructs imposed from without by the reader rather than elements that inhere within texts themselves.

Iser's conception of consistency-building has also received an unfair blow. As a phenomenologist of reading, Iser is simply accounting for what he believes most readers do, whether on a conscious or unconscious level: "fit everything together" in order to make sense.[213] Consistency-building is not necessarily a *goal* of the reading process but an activity that, at least on some level, does take place for many (though certainly not all) readers. Some readers may, for instance, empathize with a particular character, laugh or cry, "enjoy the sensuous beauty of a line," or "freely associate to a text"[214] and relegate sense-making to the periphery (if engage in it at all!). Furthermore, Iser does acknowledge that "we project" or "impose" consistency onto texts.[215] When faced with works like those of Beckett, for instance, which seem to resist comprehension and consistency, it is not uncommon for readers to "mount a massive operation of meaning-projection in order to

---

[210] *Prospecting*, 10, 21–22, 28.

[211] "The Reading Process: A Phenomenological Approach," in *Reader-Response Criticism: From Formalism to Post-Structuralism*, 55, 60–61.

[212] Ibid., 62.

[213] "The Reading Process: A Phenomenological Approach," in *Reader-Response Criticism: From Formalism to Post-Structuralism*, 58.

[214] I am here drawing upon (and quoting from) Norman Holland's criticisms of Iser's approach (*Prospecting*, 47). Cf. Wayne Booth's similar critique (*Prospecting*, 57–58).

[215] "The Reading Process: A Phenomenological Approach," in *Reader-Response Criticism: From Formalism to Post-Structuralism*, 58–59.

haul texts back within the limits of normal thinking."[216] Certainly not all readers prioritize consistency-building over empathic identification, aesthetic experience, or free association, but I must acknowledge that such a process does take place within this reader, very often "below the threshold of ... consciousness."[217] Consistency-building, therefore, will not be viewed as a goal of the reading process but a frank admission of a certain unavoidable psychodynamic within this study's reader. Nor will it be sought at the expense of hastily overwriting ambiguity or marching confidently past moments of undecidability. Consistency will not be forced.[218]

Konkretisation, for Iser, is the process of realizing the text or making explicit one of its many possible performances. As a consequence of an ongoing dialogical relationship between text and reader, we *produce* a "work," which is "more than the text" and represents the merger "of text and imagination."[219] There is one text but many works, each a reflection of "the individual mind of the reader with its own particular history of experience, its own consciousness, its own outlook."[220] Admittedly, Iser does view the resultant work as an echo of "the intention of the text,"[221] as something that lies buried or inheres within the text. Nevertheless, his notion of Konkretisation pushes readers to consider that they are entering into dialogue with someone or something other than themselves—a unique, sometimes foreign and distant, voice. Given that we have the tendency to "read the other in our own being and likeness,"[222] it is important to try as best we can to listen, even if we must simultaneously concede that *we* construct this voice with whom we are engaged. While I cannot agree with Iser's understanding of the

216 *Prospecting*, 27–28.

217 *Prospecting*, 53.

218 Admittedly, consistency-building for Iser appears to approach a goal of reading when he claims to have constructed "an idealized model of text-processing along phenomenological lines" (Ibid., 49). If his description reflects an 'ideal,' then consistency-building may indeed be something readers should pursue. However, in light of Holland's criticisms, Iser seems to allow for multiple reading experiences, some that do prioritize cognition and the solving of puzzles but others that privilege aesthetic experience or empathic identification with a character (Ibid., 53–54).

219 "The Reading Process: A Phenomenological Approach," in *Reader-Response Criticism: From Formalism to Post-Structuralism*, 50, 52, 54.

220 Ibid., 59.

221 *Prospecting*, 28.

222 Fernando F. Segovia, "Reading Readers of the Fourth Gospel and Their Readings," in *What is John? Vol. 1* (ed. Fernando F. Segovia; SBL Symposium Series 3; Atlanta: Scholars Press, 1996), 238.

text as an objective, stable object—a rigid "skeletal framework"[223] that is simply filled out in different ways by different readers—Iser's notion of Konkretisation encourages readers to see and engage a text that is truly *other*, a unique voice that may challenge, undermine, frustrate, oppress, encourage, inspire, or educate.[224] Thus, the emergent "work" stems from a genuine encounter between the reader and an *other*—in this case, a culturally and historically distant text. Konkretisation, moreover, reminds readers that any text is a "culturally produced producer"[225]—a voice shaped by its environment but one that in turn plays a part in shaping its readers. So, although Iser's conception of the text as a stable object that in some sense already "contains" its future realizations will not be retained, his emphasis on trying as best one can to "hear" a unique voice is appreciated,[226] even if the voice of this *other* is ultimately created by (and must be attributed to) the reader.[227]

---

[223] Darr, *On Character Building*, 18.

[224] I am following Fernando F. Segovia here by placing "other" in italics rather than in quotation marks as a way of "signifying a positive sense of otherness" (*Decolonizing Biblical Studies: A View from the Margins* [Maryknoll: Orbis, 2000], 97).

[225] See, e.g., Tat-siong Benny Liew, *Politics of Parousia: Reading Mark Inter(con)textually* (Boston: Brill, 1999), 39–44.

[226] Cf. Fernando F. Segovia's similar emphasis on treating ancient texts "as realities from a very different social and historical context that are to be acknowledged, respected, and engaged rather than overridden and overwhelmed" (*Decolonizing Biblical Studies*, 97). Of course, Fernando Segovia's intercultural criticism, "grounded in a hermeneutics of otherness and engagement," goes far beyond Iser's mere assertion that we are engaged with a unique voice that has the potential to unsettle, challenge, or expose the reader to new ways of seeing the world (Ibid., especially 97–115).

[227] I should add one point of clarification here. At no point will the text itself be invested with an ideological or rhetorical power of its own apart from the hermeneutical process. Yet, in order for one to initiate a dialogue, a voice of some sort must be constructed, even if such a construction has its origins in a thoroughly interested 21st century reader. Some critics today, for instance, will label books or passages in the Bible as *inherently* patriarchal, infused with an immasculating rhetoric that must be resisted. But not all readers—many of them women—would agree. A text becomes patriarchal only at the moment an interpreter labels it as such, and it remains so only for others who share a similar social location, ethical orientation, life-history, worldview, etc. A text's so-called "ideological power" is ultimately imposed from without and cannot be attributed to its very nature "independent of the shifting contexts in which it figures, the varying uses to which it is put, and the changing audiences it speaks to and for" (Wai-Chee Dimock, "New Historicism and the Reader," in *Readers and Reading*, 126). Of course, this would apply as well to interpreters who feel that many ancient texts are inherently ambiguous (such is often my experience of many of Jesus' parables). Ambiguity is *not* a textual property per se but, in all likelihood, the consequence of one's training, interpretive lens, temperament, and or worldview.

b. *Narrative Criticism and Narratology*

Biblical Narrative Criticism While narrative criticism ultimately originated within the field of Biblical Studies and "differs significantly from anything to be found in nonbiblical literary criticism,"[228] it is nevertheless indebted to literary criticism and narratology for much of its theory and terminology for describing and analyzing texts. Following American formalists, its earliest practitioners sought to offer an empirical and objective analysis of a text's formal features apart from its socio-historical context or author's intention.[229] They attended to the final form of the text without recourse to its sources, redacted layers, or compositional history and privileged *its* story-world—its settings, characters, and events—over the people and historical events upon which a narrative may have been based. Of central importance was identifying "the overall strategy of the implied author"[230] and learning how to read the text as its *implied reader*, which, though a "heuristic construct," would function as a kind of "control group in a scientific experiment" against which real readers might "compare their own responses."[231] In order to align oneself with a story's implied reader, the interpreter must attend carefully to a work's overall evaluative point of view, or "the standards of judgment by which readers are led to evaluate the events, characters, and settings that comprise the story."[232] This overall worldview operative in the story could be reconstructed based on an analysis of narration, character and plot development, rhetorical devices such as irony or symbolism, and narrative patterns such as intercalation, repetition, or chiasm.[233] For early narrative critics, therefore, the text was thought to contain a "meaning" apart from the activity of individual interpreters that could be extracted by an impartial, empirical analysis of rhetorical cues and formal features.

---

[228] Moore, *Literary Criticism and the Gospels*, xxii.

[229] Peter Merenlahti, *Poetics for the Gospels? Rethinking Narrative Criticism* (Studies of the New Testament and its World; London: T. & T. Clark, 2002), 2, 19.

[230] François Tolmie, *Narratology and Biblical Narratives: A Practical Guide* (San Francisco: International Scholars Publications, 1999), 7.

[231] Mark Allan Powell, "Narrative Criticism," in *ABD IV*, 202–03. See also Powell, *What is Narrative Criticism?* (Guides to Biblical Scholarship; Minneapolis: Fortress Press, 1990), 88–89.

[232] Powell, *What is Narrative Criticism?*, 24.

[233] Ibid., 23–34.

According to both Stephen Moore and Peter Merenlahti, narrative critics diverged from their nonbiblical counterparts by prioritizing (and often assuming) textual coherence and unity at the expense of irregularities, inconsistencies, gaps, or fissures.[234] Narratologists, for instance, generally do "not privilege or emphasize the unity of individual works" or even restrict themselves to a single text.[235] But early narrative critical studies often posited a "'*closed universe*'"[236] without first establishing a text's coherence and sought to identify "logical progressions of cause and effect"[237] between episodes even when such causation was not made explicit either by the narrator or the characters.[238] In light of recent criticisms, particularly from deconstructionists, many narrative critics today no longer assume that biblical texts are internally unified, consistent, or coherent.[239] Not only does an assumption of coherence impose monologicity while suppressing polyvalence and "multivocality," argues David Gunn, but it "leads to our ignoring or suppressing the very tensions and fractures in texts that may offer us enlivening insight or, indeed, escape from the tyranny of interpretative tradition."[240]

Present-day narrative criticism is more closely aligned with nonbiblical literary criticism in other ways as well. David Rhoads argues that narrative critics are gradually incorporating contributions from reader-response criticism, rhetorical criticism, speech-act theory, genre criticism, orality criticism, performance criticism, social-science criticism, ideological criticism, and the ethics of reading.[241] Furthermore, many have eschewed New Criticism's exclusive emphasis on the story-world

---

[234] Moore, *Literary Criticism and the Gospels*, 54–55; Merenlahti, *Poetics for the Gospels? Rethinking Narrative Criticism*, 3, 23. Merenlahti even argues that "a strong emphasis on the inherent unity of the gospel narratives must be considered the most salient single feature of narrative criticism" (23).

[235] Moore, *Literary Criticism and the Gospels*, 51–52.

[236] Ibid., 8. Moore is quoting David Rhoads ("Narrative Criticism: Practices and Prospects").

[237] Powell, *What is Narrative Criticism?*, 40–42.

[238] Admittedly, many critics viewed coherence not as inhering within texts but as something nevertheless worth pursuing. Mary Ann Tolbert, for instance, in her book *Sowing the Gospel: Mark's World in Literary-Historical Perspective*, offers "one possible 'consistent interpretation' of 'the Gospel in all its parts'" since "[t]he more coherence an interpretation can disclose in a text, the more persuasive it becomes" (3, 11).

[239] See David Rhoads, "Narrative Criticism: Practices and Prospects," 268–70.

[240] "Narrative Criticism," in *To Each its Own Meaning: An Introduction to Biblical Criticisms and Their Applications*, 226.

[241] "Narrative Criticism: Practices and Prospects," 272–85.

of the text. While critics such as Mark Allan Powell and Mary Ann Tolbert have always maintained that literary analyses are fully compatible with "historical approaches"[242] and should be informed by "the general historical, literary, and sociological matrix out of which the text comes,"[243] other early practitioners and pioneers of the approach such as D. Rhoads, who once emphasized textual autonomy, now seek to glean from the latest research on a work's social and historical context(s).[244] In a recent book that reevaluates narrative criticism's longstanding assumptions and goals, Merenlahti argues that the next generation of narrative critics must not only resituate ancient texts in context but also explore their ability to shape hearers and readers (i.e., explore their ideological power) both at their moment of production and as they have been received by others throughout the centuries.[245] Moreover, a responsible poetics, says Merenlahti, would no longer claim "objectivity and universality" but move away from its traditional focus upon tracing a work's effects upon implied readers by accounting for an interpreter's social location and ideological commitments.[246] Few narrative critical studies have yet taken Merenlahti's suggestions to heart, but more undoubtedly will. In fact, Rhoads, in his recent reconceptualization of narrative criticism, still views the narrative critic's goal in terms of enabling a text "to address us on its own terms" or allowing it to "say what it says."[247]

Narrative Criticism and Narratology as Employed in this Study Mieke Bal, in *Narratology: Introduction to the Theory of Narrative*, informs readers that she will offer "a coherent, systematic narratology" that may serve as "an instrument for making descriptions, and hence interpretations, discussable."[248] Although she acknowledges that her system is simply one among many and, like all models, always remains a construct that is both "contingent" and "deconstructable,"[249] it nevertheless enables

[242] Powell, *What is Narrative Criticism?*, 98.
[243] Tolbert, *Sowing the Gospel*, 12.
[244] "Narrative Criticism: Practices and Prospects," 268–69. See also his article entitled "Social Criticism: Crossing Boundaries," in *Mark & Method: New Approaches in Biblical Studies*, 135–61.
[245] *Poetics for the Gospels? Rethinking Narrative Criticism*, 57, 117–19, 124, 129.
[246] Ibid., 5, 117–19.
[247] "Narrative Criticism: Practices and Prospects," 284.
[248] (2d ed.; Toronto: University of Toronto Press, 1999), 3, 11.
[249] Merenlahti, *Poetics for the Gospels? Rethinking Narrative Criticism*, 29.

readers to communicate how they have internalized and structured a text. For Bal, it is only then that "the reader's share—and responsibility—can be clearly assessed."[250] For this study, too, both narrative criticism and narratology will furnish the conceptual tools and terminology for processing, describing, and analyzing the text.

There are several superb narrative critical and narratological models available today, and I have benefited enormously from many of them. Among narrative critical models, the most influential have been introductory essays by Mark A. Powell,[251] David Gunn,[252] Elizabeth S. Malbon,[253] and Robert Fowler[254] as well as more substantial expositions by Mark A. Powell,[255] François Tolmie,[256] R. Alan Culpepper,[257] and Daniel Marguerat.[258] From nonbiblical literary critical theorists, I will draw chiefly upon Mieke Bal's *Narratology: Introduction to the Theory of Narrative*, Schlomith Rimmon-Kenan's *Narrative Fiction*,[259] and Seymour Chatman's *Story and Discourse: Narrative Structure in Fiction and Film*.[260] While, as stated above, this study will employ these models in order to convey how the text is being processed and taking shape, earlier commitments to interpreting texts apart from social and historical contexts, defending or presuming textual unity and coherence, restricting subjectivity by delineating textual parameters,[261] identifying "the overall strategy of the implied author,"[262] and tracing the responses of an implied reader[263]

---

[250] *Narratology: Introduction to the Theory of Narrative*, 11.

[251] "Narrative Criticism," in *Hearing the New Testament: Strategies for Interpretation*: 239–55; "Narrative Criticism," in *ABD IV*: 201–04.

[252] "Narrative Criticism," in *To Each its Own Meaning: An Introduction to Biblical Criticisms and Their Applications*: 201–29.

[253] "Narrative Criticism: How Does the Story Mean?" in *Mark & Method: New Approaches in Biblical Studies*: 23–49.

[254] "Reader-Response Criticism: Figuring Mark's Reader," in *Mark & Method: New Approaches in Biblical Studies*: 50–83. Though Fowler is not addressing narrative criticism per se, he nevertheless discusses and illustrates concepts often employed by narrative critics (e.g., verbal and situational/dramatic irony).

[255] *What is Narrative Criticism?*

[256] *Narratology and Biblical Narratives: A Practical Guide.*

[257] *Anatomy of the Fourth Gospel: A Study in Literary Design* (Philadelphia: Fortress Press, 1983).

[258] *How to Read Bible Stories: An Introduction to Narrative Criticism* (London: SCM Press, 1999).

[259] (2d ed.; New York: Routledge, 2002).

[260] (Ithaca: Cornell University Press, 1978).

[261] Powell, *What is Narrative Criticism?*, 95.

[262] Tolmie, *Narratology and Biblical Narratives: A Practical Guide*, 7.

[263] Powell, "Narrative Criticism," 202.

will not be appropriated. Rather, in addition to working with a flesh-and-blood reader and attending to the socio-historical world of which the text speaks, an open, often ambiguous text replete with fractures and inconsistencies will be foregrounded and all narrative elements or features will be viewed as constructs imposed from without.

c. *Intertextuality*

Intertextuality in Biblical Studies Intertextual theory is typically traced to Julia Kristeva's blending and reworking of Mikhail Bakhtin's and Ferdinand de Saussure's thought[264] and, at its core, insists that every text is "shot through with references, quotations, and influences" and so "cannot exist as a hermetic or self-sufficient whole."[265] To put it differently, because texts neither emerge nor are received in a vacuum, all texts are in some way intertwined or bound up with other texts. Beyond this fundamental assertion, however, there is little agreement among practitioners in both Biblical and Literary Studies even as to what constitutes a text, whether the interpreter is restricted to tracing prior influences or whether s/he might initiate a conversation with texts from any time or culture, or what should be the goal(s) of an intertextual analysis. In Biblical Studies, for instance, one finds a wide range of philosophical assumptions and procedures represented. At one end of the spectrum are studies devoted exclusively to addressing genetic questions of influence or origin that restrict analysis to *prior* literary texts. In many cases, identification of these prior influences is designed to help further define an author's or redactor's intentions. At the other end of the spectrum are studies that place few restrictions on which intertexts an interpreter may access, assign the identification of all intertexts to the reader, and conceive of "text" in the broadest of ways so as to include not only written texts but also social mores or norms, historical information, and even the interpreter's self. This range may be illustrated by reference to three relatively recent collections of essays that address intertextual

---

[264] Graham Allen, *Intertextuality* (The New Critical Idiom; New York: Routledge, 2000), 6.

[265] Judith Still and Michael Worton, "Introduction," in *Intertextuality: Theories and Practice* (ed. Judith Still and Michael Worton; Manchester, N.Y.: Manchester University Press, 1990), 1.

analysis: *Congress Volume: Olso 1998*,[266]*Reading Between Texts: Intertextuality and the Hebrew Bible*,[267] and *Intertextuality in Biblical Writings: Essays in Honor of Bas van Iersel*.[268]

Essays in the *Congress Volume* that treat intertextuality are generally interested in exploring a work's antecedent literary texts and how they might contribute to our understanding of an author's or redactor's intentions. Antoon Schoors, for instance, conceives of the interpreter's task in terms of an impartial, scientific investigation of sources and influences that aims to establish a "trajectory from the 'source text' to the final text,"[269] and Kirsten Nielsen is interested in identifying "intertexts that the author or the editor wants us to note."[270] Patricia Tull, who draws on Bakhtin's understanding of internal dialogism, examines how an author has preserved, re-conceptualized, and re-presented prior traditions in search of "what such a recollection of memory might be *intended* to convey" (italics mine).[271] While the authors of these essays as a whole do not restrict themselves to identifying literary allusions (i.e., purposeful and explicit evocations of earlier material[272]), literary antecedents and their potential for shedding light on an intended meaning remains a primary focus.[273] In *Reading Between Texts*, one finds a fairly diverse spectrum of approaches. Jan Jaynes Granowski, for instance, identifies which intertexts from the Hebrew Bible the "implied author" of II Kings "beckons" readers to access in order to negotiate the ambiguous ending of the book.[274] Timothy K. Beal, however, who foregrounds a

---

[266] (ed. Andre Lemaire and Saebo Magne; Supplements to Vetus Testamentum 80; Boston: Brill, 2000).

[267] (ed. Danna N. Fewell; Literary Currents in Biblical Interpretation; Louisville: Westminster/John Knox Press, 1992).

[268] (ed. Sipke Draisma; Kampen: Uitgeversmaatschappij J. H. Kok, 1989).

[269] "(Mis)use of Intertextuality in Qoheleth Exegesis," 59.

[270] "Intertextuality and the Hebrew Bible," 23.

[271] "The Rhetoric of Reflection," 78.

[272] I am here paraphrasing Robert Alter's definition of allusion (*The Pleasures of Reading in an Ideological Age* [New York: Simon and Schuster, 1989], 112, 116).

[273] A similar understanding of intertextuality may be found in studies such as *Mimesis and Intertextuality in Antiquity and Christianity* (ed. Dennis R. MacDonald; Harrisburg, P.A.: Trinity Press International, 2001), *The Quest for Context and Meaning: Studies in Biblical Intertextuality in Honor of James A. Sanders* (ed. Craig A. Evans and Shemaryahu Talmon; New York: Brill, 1997), and *Intertextualitiés: La Bible en échos* (ed. Daniel Marguerat and Adrian Curtis; MDB 40; Geneva: Labor et Fides, 2000]) that focus on how a given text is re-appropriating or rereading earlier traditions. A few of the essays in *Intertextualitiés* do privilege the role of the reader in forming intertextual relations, but most tend to focus on how a work is reshaping earlier literature and for what purposes.

[274] "Jehoiachim at the King's Table," 182, 186.

surplus or diffusion of meaning and views the interpreter's job in terms of limiting this surplus by establishing intertextual relations, shifts focus upon *real* readers, whose ideological commitments ultimately determine which texts will be accessed and what role they will play in offering an interpretation.[275] Beal is also interested in transgressing well-established intertextual boundaries "in order to discover new relationships and prioritize other voices."[276] Finally, essays in *Intertextuality in Biblical Writings* generally assign the identification of all intertextual relationships to the reader. Ellen van Wolde, for instance, argues that "in an intertextual analysis or interpretation of a text it is the reader and not the writer who is center of attention, because it is the reader who makes a text interfere with other texts."[277] Gerard Luttikhuizen shares her perspective by defining intertexts broadly as "the whole of texts which *in the mind of the reader* are related to a specific text."[278] As a whole, this collection also places few restrictions on establishing intertextual relations. For example, Jean Delorme asserts that intertexts "cannot be confined to previous or subsequent texts presenting a similarity in expression or content,"[279] and James Voelz argues that in addition to drawing upon literary texts that share a common form or theme "*[t]he reader must be seen as a text, or perhaps, more accurately, the states, actions, hopes, fears, and knowledge of his life-experience.*"[280] Thus, in Biblical Studies, we find represented a wide range of approaches, each undergirded by different philosophical assumptions and goals: essays on intertextuality in the *Congress Volume* generally reflect a modernist approach that privileges prior literary intertexts, genetic questions of origin and influence, and discerning an intended meaning that inheres within a given work; the contributions in *Reading Between Texts* are diverse, including a semi-modernist exploration of what "implied authors" "beckon" readers to see and postmodernist analyses that place full interpretive authority in the hands of committed, real readers; and the essays in *Intertextuality in Biblical Writings* generally reflect a postmodernist perspective that shifts full responsibility for establishing intertextual relations to readers and

---

[275] "Ideology and Intertextuality: Surplus of Meaning and Controlling the Means of Production," 27–28, 32.

[276] Ibid., 36.

[277] "Trendy Intertextuality?," 47.

[278] "Intertextual References in Readers' Responses to the Apocryphon of John," 117.

[279] "Intertextualities about Mark," 36.

[280] "Multiple Signs and Double Texts: Elements of Intertextuality," 31.

significantly broadens the range of intertexts with which the interpreter might enter into conversation.

Intertextual Theory as Employed in this Study All texts are profoundly dialogic[281] in that they draw upon prior and contemporaneous voices "from the innumerable centres of culture"[282] and therefore constitute "part of the *already written*, the *already said*, the *already read*."[283] When a text raises a certain theme or issue (e.g., wealth and possessions), it is "always entangled in someone else's discourse about it,... already present with qualifications... [and] still warm from... struggle and hostility."[284] That is, no text emerges in a vacuum: it is born in the midst of an already existing conversation, incorporates views that have already been expressed, and offers a response of its own. Texts, in short, "do not exist without other texts"[285] and therefore do not constitute closed systems. Rather, they are open and super-abound with meaning. For the interpreter who foregrounds an open text and a surplus of meaning, part of the hermeneutical task involves limiting a text's "innumerable intertextual possibilities,"[286] or, to borrow Roland Barthes's terminology, structuring its polysemeity.

But invoking certain intertexts while ignoring or suppressing others is a profoundly reader-oriented enterprise. As we read, we constantly recall and interact with texts previously encountered in order to interpret or make sense of what lies in front of us,[287] but at no point can we be confident that we are accessing literature that an author or editor wished readers would access. All intertexts are ultimately selected by situated, ideologically committed readers so that "what is produced at the moment of reading is due to the cross-fertilization of the packaged

---

[281] Mikhail Bakhtin, "The Problem of the Text in Linguistics, Philology, and the Human Sciences: An Experiment in Philosophical Analysis," in *Speech Genres and Other Late Essays* (trans. Vern W. McGee; Austin, TX: University of Texas Press, 1986), 125.

[282] Roland Barthes, "The Death of the Author," in *Image, Text, Music* (trans. Stephen Heath; New York: Hill and Wang, 1977), 146.

[283] Graham Allen, *Roland Barthes* (Routledge Critical Thinkers Series; New York: Routledge, 2003), 92.

[284] Mikhail Bakhtin, "Heteroglossia in the Novel," in *Bakhtinian Thought: An Introductory Reader* (ed. Simon Dentith; New York: Routledge, 1995), 223–24.

[285] Ellen van Wolde, "Introduction," in *Intertextuality in Biblical Writings*, 7.

[286] Timothy K. Beal, "Ideology and Intertextuality: Surplus of Meaning and Controlling the Means of Production," 36.

[287] Gerard Luttikhuizen, "Intertextual References in Readers' Responses to the Apocryphon of John," 117.; Ellen van Wolde, "Introduction," 7.

textual material (say, a book) by all the texts which a reader brings to it."[288] Intertextual reading may therefore be described as "aggressive participation."[289] Since interpreters cannot assume that certain intertexts are simply self-evident or implied (unless an explicit allusion to an antecedent is present), part of the critic's job, I believe, is to make explicit this process of selecting and engaging intertextual partners. Indeed, as D. Fewell observes, because accessing certain intertexts over others may dramatically alter one's reading,[290] mapping one's intertextual decisions should be a key component of the hermeneutical process.

This study will employ a hypertext model, which allows readers to temporarily "break the linear flow" of reading in search of other material that may help shed light on the focal text.[291] Just as a web user might click on underlined or highlighted words and phrases in web documents to gain access to additional information, so may interpreters halt the reading process momentarily and explore similar "links" that can, for instance, add depth to one's construction of a character or introduce other views on a given issue or theme. While in practice many web users will follow a trail of hypertextual links without returning to the original document,[292] such will not be the case here given a commitment to an attentive and respectful hearing of the focal text as *other*. Hypertextual explorations are thus *momentary* disruptions in a sequential reading process.

Many have noted that intertextual analyses often call exclusively upon literary texts while overlooking a work's historical and socio-political dimensions.[293] In this study, "intertext" will be defined broadly so as to include not only intra- and extra-textual literature but historical information as well as social mores and norms. As a way of respecting the social, cultural, and historical otherness of the Gospel,[294] the reader

[288] Still and Worton, "Introduction," in *Intertextuality: Theories and Practice*, 1–2.

[289] Ibid., 11.

[290] "Introduction," in *Reading Between Texts*, 19.

[291] Allen, *Intertextuality*, 202.

[292] Ibid.

[293] See, e.g., Liew's criticism of most literary approaches to the Gospel of Mark in *Politics of Parousia: Reading Mark Inter(con)textually*, 22, 32–33. Cf. J. Frow, "Intertextuality and Ontology," in *Intertextuality: Theories and Practices*, 54.

[294] Inspiration for this aspect of the approach comes from Fernando F. Segovia (*Decolonizing Biblical Studies*, 97–115) and, to some extent, H. R. Jauss (see "The Identity of the Poetic Text in the Changing Horizon of Understanding," in *Reception Study: From Literary Theory to Cultural Studies* [ed. James L. Machor and Philip Goldstein; New York: Routledge, 2001]: 7–28). Jauss, for instance, writes: "Literary understanding

in this study will prioritize the literary and cultural repertoire of (or available to persons in) the first century Mediterranean world.[295]

4. *Delineating the Reader-Position*

Introduction

In keeping with the recent shift in Literary and Biblical Studies away from universal reader constructs toward real, situated, perspectival readers, the reader in this study is a flesh-and-blood reader. Specifically, this reader is a citizen of the United States who has elected to foreground two features of his own social and historical context at the beginning of the twenty-first century: rampant overconsumption and unprecedented personal wealth. In view of the fact that nearly half of the world's population lives on less than two dollars a day and billions still lack access to basic medical care, safe drinking water, and adequate food and sanitation, I consider these two features troubling.

As a member of a Christian community who is encouraged to prioritize dialogue with the canonical books of the First and Second Testaments when reflecting critically upon and formulating a response to our present situation in the world, I have enlisted the Gospel of Luke as a principal conversation partner. While it is hoped that the Gospel will prove to be an insightful, challenging interlocutor, it is certainly only one of many possible options, and readers who desire to further reflect upon overconsumption and wealth would undoubtedly benefit from a wide spectrum of past and present voices. For the author of this study, it is anticipated that the ensuing encounter with this Gospel will constitute only the beginning of a much larger and far-reaching dialogue on these issues.

Of course, one need not be a member of a Christian community either to engage Luke's story of an itinerant teacher and healer from Galilee or to share this reader-position. Indeed, it is this author's hope that anyone who is troubled by overconsumption and extraordinary

becomes dialogical only when the otherness of the text is sought and recognized from the horizon of our own expectations, when no naïve fusion of horizons is considered, and when one's own expectations are corrected and extended by the experience of the other." [9]).

[295] Cf. Darr, *On Character Building: The Reader and the Rhetoric of Characterization in Luke-Acts*, 170–71.

personal wealth and longs for a more just and humane social order may benefit from the reading presented here.

Consumption and Wealth in the United States

Although home to less than 5% of the world's population,[296] the U.S. consumes a disproportionate share of the earth's resources, and there is no sign that this trend will soon abate. Indeed, driven by an economic system that depends upon sustained growth for its very survival, we continue to manufacture and find ways to fulfill our desires for more. Our present consumption habits are not only depleting nonrenewable resources at alarming rates but having disastrous effects on our planet's fragile ecosystems.

According to Personal Consumption Expenditures (PCE)[297] between 1946 and 1995, per capita consumption in the U.S. "grew significantly" in spite of a "decrease in average household size" during this same period from 3.2 persons to 2.4 persons per household. While PCE includes expenditures on food, housing, durable goods, medical care, energy, transportation, education, and recreation, recent increases in consumption are particularly visible in the housing, energy, and food sectors. A brief statistical summary of each of these sectors will therefore be provided below.

<u>Housing Sector</u>: According to the National Association of Home Builders Report (2005), the average size of homes constructed in the U.S. more than doubled between 1950 and 2003 from 983 sq. ft. to 2,330 sq. ft.[298] During the same period, homes with four bedrooms multiplied exponentially (from 1% in 1950 to 37% in 2003) as did homes with 2 ½ bathrooms or more (from 1% in 1950 to 56% in 2003). Finally, while 53% of homes did not have either a garage or a carport in 1950, 82% of newly constructed homes in 2003 included *at least* a two-car garage.[299]

[296] According to the Population Reference Bureau, the U.S. population was roughly 293.6 million in mid-2004.

[297] According to Daniel Slesnick, Personal Consumption Expenditures "are the most widely used source of aggregate data" employed by researchers today in measuring spending habits on goods and services for the household sector (*Consumption and Social Welfare: Living standards and their distribution in the United States* [New York: Cambridge University Press, 2001], 45–46).

[298] "Housing Facts," NAHB (January, 2005): 1–9.

[299] Ibid., 7.

Energy Sector: According to the BP Statistical Review of World Energy (2004), in 2003 the United States accounted for nearly one quarter of the world's primary energy consumption, which includes energy derived from oil, natural gas, coal, and nuclear and hydroelectric sources.[300] The U.S. Energy Information Administration's Annual Energy Outlook for 2005 has forecasted increases in consumption of energy derived from all sources except coal, and consumption of both petroleum and natural gas (two nonrenewable fuels) is expected to grow significantly.[301]

One reason for high petroleum consumption in the U.S. is the current popularity of large SUVs and full-size pickup trucks, most of which get below 20 miles per gallon in the city. Many of these models have been introduced just within the last decade or so. Ford, for instance, recently introduced its two largest SUV models: the Expedition (1997) and its massive cousin, the Excursion (2000). On its website, Ford discloses that the 2005 Expedition (4 × 2) was rated at 14 mpg in the city but, not surprisingly, refuses to divulge mpg-ratings for the Excursion. Hummer, a subsidiary of General Motors, recently added two new vehicles to its line to complement the much more expensive Hummer 1: H2 (introduced in 2003) and H3 (introduced in 2006). Tellingly, Hummer does not publish mpg-ratings for any of its vehicles on its website. Even Toyota and Honda, companies that built their reputations in part on engineering fuel-efficient automobiles, have followed suit by introducing similar vehicles. Toyota, for instance, recently debuted both a full-size pickup truck (Tundra; 2000)[302] and an oversized SUV (Sequoia; 2001)[303] to compete with Ford and GM in the U.S. marketplace. Honda only very recently introduced its first large SUV (Pilot; 2003)[304] and full-size truck (Ridgeline; 2006).[305] For decades, environmentalists have been trying to persuade Congress to require tougher mpg-ratings from all U.S. automobile manufacturers, but gas-guzzling vehicles continue to roll off the assembly lines, even from foreign car companies that historically have taken the lead in reducing fuel consumption and emissions.

---

300 "Energy in Focus," BP Statistical Review of World Energy (June, 2004): 1–40. See especially the table on p. 37.

301 U.S. Energy Information Administration, "Annual Energy Outlook 2005." Online: http://www.eia.doe.gov/oiaf/aeo/forecast.html.

302 Mpg-ratings for the 2005 model: 17 city/22 highway (V6 Manual Transmission; Regular Cab).

303 Mpg-ratings for the 2005 model: 15 mpg city/18 mpg highway.

304 Mpg-ratings for the 2005 model: 17 mpg city/22 mpg highway.

305 Mpg-ratings for the 2005 model: 16 mpg city/21 mpg highway.

Food Sector: Finally, studies show that food portion sizes both in restaurants and at home have increased in the U.S. between 1977 and 1998.[306] Consequently, during a similar period (1971–2000), we have witnessed a rise in overall caloric intake[307] and a rather rapid increase in obesity (from 14.5% to 30.9%),[308] a trend now affecting even young children.

Of course, these consumption habits are possible only because the U.S. is an extraordinarily wealthy nation—in fact, the wealthiest in the world. In addition to posting the highest GDP in 2004,[309] U.S. government, businesses, and citizens command a significant portion of the world's capital. This year (2005), for instance, eight of the top ten companies ranked by market value are based in the U.S.,[310] and nine of the wealthiest fifteen persons in the world ranked by net worth are U.S. citizens.[311] The Shared Capitalism Institute observes that in 1999 three U.S. citizens—Microsoft co-founders Bill Gates and Paul Allen and Berkshire Hathaway's Warren Buffet—possessed a net worth that exceeded the combined GDP of the world's 41 poorest nations.[312]

But wealth within the U.S. is far from evenly distributed. Among industrialized nations, the U.S. exhibits the highest level of wealth inequality. According to economist Edward Wolff, the richest 1% of U.S. households owns approximately 38% of the nation's wealth, and the richest 20% owns a staggering 80%![313] Moreover, incomes of the so-called "hyper-rich" (the wealthiest 0.1%) are continuing to grow at

---

[306] See, e.g., Samara Joy Nielsen and Barry M. Popkin, "Patterns and Trends in Food Portion Sizes," *JAMA* 289 (2003): 450–53.

[307] "Trends in Intake of Energy and Macronutrients, United States, 1971–2000," *Morbidity Mortality Weekly Report* 53 (2004): 80–82.

[308] K.M. Flegal, M. D. Carroll, C. L. Ogden, and C. L. Johnson, "Prevalence and Trends in Obesity among U.S. Adults, 1999–2000," *JAMA* 288 (2002): 1723–27.

[309] Both the World Bank and the International Monetary Fund list the U.S. as having the highest GDP for 2004 (the European Union ranks second). U.S. nominal GDP accounts for roughly one quarter of world GDP.

[310] "The Forbes Global 2000." Online: http://www.forbes.com/2005/03/30/05f2005land.html.

[311] Online: http://www.forbes.com/billionaires.

[312] Online: http://www.sharedcapitalism.org/scfacts.html. The Institute obtained its data from "Rich Comparison," *The Wall Street Journal* (July 30, 1999), 1.

[313] "The Wealth Divide: The Growing Gap in the United States Between the Rich and the Rest. An Interview with Edward Wolff," *Multinational Monitor* 24 (2003). Online: http://multinationalmonitor.org/mm2003/03may/may03interviewswolff.html.

exponential rates,[314] in part because of tax cuts awarded by the Bush administration, while many low and middle income workers' wages remain stagnant and unable to keep pace with recent increases in health care and housing costs. Many CEOs would, of course, be included among this expanding group of the "hyper-rich." A recent comparison of salaries received by "the top tier of American CEOs" with wages earned by American manufacturing employees yields a ratio of 475:1 "and would be vastly greater if assets, not income, were taken into account. By way of comparison, the ratio in Britain is 24:1, in France 15:1, in Sweden 13:1."[315]

Astonishingly, in spite of such wealth, the U.S. ranked "dead last among 22 top donor countries" in giving for 2003.[316] Indeed, while the European Union "gave away 36.5 billion in development aid in 2003," we "managed just one third that amount—and much of that foreign aid either went to Israel or else came with strings attached."[317] Private charitable donations in the U.S. do not add much to the overall total. In fact, when private contributions are included, the U.S. moves up the ladder of top donor countries only one notch.[318]

5. *Procedure*

Though this study will focus on four parables in Luke's Travel Narrative (12:16–21; 15:11–32; 16:1–13; 16:19–31), their co-texts will play a part in the analysis as well. Each close-reading of a parable will be prefaced with a brief synopsis of initial impressions to Jesus' prior instruction on wealth and possessions. For the first parable, a record of these impressions will begin at the start of the Travel Narrative, when Jesus "set his face to go to Jerusalem" (9:51). Included also will be a discussion of the narrator's introductory remarks, concluding applications, and any nimshalim added by the parabler.

[314] See, e.g., David Cay Johnston, "Richest are Leaving Even the Rich Far Behind," *The New York Times* (June 5, 2005). Cf. Arthur B. Kennickell, "A Rolling Tide: Changes in the Distribution of Wealth in the U.S., 1989–2001" (Annandale-on-Hudson, NY: Levy Economics Institute, 2003), 47–49.

[315] Tony Judt, "Europe vs. America," *The New York Review of Books* 52 (February 10, 2005).

[316] Nicholas D. Kristof, "Land of Penny Pinchers," *The New York Times* (January 5, 2005). The figures he discusses are based on recent OECD calculations.

[317] Judt, "Europe vs. America."

[318] Kristof, "Land of Penny Pinchers."

Following Roland Barthes's procedure in *S/Z*, each parable will be "starred" into "manageable reading units" called *lexias*. These lexias, which may consist of a phrase, sentence, or even just a word, are a "matter of convenience" and may therefore appear arbitrary and not accord with the "natural" divisions of the text.[319] The reading will proceed slowly and sequentially and give special attention to whether expectations are confirmed or shattered, how characters take shape and whether they elicit approval or disapproval, surprising plot developments that may take the reader off-guard, and ambiguous constructions (or moments of "undecidability") that simultaneously unsettle and draw the reader yet further in. Literary and socio-cultural intertexts will be evoked and engaged, and gaps will be identified and filled with recourse to the literary and cultural repertoire available to persons of the first century Mediterranean world. Finally, reading will halt occasionally to allow for reflection on how larger units are unfolding and affecting the reader.

[319] (trans. Richard Miller; New York: Hill and Wang, 1974), 13–15.

CHAPTER TWO

CHALLENGING OVERCONSUMPTION

A. The Parable of the Wealthy Landowner (12:16–21)

1. *Exploring the Pre-text: Impressions of Jesus' Teaching on Wealth and Possessions in 9:51–12:12*

Shortly after setting his face to go to Jerusalem (9:51),[1] Jesus reminds any who would follow him "along the way" (ἐν τῇ ὁδῷ)[2] that a firm break with the past and an unwavering commitment to proclaiming the good news of God's kingdom will be required (9:57–62). Because disciples will constantly be on the move, they must forgo stability and security (9:57–58), and mission objectives must take precedence over familial relationships (9:59–62). Those selected to journey from town to town in pairs will be asked to carry "neither purse, nor bag, nor sandals" (10:4) and depend solely upon their hosts for shelter and nourishment (10:7–8).[3] Disciples are also asked to seek only what they really need (11:3),[4] set their debtors free (11:4),[5] and trust that God will provide for them (11:5–12). In the midst of his instruction to disciples,

[1] The narrator's statement in 9:51 delineates the beginning of Luke's "Travel Narrative."

[2] While Jesus and his disciples are literally making their way along a road (ἐν τῇ ὁδῷ) toward Jerusalem, readers may also wish to treat the phrase as a symbol for Christian discipleship and so render ὁδός more generally as "way" (as here).

[3] Even though those appointed for this second missionary journey give up basic provisions (10:4) and look to others for sustenance (10:7–8), they nevertheless return "with joy" (10:17). Thus, their rigorous, ascetic lifestyle does not prevent them from finding joy in their task.

[4] Because the adjective ἐπιούσιος is unattested prior to its appearance in Luke and Matthew, translators have little choice but to look to its etymology and narrative context (Fitzmyer, *The Gospel According to Luke X–XXIV*, 904–6). I prefer to render it as "essential," which seems to fit well with Jesus' previous call to ascetic itinerancy (9:57–10:12), and thus follow Origen, John Chrysostom, and Jerome (for all options, see *BDAG*, 376–77).

[5] ὀφείλω may connote debt in a financial or social/moral sense (*BDAG*, 473). Both associations may be retained given the Gospel's interest in relief for the poor (see, e.g., the jubilee themes introduced in 4:18–19) and in forgiveness from sins (1:77; 24:47).

Jesus pauses to address outsiders[6] as well: they are strongly encouraged to give whatever they have in order to help those in need (10:25–37). Thus, the overall impression by 12:1 is that true discipleship comes only at the greatest personal cost. It will require a firm break with one's prior commitments, a willingness to seek and consume only what is needed (which, for those journeying in pairs from town to town, will be provided through the generosity of others), and an obligation to setting debtors free.

The two-fold theme of trusting God for material needs and renouncing stability and prior commitments recurs in 12:4–12, just prior to Jesus' encounter with the man from the crowd (12:13–15) and his narrating of the parable about the rich man (12:16–21). While Jesus does promise his disciples that God has every hair on their heads counted and encourages them not to worry (12:7, 11), he also reminds them about future trials before "rulers and authorities," when many will be tempted to deny their association with the movement (12:8–12). God will indeed provide, but the cost of following Jesus will be great.

Setting the Stage: Jesus' Encounter with a Man from the Crowd (12:13–15)

The sudden interjection from an unnamed person in the crowd provides welcome relief from the mounting emotional weight of the preceding warnings in vv.8–12. Though Jesus encourages his disciples at the end of his speech not to worry (μή μεριμνήσητε; v.11), the punishments for denying Jesus or blaspheming the Holy Spirit before "rulers and authorities" seem unbearable (vv.8–10). The cost of following Jesus is already high, and a reminder of human frailty under pressure only increases fear of what lies ahead. The narrator's voice is indeed a welcome interruption, and the introduction of a new episode in v.13 eases readers' growing anxiety over whether or not they will be strong enough to continue "along the way."

The narrator does not indicate whether the man from the crowd (an enormous throng consisting of thousands; see 12:1) rudely interrupts Jesus or merely takes advantage of a pause and seizes the moment to advance his request. In fact, the narrator declines to offer any descriptive tags that might prejudice readers against or in favor of this man

[6] Given the narrator's negative assessment of the lawyer's motives in 10:25, 29 ("[he] stood up in order to test him"; "But, wishing to justify himself..."), it does not appear that he has any intention of actually joining Jesus and his disciples "on the way." I therefore consider him to be a representative of those on the "outside."

and immediately turns the stage over to him, inviting readers to begin forming an impression for themselves: "Teacher, tell my brother to divide the inheritance with me!" (12:13) The motivation behind his request is not disclosed. Has he been cheated by a brother who has usurped the family inheritance all for himself, or is he seeking property that really does not belong to him? According to Deuteronomic legislation, the eldest son should receive a "double portion"[7] of his father's inheritance (Deut 21:17).[8] It is impossible to know whether his family sought to abide by this legislation, but if so, this man may either be contesting the fairness of the law itself and therefore asking that he receive an equal distribution or claiming that a greedy and devious elder bother found a way to corral all of his father's property for himself. In either case, the man's request seems reasonable, and we may be inclined to believe that Jesus will take up his cause. After all, he is not asking for the full inheritance but only a portion (εἰπὲ τῷ ἀδελφῷ μου *μερίσασθαι* μετ' ἐμοῦ).[9]

Jesus, however, refuses to entertain the man's request, and his abrupt, dismissive retort in the form of a rhetorical question comes as a surprise: "Who appointed me judge or divider over you?" (v.14). What are we to make of Jesus' refusal to engage this man's appeal? J. Duncan M. Derrett argues that the "arbitral award" of a popular teacher and healer like Jesus is often highly regarded in traditional societies "where litigation is costly and unpredictable."[10] This man's brother, as well as the townspeople, may therefore have taken Jesus' judgment seriously if it had been offered. However, hostility to Jesus has been mounting rapidly since he was first rejected by the people of Nazareth (4:16–30). At the end of Chapter 11, the narrator reminds readers just how strong the opposition is to Jesus, especially among the religious authorities: "The scribes and the Pharisees began acting in a hostile manner and

---

[7] Literally, "two-thirds."

[8] See W. O. E. Oesterley, *The Gospel Parables in the Light of Their Jewish Background* (New York: MacMillan Company, 1938), 168–69.

[9] Joel Green argues that the younger brother, through the acquisition of at least part of the family's land, may have been seeking greater power and influence in the community (*The Gospel of Luke*, 489). Herman Hendrickx similarly argues that by acquiring a share of the inheritance he sought "to become independent" whereas his brother wisely sought to keep his father's property undivided (*The Parables of Jesus*, 98). At this point, however, readers need not rule out the possibility that he, much like the widow in 18:1–8, was seeking justice in light of a recent wrong.

[10] "The Rich Fool: A Parable of Jesus Concerning Inheritance," *HeyJ* 18 (1977), 132.

interrogating him closely about many things while lying in wait to catch something from his mouth" (vv.53–54). Thus, at this point in the story, it is highly unlikely that the religious authorities would have heeded Jesus' judgment, and if they were to refuse their consent, the man would have little chance of actually receiving part of his family's inheritance. Furthermore, since no one has in fact "appointed" (v.14) Jesus to serve as arbitrator, neither the local authorities nor the elder brother would have good reason to view Jesus' judgment as binding. In v.14, Jesus may therefore be stating a simple fact (i.e., he does not have authority to render a judgment), revealing a bit of frustration over having no official standing in the religious community, or responding angrily to a request stemming from a misguided motivation like greed. Thus, at this point in the dialogue, neither the motivation behind Jesus' abrupt reply nor the rationale for the man's request is evident. Can readers penetrate (at least in part) the opacity of this terse exchange?

Some early Christian scribes saw an allusion in Jesus' rhetorical question to Exod 2:14,[11] where Moses is the recipient of a similar retort from a fellow Hebrew. After killing an Egyptian for oppressing one of his kinsmen and burying his body in the sand, Moses stumbles upon two men who are fighting. He tries to reconcile them, but one of the men, who already knows that Moses murdered a man, interjects: "Who made you ruler and judge (ἄρχοντα καὶ δικαστὴν) over us?[12] Do you mean to kill me as you killed the Egyptian?" (2:14). Those familiar with the remainder of Exodus may see irony at work here, for a few verses later Moses is in fact called by God and appointed leader of his people (3:1–22). Later, he will function as judge as well. While his fellow kinsman is unaware of Moses' divine election as Israel's new leader, readers know that he will soon assume both roles as ruler and judge. A similar irony may be found in Luke 12:13–14. Jesus has not been appointed judge or divider in the traditional sense, so his ruling would carry little if any weight with the man's elder brother or the local authorities. However, like Moses, he has been appointed by God to a place of prominence among the people, though his true identity is currently known only to a few. By the conclusion of the infancy nar-

---

[11] See also Acts 7:27.

[12] The account in the LXX also makes use of the verb καθίστημι: Τίς σε κατέστησεν ἄρχοντα καὶ δικαστὴν ἐφ' ἡμῶν; Several manuscripts, it appears, substituted ἄρχοντα, δικαστὴν, or both for κριτὴν ἤ μεριστήν in order to make explicit an allusion to Exod 2:14.

rative, Jesus is already endowed with the titles "Son of the Most High" (1:32), "Son of God" (1:35), "Savior" (2:11), and "Messiah" (2:11), and it is made known that he will preside over an eternal kingdom (1:33) and possess unusual acumen (συνέσει; 2:47). In Chapter 10, the narrator allows readers to overhear a prayer in which Jesus discloses that the Father has handed everything (πάντα) over to him (v.22), hinting at his role as *cosmic* judge and divider.[13] For readers who, based on his impressive credentials thus far, infer that Jesus has received such a role (or that it will be confirmed later),[14] Jesus' dismissive retort may prove ironic and serve to further enhance his ethos. While he has not been awarded earthly authority as a judge or divider by his fellows, God has already designated him as such in a cosmic sense.

Having reconstructed the irony of the rhetorical question, readers are further instructed as to Jesus' true identity, reminded of his divinely sanctioned authority (which, in Luke, contrasts markedly with the fragile authority claimed by the religious authorities), and thus fully prepared to receive the strong warning against πλεονεξία in v.15. Shifting his attention outward to all in earshot (πρὸς αὐτούς; v.15), it appears that Jesus has completely written-off the man's request, the motivation of which is still unclear. The man disappears from the scene, and Jesus uses the occasion to instruct the crowd, first with a firm, uncompromising apostrophe (v.15) and then with a supporting proof in the form of a parable (vv.16–21).

Jesus prefaces his *apostrophe* with a strong double-imperative unparalleled elsewhere in the Gospel:[15] "Take care and be on guard against (ὁρᾶτε καὶ φυλάσσεσθε) every kind of πλεονεξία." The man's request has elicited a powerful emotional reaction from Jesus, which assists readers in further narrowing motivational possibilities behind his former dismissive retort. Jesus, it seems, assumes that the man's request, even if a contestation of Deuteronomic legislation that favored the elder sibling, is ultimately motivated by greed.[16] The apostrophe itself is inclusive of

---

[13] "Divider" in the sense of a judge who separates the righteous from the wicked.

[14] Not surprisingly, this role is later confirmed, particularly when Jesus speaks about the role the Son of Man will play in ushering in a new era (e.g., 17:22–37; 21:27, 34–36; 22:69).

[15] See Seccombe, *Possessions and the Poor in Luke-Acts*, 139; Hendrickx, *The Parables of Jesus*, 98–99.

[16] As God's Son and Messiah, who is endowed with unique powers and knowledge, readers wishing to align themselves as best they can with the narratee are to trust that his judgment is correct, even if it seems hastily drawn and not based on verifiable

every kind (πάσης) of πλεονεξία, but the *ratio* that follows, in addition to providing a reason why one should avoid πλεονεξία, delineates its object with greater specificity: "For one's life does not consist in one's *possessions*, even when they abound." In the ratio, Jesus narrows the scope of πλεονεξία to material possessions, presumably the object of the man's desire as well.

Though this is its only occurrence in the Gospel, the term πλεονεξία was widely known in the Greco-Roman world.[17] Plutarch defines it generally by appealing to its etymology: "πλεονεξία never rests from acquiring τὸ πλέον."[18] At its core, for Hellenistic philosophers the term entails an insatiable desire for more that exceeds normal levels of consumption and disrupts social and even cosmic harmony.[19] Most Hellenistic philosophers prized moderation above all else,[20] and therefore πλεονεξία was widely regarded "as a form of depravity."[21] For instance, Diodorus Siculus called it "the metropolis of all evil deeds,"[22] and Dio Chrysostom referred to it as "the greatest evil."[23] In many places, however, πλεονεξία was also associated with an aggressive, ruthless, and sometimes violent grasping for power or honor *at the expense of others*.[24] This association may be found in the LXX (e.g., Ezek 22:27), first century Jewish writers such as Josephus (B.J. 7.256) and Philo (*Mos.* 1.56; *Agr.* 83), and among Greek philosophers such as Plato (e.g., *Leg.* X, 906c; *Resp.* II, 362b; 365d) and numerous other Greco-Roman writers such as Diodorus Siculus (17.70.5), Thucydides (3.45.4), and Dio Chrysostom (67.9).[25] If we assume not only the more general

---

evidence. To be sure, readers may feel that Jesus has not given this man a fair hearing and wish to contest or resist his judgment, but his assessment of other characters contributes to the overall evaluative point of view of the Gospel, which the narrator hopes his narratee will eventually share (1:1–4). Whenever Jesus becomes the focalizer, even if his perception seems unfounded or his reaction rash, a powerful rhetorical device is deployed.

[17] The term also appears in numerous New Testament vice-lists (e.g., Mark 7:22; Rom 1:29; Eph 4:19; 5:3).

[18] *On the Love of Wealth* 1 (Mor. 523 E) as quoted in Johnson, *The Gospel of Luke*, 198.

[19] Delling, "πλεονέκτης, πλεονεκτέω, πλεονεξία," in *TDNT* VI, 266–69.

[20] John R. Donahue, *The Gospel in Parable* (Philadelphia: Fortress Press, 1988), 177.

[21] Green, *The Gospel of Luke*, 489.

[22] Ibid.

[23] *Or.* 67.7. See Delling, "πλεονέκτης, πλεονεκτέω, πλεονεξία," 268.

[24] See Spicq, "πλεονεξία, pleonexia," in *TLNT* III, 117–18; Delling, "πλεονέκτης, πλεονεκτέω, πλεονεξία," 266–70.

[25] See especially Spicq, "πλεονεξία, pleonexia," 117–18; Delling, "πλεονέκτης, πλεονεκτέω, πλεονεξία," 266–69.

connotation of an insatiable desire for more that exceeds typical levels of consumption but attribute to πλεονεξία a rapacious will-to-power that seeks one's own advantage without regard for the interests of others, Jesus appears to have associated the man from the crowd with other ruthless elite who, while steadfastly determined to advance their own interests, show no concern whatsoever for the poor. In view of his commitment and mission to the poor (4:18–19), his angry rejoinder in v.14 would then appear to be a fitting response.[26] Simple greed or covetousness is one thing, but an aggressive desire to advance one's interests at the expense of others is another and would stand in direct opposition to Jesus' mission to improve conditions for the poor. Because πλεονεξία occurs only here in Luke[27] and the motivation behind Jesus' and the man's terse exchange has proven so elusive, it is difficult to render a decision as to which of the two associations to embrace. For now, we must be content with the awareness that both associations are available and move forward.

2. *Reading the Parable: 12:16–21*[28]

And he spoke a parable to them, saying, "The land of a certain rich man yielded well."

The narrator intrudes very briefly to inform readers of a shift to parabolic discourse and immediately withdraws. Jesus, who assumes the role of an embedded or intradiegetic narrator, now offers a parable as proof for the succinct proposition and ratio in v.15. If heard within the context of the Greco-Roman rhetorical tradition, Jesus' parable will be expected to further clarify the proposition,[29] but there is certainly no

[26] The narrator refuses to offer descriptive labels, but perhaps this man was accompanied by an entourage of servants or, like those who live in royal palaces, was dressed in "soft robes" and "fine clothing" (μαλακοῖς ἱματίοις…ἱματισμῷ ἐνδόξῳ; see 7:25), external factors that may have contributed to an overwhelmingly negative visceral reaction. At the level of discourse, it remains difficult to assess motivation, so readers may wish to construct a visual image of the incident in search of other possibilities at the level of story (admittedly hypothetical) that may help explain the puzzling exchange.

[27] I.e., there are no other occurrences with which to compare it.

[28] Having explored the pre-text, it is at this point that the text will be broken into lexias (manageable reading units) and the hypertext model outlined in the first chapter will be employed.

[29] See, e.g., Mack and Robbins, *Patterns of Persuasion in the Gospels*, 147–48; George A. Kennedy, *New Testament Interpretation through Rhetorical Criticism* (Chapel Hill: The University of North Carolina Press, 1984), 21–22.

guarantee that the embedded story will accomplish its goal. The new story deserves a hearing in its own right and may elicit numerous unintended associations, thereby sending readers in multiple directions, possibly even detracting from the clarity of the initial proposition.

Remarkably, with only five words Jesus introduces a protagonist ("a certain rich man"), provides a setting (ἡ χώρα), and summarizes many months of nature's activity (εὐφόρησεν). Though the man from the crowd in v.13 was characterized only indirectly through his verbal request, the protagonist here is characterized directly, indeed *defined* exclusively by his wealth. Readers have likely internalized a negative evaluation of wealth by this point in the narrative. For instance, as early as Chapter 1, Jesus' mother Mary affirms in a hymn of praise that God has scattered the proud, brought down the powerful from their thrones, and sent out the rich (πλουτοῦντας) empty-handed (1:51–53). Moreover, in his Sermon on the Plain, Jesus pronounces the first of his three woes against the rich: "But woe to those who are rich (τοῖς πλουσίοις), for you are receiving in full (ἀπέχετε) your consolation" (6:24). The setting (ἡ χώρα) further contributes to our initial portrait of this man: he owns not a small field or plot of land, typically designated by the Greek word ἀγρός, but probably "a large country estate."[30] While χώρα essentially indicates dry land as opposed to water, in the Gospels it is generally used with reference to the open country or large tracts of land such as a district or region.[31] This is no tenant farmer: probably a wealthy landowner with many slaves and laborers, he looks out over enormous acreage. Notably, he is not identified by his occupation as cultivator or farmer (e.g., γεωργός) but by his economic status/class. Indeed, as Mary Ann Beavis has argued, Jesus has probably introduced us to an absentee landlord who resided in the city and only occasionally visited his property to make sure his managers were doing their job.[32] In light of the negative evaluation of the rich in the Gospel thus far, it will be difficult to identify with this man. Has Jesus preconditioned us to

---

[30] Charles Hedrick, *Parables as Poetic Fictions: The Creative Voice of Jesus* (Peabody, MA: Hendrickson Publishers, 1994), 154.

[31] *BDAG*, 1093–94.

[32] "The Foolish Landowner (Luke 12:16b–20)," in *Jesus and his Parables: Interpreting the Parables of Jesus Today* (ed. V. George Shillington; Edinburgh: T & T Clark, 1997), 64.

judge this man negatively before he even has an opportunity to speak or act?[33]

"And he began reasoning to himself, 'What will I do? For, I do not have space where I may gather my crops.'"

After a short summary covering many months, the story decelerates rapidly and focuses on the moment when the landowner becomes aware of the magnitude of the year's harvest and his subsequent attempt to resolve his dilemma. Jesus invites readers into this man's thought processes by making explicit his internal monologue. Strikingly, from this point forward nothing will transpire outside of the landowner's mind. The parable is entirely phonodramatic and therefore lacking in perceivable action visible to the mind's eye. We may, of course, visualize a large country estate with fields full of grain and a landowner gazing out over his many acres in deep reflection. But beyond this provisional image, nothing will actually "happen." Furthermore, Jesus shows no interest whatsoever in this man's past or character. He may, for instance, have been stingy and habitually underpaid his hired hands and underfed his animals, or he may just as well have been exceedingly generous and kind to his slaves and seasonal employees. Jesus assigns a single socio-economic label ("rich") and proceeds immediately to his internal ruminations.

The landowner's bountiful yield, while certainly good news, takes him by surprise: his present facilities are not equipped to handle the harvest. As Philip Sellew observes, he faces a practical rather than a moral dilemma.[34] Understandably concerned that the harvest not go to waste, he will consider his options. At this point, readers may hear the landowner's question, "What shall I do?," as an invitation to enter the situation, entertain a variety of responses, and even begin formulating possible solutions.[35] With the landowner, we too may ask: "What would

---

[33] If we ascribe to πλεονεξία in v.15 the added negative valence of acquiring advantage at the expense of others and assume that Jesus saw this quality in the man from the crowd, there is even less of a chance that readers will identify with the protagonist. Given that parabolic discourse implies a comparison of some kind (παραβολή = "a casting alongside"), many readers will infer a comparison between the man from the crowd and the rich man in Jesus' parable.

[34] "Interior Monologue as a Narrative Device in the Parables of Luke," *JBL* 111 (1992), 244.

[35] See Denis Marion, "Paraboles of Crise: Le Riche Insensé; Le Riche et Lazarus," *Esprit et Vie* 106 (1996), 227.

I do? Would I give what will not fit in my barns to those in need? Would I seek at least a nominal profit by selling the surplus to nearby landowners whose facilities can accommodate more? Would I consider expanding my facilities?" The problem, in any case, introduces an element of suspense, eliciting readers' curiosity and awakening anticipation. What course(s) of action will the landowner consider?

"And he said, 'This I will do! I will tear down my barns and build bigger ones, and I will gather everything there—my grain and good things.'"
The presence of the καὶ εἶπεν (v.18) separating the landowner's initial question from the beginning of his resolution indicates that some time has elapsed, though readers are not told how much. The span of the ellipsis—minutes, hours, days?—remains unknown. What is clear, however, it that his resolution is offered with firm resolve: "*This* I will do!" He may have mulled over several possibilities and vacillated for some time, but any misgivings have now receded.

Although this first part of the resolution is replete with first person pronouns,[36] one need not see egoism at work, for both positive and negative responses are possible. Bernard Brandon Scott, for instance, suggests that the man's decision may thus far call to mind either Joseph's prudence and concern for sustaining his people during the lean years (Gen 41:35–36) or the Israelites' gathering of twice as much manna at the end of the week so that they would not go hungry on the Sabbath.[37] These two familiar stories from the Hebrew Bible constitute a conceivable "repertoire" from which readers might draw in assessing the man's thought processes.[38] Furthermore, argues Scott, if one assumes from the perspective of Israel's wisdom tradition that "wealth implies social responsibility,"[39] "an audience judges the rich man prudent and wise, preparing for the lean years ahead for both himself and his people."[40] However, for someone influenced primarily by Israel's prophetic tradition or the later apocalyptic tradition, such resolve to gather

---

36 "I" as subject of the verb occurs four times; "my" as a genitive of possession is found twice.

37 *Hear Then the Parable: A Commentary on the Parables of Jesus* (Minneapolis: Fortress Press, 1989), 133.

38 Ibid., 134. To Joseph's storing of food for leaner years, one might also add Proverbs' example of industry and prudence drawn from the natural world: ants, though "without strength," are nonetheless "exceedingly wise" in preparing (ἑτοιμαζονται) food in the summer (30:25).

39 See, e.g., Sir 31:5–11.

40 Ibid., 135.

and store may trigger images of a corrupt and wealthy elite who have no regard for the welfare of others.[41] Several commentators therefore attribute self-interest to the rich man's opening reflections. Joel Green, for example, suggests that he "does not plan to contribute to the current year's saturation of the market with his surplus, but will hold his harvest back in order to achieve a higher price when the market is not glutted," a decision that both hurts the local economy and enhances "his economic power and position of status in the village as others are made more and more dependent on him."[42] Charles Hedrick raises this possibility as well: the landowner might be saving his grain, which Varro says can be stored for 50–100 years, in order to maximize his profit margin when supply is down and demand is up.[43] Mary Ann Beavis also ascribes to this man the malicious intent of hoarding grain until a shortage drives up the price.[44]

At this point in his monologue, however, I would argue that it is difficult to defend an overly negative evaluation of the landowner. Selfishness and malicious intent must be inferred based on prior intertextual associations, since the motivation behind his decision to tear down his existing facilities and build new ones is not yet made explicit.[45] To be sure, the man's preliminary reflections may make readers uneasy, but a decisive judgment for or against this man is not yet prudent. Two aspects of his decision, however, seem amiss and may at least be hinting at incompetence: 1) tearing down existing structures with a bumper crop awaiting immediate harvest and building entirely new facilities; 2) gathering not only his grain in these new facilities but his ἀγαθά (lit. "good things/goods"). The landowner proposes an outrageous, almost laughable plan of dismantling old barns and constructing larger ones with fields full of mature grain. Can he possibly manage to accomplish this task in time to store his surplus? Consequently, Charles Hedrick wonders: "[I]s the narrator simply having a little fun with the audience

[41] See, e.g., Ezek 43; 1 En. 92–105; Rev 18. George W. E. Nickelsburg offers an excellent analysis of these traditions in the Epistle of Enoch ("Revisiting the Rich and the Poor in I Enoch 92–105 and The Gospel According to Luke," in *SBL 1998 Seminar Papers* 37 [Missoula, MT: Scholars Press, 1998], esp. 579–95).

[42] *The Gospel of Luke*, 490–91.

[43] *Parables as Poetic Fictions*, 156–57.

[44] "The Foolish Landowner (Luke 12:16b–20)," 64.

[45] After attaching to this man a single socio-economic label ("rich"), Jesus turns the process of character construction over to readers. By "showing" readers this man's internal thought processes (a risky, less precise means of characterization), Jesus invites hearers/readers to begin constructing a portrait for themselves.

at the farmer's expense?"[46] Moreover, the addition of τὰ ἀγαθά μου to σῖτον ("grain") at the end of his statement is indeed strange and a bit surprising given that the neuter plural elsewhere is generally used to describe material possessions.[47] Several scribes appeared to have been troubled by this as well and so substituted either τὰ γενήματά μου ("my produce/yield")[48] or τοὺς καρπούς μου ("my crops").[49] If one is to take the landowner's proposition at face value, it appears that he plans to put not only his grain (σῖτον) in his new barns but all of his "goods" or "possessions" as well. Is he foolishly electing to expose nearly everything he owns to thieves and the elements of nature? Neither the decision to build larger barns with a bumper crop awaiting harvest nor his desire to store all of his "possessions" in barns seems to make much sense. Surely something about the landowner's initial ruminations is amiss. If Jesus is hinting at a future criticism of this man, it may not cohere in kind with what has been presented in 1:53 and 6:24. In sum, while a *moral* critique of the rich man's plan is difficult to establish at this point, his proposals do seem odd and may very well foreshadow some sort of negative evaluation that will soon emerge with greater clarity.

"'And I will say to my soul, "Soul, you have many good things laid up for many years."'"

Thus far, the rationale behind this man's plan has remained hidden. We did not know whether he was wisely storing produce for leaner years or seeking to grow his wealth. With this statement, however, Jesus seems to be characterizing him in much the same way he characterized the man from the crowd: as one whose desire-for-more (πλεονεξία) has a self-serving end. The landowner views this surprisingly abundant harvest as an opportunity to alleviate some anxiety over the future and find solace in knowing that, even if people in his region should face food shortages due to famine or other environmental or political factors, *his* barns will be full of "many good things" (πολλὰ ἀγαθὰ). His primary reason for building larger storage facilities is to establish some measure of security in a stubbornly unpredictable world. Furthermore, in view

---

[46] *Parables as Poetic Fictions*, 158.

[47] See, e.g., Luke 1:53; 12:19; 16:25. *BDAG* does indicate that ἀγαθά in extent literature can refer to crops on occasion (e.g., Diodorus Siculus 3.46.1 and 19.26.3), but this would be its only such use in Luke.

[48] א* D it (sy$^{s.c}$). See *BDAG*, 193.

[49] a c d e. See *BDAG*, 509–10.

of how he constructs his self-address ("I will say to *my* soul...*you* [sg.] have many goods laid up"), it is clear that his efforts are focused solely on providing for *his* own welfare. No one else is in view—no family members, friends, servants, hired laborers, or other persons in the community. Already wealthy (v.16), he hopes to further increase his wealth, which he believes in coming years will allay anxiety and offer consolation in the event that unforeseeable environmental or political changes should arise. Others who have not been so fortunate will have to fend for themselves.

For Bernard B. Scott, this is the moment readers unexpectedly discover that the rich man "is surely no Joseph in Egypt preparing to protect his people from hard days ahead."[50] Having devised a plan that serves only his needs and refuses to consider those in the community of which he is a part, he "mismanages the miracle."[51] Certainly he is out of step with what Jesus requires of his followers, who are asked only to pray for and consume food that is "essential" (ἐπιούσιον; 11:3). Additionally, in seeking an exemption from the divinely appointed task of working for one's daily sustenance (Gen 3:17–19; cf. Sir 40:1)—an option not available to small landholders and tenant farmers—he will be isolating himself from many of the common struggles that bind people together. In effect, while adding stone and mortar to his fortress in hope of greater security, he will banish his neighbor from view and further withdraw into an exclusive, private kingdom of abundance.

A self-serving motive is indeed beginning to emerge,[52] but shall we condemn his thought processes as malicious or chuckle at his unwarranted self-assurance that "many good things" will indeed be available to him for "many years" (ἔτη πολλά)? Barns, for instance, are hardly secure; their contents are vulnerable to thieves, rodents, and insects. Furthermore, in a volatile political and economic environment like first century, Roman-occupied Judea, any resident would be hard-pressed to say with certainty that s/he could count on retaining possession of both land and property for many years to come. Given hints of gross incompetence in the man's previous ruminations (v.18), should we evaluate his self-address here as merely foolish and refrain from

---

[50] *Hear Then the Parable*, 135.

[51] Ibid., 136–37.

[52] The disclosure of his true motive behind the construction of new barns may distance this already "rich" character from many (if not most) readers.

characterizing him as callously self-serving and indifferent to the plight of his neighbor?

Again, it depends entirely upon whether one is working primarily from within Israel's wisdom tradition or the prophetic or later apocalyptic traditions. An intertext such as Sirach 11:1–28, a passage from Israel's wisdom tradition (and one commonly referenced by commentators as a fitting parallel to this parable),[53] may encourage readers to judge him as a mere fool who has not grappled sufficiently with life's unpredictability, while smugly assuming that his πολλὰ ἀγαθὰ will offer him some security and solace. In Chapter 11, Ben Sira first reminds readers that God alone controls fortunes (v.6) and doles out "good things and bad, life and death, poverty and wealth" (v.14; *NRSV*) and then offers the following advice to any who might stumble into wealth: "Do not say, 'I have self-sufficiency/independence (αὐτάρκη). From now on, what harm can come to me?'" (v.24). Ben Sira, in effect, steers readers away from naïve self-confidence and toward a healthy respect for life's transience and frailty. If Jesus' parable is read in conjunction with Ben Sira's instruction, then we are presented with a fool whose confidence is misguided, baseless, and self-deceiving (i.e., he hurts only himself).[54] However, if we juxtapose passages from the Epistle of Enoch (1 En. 92–105) that passionately condemn the accumulation of wealth and view it largely as a product of subjugation and exploitation of the poor, then Jesus has created a character-type who stands in direct opposition to his mission (4:18–19).[55] It is difficult to decide at this point whether to characterize him as mere fool or as callous, self-serving antagonist to the good news; we must await the final installment of his internal monologue.

"Relax, eat, drink, and be merry!"[56]

In addition to seeking an exemption from labor and a panacea for his anxiety over the future, this man hopes to enjoy life to the full. Sig-

---

[53] E.g., Hedrick, *Parables as Poetic Fictions*, 149.

[54] Commentators who look primarily to Israel's wisdom tradition as a backdrop include, e.g., H. Hendrickx (*The Parables of Jesus*, 104), J. Dupont (*Les béatitudes* III [Paris: Gabalda, 1973], 183), and R. Meynet (*L'Evangile Selon Saint Luc*, 144).

[55] One commentator who appears to foreground Israel's prophetic and apocalyptic traditions is Mary Ann Beavis ("The Foolish Landowner [Luke 12:16b–20]," 64–66).

[56] Interestingly, Codex Bezae only retains ἀναπαύου, thus entirely omitting, "Eat, drink, and be merry!" However, only Westcott-Hort's edition of the GNT places MS. D's reading in the main text.

nificantly, eating and drinking (φάγε; πίε) are bracketed by two present imperatives (ἀναπαύου; εὐφραίνου), which suggests that he is proposing not a single celebration after the harvest but a lifestyle characterized by rest and merriment. However, does his final statement provide readers with enough information to ascribe the charge of hedonism to him?

Charles Hedrick suggests that the statement in itself suggests nothing "of the grotesque self-indulgence and dissipation that has come to characterize the Rich Farmer under the influence of Luke's reading of the story."[57] He draws attention to similar formulaic statements in Tobit 7:9–11 and Ecclesiastes 8:15,[58] neither of which is presented with negative overtones. In fact, in both passages, he argues, the injunction to eat, drink, and enjoy oneself is framed as a fully appropriate response to God's gifts in creation. In Tobit 7, however, this exhortation (φάγε καὶ πίε καὶ ἡδέως γίνου; v.10) is spoken in the context of a special celebration before marriage and not offered as a way of life to be pursued with regularity. In Ecclesiastes 8:15, the Teacher offers a similar injunction (τοῦ φαγεῖν καὶ τοῦ πιεῖν καὶ τοῦ εὐφρανθῆναι) in view of life's vanity (ματαιότης; v.14) and for the purpose of counterbalancing or easing our daily toil (μόχθῳ; v.15). Indeed, as Hedrick argues, there is no indication that the Teacher is recommending a life of self-indulgence and dissipation. However, nowhere does he, like the landowner, entertain the option of forgoing work altogether and leaving others behind in their struggle for sustenance and shelter. In fact, the Teacher assumes the very opposite to be true: human beings are imprisoned by labor and vanity throughout their lives and can escape neither one until death (see 9:10). In view of the many demands and perplexities life presents to us, says the Teacher, at least we can gather occasionally and enjoy the fruits of our labor and one another's company.[59] The landowner's self-address, however, differs in two respects, neither of which is paralleled in Tobit 7:10 or Ecclesiastes 8:15: 1) he proposes ongoing rest (ἀναπαύου) from the divinely appointed task of labor; and 2) he hopes that both rest and celebration will become a way of life rather than remain occasional or intermittent.

The landowner's final remark need not raise entirely negative associations, as Hedrick argues, but his unique formulation of the phrase does

---

[57] *Parables as Poetic Fictions*, 150.

[58] Cf. 2:24; 3:12–13.

[59] All three verbs in 8:15 are in the aorist tense; there is therefore no indication that Qoheleth recommends such celebration with regularity.

diverge from similar injunctions in Tobit and Ecclesiastes, at least *suggesting* hedonism. The present imperatives in the landowner's self-address contrast markedly with the aorist imperatives in Hedrick's intertexts and hint not at sporadic but ongoing festivity. Consequently, Bernard B. Scott believes that his wish is better aligned with Epicurean thought, which recommends merriment in view of life's brevity and "the inescapable fate of death,"[60] and Abraham J. Malherbe situates his final remark alongside others that convey greed and hedonistic self-interest, both strongly condemned by the Greco-Roman rhetorical and philosophical traditions.[61] Valuable resources, it seems, will be consumed regularly and rapidly—and all by one individual. The landowner appears to be planning not a special celebration to which many in the community are invited but a never-ending party for himself. Already rich (v.16), he plans both to grow his wealth and to increase his level of consumption. Moreover, he is to be the sole beneficiary of the surprisingly high yield, which, interestingly, is largely due to natural processes and not his own ingenuity and hard work.

"But God said to him,"

This is the only parable in which God directly intervenes as a character. Alongside Jesus' and the narrator's words, God's voice contributes to what John Darr has called the Gospel's "'*divine*' frame of reference,"[62] or the overall evaluative point of view by which other characters, actions, and speech may be judged.[63] For readers seeking to align themselves with this perspective (and thus with the Gospel's narratee), God's subsequent address and assessment of the rich man's ruminations will be received as fully trustworthy and accurate. In fact, although heard only infrequently,[64] there is no more authoritative voice in the Gospel. It is still unclear, however, whether Jesus is introducing direct discourse that is presented to the landowner either audibly or by means of a dream[65]

[60] *Hear Then the Parable*, 137. Cf. Paul's reference to Epicurean thought in 1 Cor 15:32.

[61] "The Christianization of a Topos (Luke 12:13–34)," *Novum Testamentum* 38 (1996), 123–135.

[62] *On Character Building: The Reader and the Rhetoric of Characterization in Luke-Acts*, 51. The italics are his.

[63] See Powell, *What is Narrative Criticism?*, 24.

[64] E.g., 3:22; 9:35.

[65] See, e.g., Fitzmyer, *The Gospel According to Luke X–XXIV*, 973.

or whether what follows is an aside only for hearers/readers and to which the rich man therefore does not have access.[66]

"'Fool!'"[67]

God's characterization of this man as a "fool" is striking and encourages a reevaluation of prior reflections entertained from the perspective of Israel's prophetic and apocalyptic traditions. Has God attended only to those aspects of his ruminations that hint at gross incompetence and carelessness? Are readers now encouraged to assess his thought processes primarily from the perspective of Israel's wisdom tradition and refrain from considering what impact his decisions might have upon the local economy and community? Initially, at least, God appears not to characterize him as profoundly self-centered and determined to stockpile limited resources, further increase his level of consumption, and pursue a life of pleasure. Rather, he emerges as a mere "fool" who either risks losing his bountiful harvest while awaiting the construction of his new facilities, jeopardizes his many "good things" by exposing them to thieves and the natural elements, or naively assumes that this recent windfall can guarantee the rest, merriment, and security for which he longs.

"'This very night they[68] *are demanding your soul back from you. And the things that you prepared, to whom will they belong?'"*

Although the rich man has formulated a plan, Jesus does not inform us that he has taken any action, so God's announcement of the man's

---

[66] Both Hedrick (*Parables as Poetic Fictions*, 147, 149) and Hendrickx (*The Parables of Jesus*, 103) argue for this position.

[67] Denis Marion observes alliteration here: ἄφρων phonetically mimics the final word in the landowner's monologue, εὐφραίνου ("Paraboles de crise: Le riche insensé; le riche et Lazare," 227).

[68] Fitzmyer prefers to view ἀπαιτοῦσιν as an indefinite, impersonal 3rd plural and therefore as a substitute for the divine passive (*The Gospel According to Luke X–XXIV*, 974). Other examples may be found in 6:38; 16:9; 23:31. I much prefer a more literal reading. Angels escorting human beings (or their "souls") either to Hades or to Heaven is a popular motif in some first century Jewish literature (e.g., *The Testament of Abraham*). Furthermore, in the Gospel itself, one character (Lazarus) will be carried "by angels" to "Abraham's bosom" after he dies (16:22). Mary Ann Beavis, when reflecting on Jesus' parable apart from the frame provided by the diegetic narrator, suggests that the subject of the verb may be a group of angry peasants who come and kill the landowner. The landowner, therefore, would ultimately bring about his own death ("The Foolish Landowner [Luke 12:16b–20]," 64–66). Others have suggested that the subject of the verb constitutes his many possessions (see, e.g., R. Wayne Stacy, "Luke 12:13–21: The Parable of the Rich Fool," *Review and Expositor* 94 [1997], 288).

death is unexpected and unsettling. Can God really be pronouncing a death sentence as a direct result of his ruminations?[69] In view of God's forbearance toward "sinners" elsewhere in the Gospel, such a position may be difficult to defend. Nowhere else is a character sentenced to death for misguided internal reflections. Two other options, however, do seem plausible. Either we can: 1) posit an ellipsis between the conclusion of the man's internal monologue and God's announcement during which he actually implemented his proposals and began to realize his dream; or 2) infer that his appointed time of death unfortunately coincided with a spectacular harvest and that God is simply informing him of this tragic twist of fate only hours before he is to die.

The reader reaches a moment of undecidability here, for while the formulation "this very night" (ταύτῃ τῇ νυκτὶ; v.20) suggests that God responded almost immediately, the way in which the concluding rhetorical question has been formulated ("The things that you prepared [ἡτοίμασας; v.20], to whom will they belong?") seems to indicate that the rich man has already had time to realize his dream. In fact, if we do not posit a fairly significant ellipsis spanning several months, it is difficult to account for why ἡτοιμάζω is found in the aorist tense. We can, of course, suppose that God speaks to the landowner on the eve of his enthusiastic ruminations, but then "the things that you prepared" (ἃ... ἡτοίμασας) would refer not to what he plans to amass but to the wealth he already possesses at the beginning of the parable (v.16). In other words, God would be judging him for his wealth and not his misguided plans. This, it seems, would render Jesus' disclosure of the man's thought processes in vv.17–19 superfluous. Thus, a tentative decision in favor of an ellipsis of several months is best: Because God assumes that the landowner has already brought his plan to fruition, the divine pronouncement in v.20 is offered only at some point *after* the rich man is able to construct new facilities and fully embrace his idyllic life of rest and merriment.

God's final rhetorical question may leave readers who constructed a profoundly self-centered character bent on increasing both his wealth and level of consumption a bit confused. Indeed, it initially appeared

[69] In view of how the parable has been framed by the Gospel's author, Mary Ann Beavis believes this is exactly what God does. For her, because "God is the agent of the man's demise," readers are presented with a violent and "punitive God," a portrayal that ultimately frustrates readers' attempts to open-up liberative possibilities for the parable ("The Foolish Landowner [Luke 12:16b–20]," 67–68).

that his plans, which included no one else and were designed entirely for the purpose of allaying *his* anxiety and gratifying *his* desires, were detrimental to the community and stood in direct opposition to Jesus' mission to the poor (4:18–19). Surprisingly, when God does intervene, none of these issues are brought to the fore; rather, the focus is upon this man's failure (as "fool") to realize that a storehouse of possessions can guarantee neither the kind of life he envisioned nor even the continuation of life itself.[70]

(")So it is for the one who treasures-up for him/herself and is not rich toward God.(")

The parable's concluding application (possibly spoken either by the diegetic or intradiegetic narrator)[71] works against the grain of God's prior pronouncement. While God characterizes the landowner as foolish and naïve for presuming that "many good things" should guarantee "many years" of rest and merriment, the application draws attention to his desire to "treasure-up for himself" (θησαυρίζων ἑαυτῷ) and so frames him in more negative terms as self-serving and intent on growing his estate. Whose characterization takes precedence? To whom shall we listen? If we were to follow MSS D it^{a,b,d}, all of which omit v.21, then God's voice is the last we hear and readers are encouraged to judge him as mere "fool." If we follow, however, the majority of manuscripts and therefore heed the voice of the narrator, our inclination is to affirm the portrayal that emerged at the end of the monologue of a profoundly self-centered individual "treasuring-up" for the purpose of increasing both his wealth and level of consumption.

Since the omission of v.21 is confined to a single manuscript tradition and appears to be accidental,[72] I would propose following the vast majority of textual witnesses here and therefore allowing the narrator (whether diegetic or intradiegetic) to have the final word. To be sure, as God said, this man was indeed a "fool" first to assume that his "many good things" would be safe in barns from thieves, rodents, and insects and then to suppose that a full storehouse could guarantee a long life of rest and merriment. He is, however, ultimately defined by the narrator

[70] Some manuscripts conclude the episode here and do not add Jesus' (or possibly the narrator's) application in v.21 (D it^{a,b,d}).

[71] The parentheses around the quotation marks signal this ambiguity.

[72] See, e.g., Bruce Metzger's brief comments (*A Textual Commentary on the Greek New Testament* [2d ed.; Stuttgart: Deutsche Bibelgesellschaft, 2001], 135).

as "one who treasures-up for himself"—the final label attributed to him and therefore the one that will linger on in the minds of readers, perhaps even trumping earlier tags of "rich" (v.16) and "fool" (v.20). The landowner, already wealthy, corrals a stockpile of grain in hope of growing his wealth, allaying his anxiety over the future, and claiming a permanent exemption from the divinely appointed task of struggling for his sustenance. Increasing his level of consumption, he will withdraw even further from his community into an exclusive, private realm of rest, abundance, and merriment.

Nowhere does Jesus or the narrator inform us of the landowner's fate. Admittedly, since God as character is to be trusted, many readers will assume the rich man died later that evening, only hours after the divine announcement. However, might he have acknowledged his error and pleaded with God to spare his life? According to the *Testament of Abraham*, Abraham was able to forestall his death. When the time came for the patriarch's soul to be taken up into heaven, the archangel Michael pursued him relentlessly without success. Finally, God resorted to sending Death, who, after being rebuffed by Abraham as well, was forced to disguise himself and trick the patriarch into kissing his right hand. With this kiss, the battle for Abraham's soul was finally over, and angels escorted him into heaven (20:12; Recension A). Although not written down until after the composition of the Gospel, some rabbinic traditions affirm that repentance and divine reconciliation always remain a possibility as long as a person is still alive, even moments before death.[73] In any case, the landowner's death is not narrated. As with many of Jesus' parables, the "true 'end of the story'...remains untold."[74]

[73] See, e.g., *Tosefta Qiddushin* 1.14: "Rabbi Simeon deduced from Ezekiel xxxiii 12–14: 'If a man was wholly wicked all his days, and repented in the end, the Omnipresent receives him" (Quoted in E. E. Urbach, *The Sages: Their Concepts and Beliefs* Vol. I [trans. Israel Abrahams; Jerusalem: The Magnes Press, 1975], 467). See also *Ruth Rabbah* 3.3: "*In this world, he who is crooked can be made straight*, and he who is straight can become crooked, but in the hereafter he who is crooked cannot be made straight, nor he who is straight crooked" (Italics mine. Quoted in Brad H. Young, *The Parables: Jewish Tradition and Christian Interpretation* [Peabody, MA: Hendrickson Publishers, 1998], 281).

[74] Stephen Wright, "Parables on Poverty and Riches (Luke 12:13–21; 16:1–13; 16:19–31)," in *The Challenge of Jesus' Parables* (ed. Richard N. Longenecker; Grand Rapids: Eerdmans, 2000), 218.

3. *Summary*

Although the landowner's prior wealth (v.16) does not receive an explicit critique either in God's announcement (v.20) or in the narrator's concluding application (v.21), his desire to grow his wealth and secure a lifestyle marked by overconsumption and indulgence does. In fact, his very first resolution of tearing down old facilities and constructing new ones suggests to the reader that he is careless and wasteful. Would it not have been more appropriate to expand his existing facilities? This early hint is confirmed most clearly in the landowner's final self-exhortation: "Relax, eat, drink, be merry!" (v.19). The landowner's unique formulation differs significantly from similar injunctions in Tobit and Ecclesiastes, neither of which advocates merriment as a way of life or encourages ἀνάπαυσις. The present imperatives in the landowner's self-address (ἀναπαύου; εὐφραίνου) do suggest hedonism, i.e., a way of life defined primarily by rest and celebration. Furthermore, he proposes to gather and store the harvest in order to satisfy only *his* desires; no one else is in view. Presumably, while he can feel secure in his surplus[75] and opt out of labor altogether, others in his community will have no choice but to continue working the land and to fend for themselves in the event of environmental or political changes.

The parable itself, if read apart from its context, does not seem to offer the overtly negative portrayal of the landowner foreshadowed in Jesus' opening apostrophe (v.15) and confirmed in the concluding application (v.21). In fact, only with the landowner's final self-exhortation in v.19 ("Relax, eat, drink, be merry!") can readers begin attributing self-indulgence and overconsumption to him—a portrayal that, surprisingly, is not confirmed by God's announcement in v.20. God does not criticize him for proposing a way of life marked by self-indulgence but focuses on his failure as "fool" to realize that his many possessions ultimately cannot the offer the security and solace he desires. If readers were to stop here (as readers of MSS D it[a,b,c] once did), an overwhelmingly negative evaluation would be difficult to defend, for his only real flaws are incompetence and failing to account for life's fragility and transience. Rather, it is primarily the parable's context that encourages

[75] The reader may be reminded here of Jesus' words in the Sermon on the Plain: "But woe to you who are rich, for you are receiving in full your consolation" (6:24). The landowner's surplus will indeed provide 'consolation in full,' though it will not last (see 12:20).

readers to confirm the suggestion of overconsumption and hedonism in his final self-exhortation (v.19) and view him both as an example of πλεονεξία and as "one who treasures-up for himself" (v.21) Moreover, if readers chose in v.15 to ascribe not only greed but a rapacious and aggressive desire to advance one's interest at the expense of others to πλεονεξία, the landowner may very well be associated with a class of ruthless elite who show no concern whatsoever for the poor and disenfranchised. Jesus' parable would then be an instance of dramatic irony in which readers, already set against the "rich" (see 1:53; 6:24), view the landowner as a hopelessly tragic character from the outset (v.16), predictably formulating a plan that stands in direct opposition to Jesus' mission to the poor.[76]

B. The Parable of the Father and his Two Sons (15:11–32)

1. *Impressions of Jesus' Teaching on Wealth and Possessions in 12:22–15:10*

At the conclusion of the parable, Jesus turns to address his disciples (12:22–34), building upon his former remarks to the crowd (διὰ τοῦτο; v.22). While the rich man was excessively preoccupied about the welfare of his "soul" (ψυχή; v.19), Jesus encourages disciples not to worry about theirs (μεριμνᾶτε τῇ ψυχῇ; v.22). As a contrast to the rich man, Jesus turns to the natural world in search of a positive example for discipleship. Ravens neither sow nor reap nor store away in barns as the rich man did, yet God provides for them; lilies neither toil nor spin, yet not even Solomon, surely far wealthier than the protagonist in Jesus' parable, was "clothed like one of these" (v.27). Because God already knows what the disciples *need* (χρῄζετε; v.30; cf. 11:3), they need not worry like the landowner about securing food and drink (τί φάγητε καὶ τί πίτηε; v.29) and are therefore free to seek God's kingdom (vv.30–31). The rich man stockpiled far more than he needed, amassing a treasure here on earth. By contrast, disciples are not to accumulate but sell and give alms, thereby acquiring an inexhaustible treasure in heaven that cannot be sabotaged by thieves or decay (vv.33–34). For those who are "on the way," "treasuring-up" (v.21), a product of the inner drive for

[76] For a brief but helpful discussion of dramatic irony, see Robert Fowler, "Reader-Response Criticism," 65–70.

more and more (πλεονεξία; v.15), is to be supplanted by selling and giving (v.33). With no tangible form of security, disciples are to live by "the wisdom of insecurity,"[77] trusting that (somehow) God will provide, much as he does for the ravens and lilies.

In 14:25–33, Jesus reminds any would-be followers in the crowds of the rigorous, unrelenting demands of discipleship (vv.26–27, 33) and encourages them to consider the personal costs before joining him "on the way" (vv.28–32). Discipleship will require "hating" not only family members but one's very "life" (τὴν ψυχὴν ἑαυτοῦ) and may even involve following Jesus to the death (vv.26–27). Indeed, unless they "say good-bye" (ἀποτάσσεται) to all of their possessions, they cannot be his disciples (v.33).

The overall impression remains that following Jesus will demand both a firm break with possessions and prior commitments as well as a willingness to trust God only for what one really needs. Jesus' disciples are not to worry about their "lives" but "hate" them; they are not to store excess but sell and give. Like ravens and lilies, they are to depend entirely upon God to provide what they need.

Setting the Stage: 15:1–10

The narrator intrudes briefly to inform us that "all the tax collectors and sinners were drawing near to hear [Jesus]," whose willingness to welcome them elicits "grumbling" from Pharisees and scribes (vv.1–2). Jesus replies with two short parables:[78] The Parable of the Lost Sheep and the Parable of the Lost Coin (vv.3–10). In each, when something lost is found, a protagonist invites friends and neighbors to rejoice. The lost sheep and coin are compared to sinners, and the joy that follows their recovery represents joy in heaven over their repentance (vv.7, 10). Strikingly, the sheep and coin play no part whatsoever in their recovery but are passive recipients of the shepherd's and the woman's efforts.

---

[77] This phrase is borrowed from the title of Alan Watts's book, *The Wisdom of Insecurity: A Message for an Age of Anxiety* (New York: Vintage Books, 1951).

[78] The parables' primary audience is ambiguous: Does αὐτοὺς in v.3 refer to "Pharisees and scribes," "tax collectors and sinners," or possibly to both groups? Since "Pharisees and scribes" is the most immediate antecedent, many commentators believe Jesus directs the following parables to them (see, e.g., Hendrickx, *The Parables of Jesus*, 139, 142; C. D. Cloete and D. J. Smit, "Rejoicing with God... [Luke 15:11–32]," *Journal of Theology for Southern Africa* 66 [1989], 63). Of course, Jesus' audience for all three parables may include both groups (see, e.g., John J. Killgallen, "Luke 15 and 16: a Connection," *Biblica* 78 [1997], 371).

Both parables therefore frustrate traditional notions of repentance that place the burden for reorientation and reform upon the sinner.

While both of these parables, joined by the conjunction ἤ (v.8) and punctuated with virtually identical applications (vv.7, 10), are to be read together, the narrator interrupts afterward with εἶπεν δέ (v.11), which encourages readers to consider whether the following parable should be read alongside the previous two or in tandem with what follows. Presumably, Jesus' audience still consists of tax collectors, sinners, Pharisees, scribes, and disciples, but it is unclear whether the subsequent parable will address the very same themes found in vv.3–10, explore them from a different angle, or perhaps even introduce a new topic.

2. *Reading the Parable: 15:11–32*

"A certain man had two sons."

When introducing the three main characters, Jesus refrains from assigning labels that may prejudice his audience against or in favor of one in particular. Furthermore, neither socio-economic status nor occupation—elements that were disclosed in the opening line of the previous parable (12:16–21)—is apparent here. Even the locale remains hidden. Readers, it seems, will have to construct both the setting and the characters as they progress through the narrative.

For Bernard B. Scott, the introduction recalls Israel's two-sons mytheme, an ancient folklore motif in which both younger and elder sons play stereotyped roles.[79] Typically, the elder son is a relatively flat, uninteresting character who is dutiful yet boorish. By contrast, the younger son is a round, appealing character with whom readers are inclined to sympathize or even identify. In addition to being his parents' favorite, there is generally something scandalous, off-color, or roguish about his behavior.[80] He may journey far from home, encounter many trials, and employ underhanded or deceitful tactics to get what he wants, but inevitably things turn out well for him. For Scott, then, with these first few words Jesus evokes a common motif that elicits the

[79] *Hear Then the Parable*, esp. 109–13. Examples from the Hebrew Bible include the stories of Cain and Abel, Ishmael and Isaac, and Esau and Jacob. Closely related are stories in which the youngest of several brothers is favored and, against all odds, ultimately triumphs or rises to a place of prominence. Joseph, Benjamin, David, and Solomon all fit within this paradigm. Many believe that this ancient motif originally served to legitimate Israel's place as God's chosen among the nations.

[80] Ibid., 112, 123.

expectation of scandalous, roguish behavior from a favored younger son and boorish behavior from the elder. Moreover, although the younger son may initially encounter trial or tragedy, we ultimately expect him to triumph.[81]

"And the younger of them said to his father, 'Father, give me the share of the property that falls to me!' And he divided [his] means for life between them." Assuming this family sought to follow inheritance legislation as prescribed in the Torah, the older son would receive two-thirds of his father's estate while the younger son would receive the remaining third (see Deut 21:17). Since our primary sources for inheritance law post-date the time of Jesus, it is very difficult to move beyond this general assertion to discern with greater specificity which regulations and customs were commonly practiced in first century Judea.[82] Commentators, however, generally do not hesitate to venture a tentative reconstruction, and a consensus appears to have emerged, even if based largely on later Mishnaic material.[83] While the oral law does allow for a father to distribute an inheritance before his death, he would typically retain usufruct rights throughout the remainder of his life. Moreover, if a son should choose to sell his property, the buyer could not take possession of it until the father had died. Kenneth Bailey and Brad Young emphasize that within the context of traditional Middle Eastern culture a son's premature request for a portion of the inheritance would be received as a grave insult and tantamount to proclaiming the father already dead.[84]

---

[81] Others foreground this mytheme as well. See, e.g., François Bovon, *L'Évangile Selon Saint Luc 15,1–19,27* (Commentaire du Nouveau Testament IIIc; Genève: Labor et Fides, 2001), 44; Buetubela Balembo, "Lecture Africaine de la Bible: Essai sur l'exégèse symbolique de Lc 15, 1–32," in *Théologie Africaine: Bilan et Perspectives. Actes de la Dix-septième Semaine Théologique de Kinshasa 2–8 avril 1989* (Kinshasa: Facultés Catholiques de Kinshasa, 1989), 235; Arie Troost, "Reading for the Author's Signature: Genesis 21.1–21 and Luke 15:11–32 as Intertexts," in *A Feminist Companion to Genesis* (ed. Athalya Brenner; The Feminist Companion to the Bible 2; Sheffield: Sheffield Academic Press, 1993), 264–67. Kenneth E. Bailey, however, dismisses this mytheme as appropriate literary repertoire for the parable (*Finding the Lost: Cultural Keys to Luke 15* [St. Louis: Concordia Publishing House, 1992], esp. 118–19).

[82] See Fitzmyer's brief word of caution against relying on reconstructions of first century Palestinian inheritance law (*The Gospel According to Luke X–XXIV*, 1086).

[83] See, e.g., Joachim Jeremias, *Rediscovering the Parables* (New York: Charles Scribner's Sons, 1966), 101; Young, *The Parables*, esp. 138–39; Bailey, *Finding the Lost*, esp. 109–17; Scott, *Hear Then the Parable*, 109–11; Fitzmyer, *The Gospel According to Luke X–XXIV*, 1087.

[84] Bailey, *Finding the Lost*, 109; Young, *The Parables*, 138–39.

Therefore, by requesting a portion of the inheritance, the younger son in this parable is essentially "telling his father that he wanted him to die."[85] Strikingly, instead of adamantly refusing his son's request and exploding in anger (which was to be expected),[86] this father acquiesces. For good reason, Ben Sira strongly advises against a premature dispersal of the estate (33:20–24).[87] After all, one never knows how it will fare in the hands of children or if one might still need access to it. Ben Sira urges all fathers to distribute their inheritance only at the hour of death, not before (v.24). Thus, while certainly not outside the range of accepted practice, both the son's bold request and the father's surprisingly conciliatory response are unusual.

Though Jesus has not provided any descriptive tags for the characters, because the younger son's request echoes an earlier request for a portion of the family estate (12:13–14), the younger son is immediately framed in negative terms. The motive of the man's request may not have been clearly stated, but Jesus, whose perspective contributes to the Gospel's evaluative point of view, saw him as greedy (πλεονεξία; 12:15) and one who, by seeking a share of the inheritance, sought to "treasure-up for himself" (12:21). Readers will be inclined to view the younger son similarly. Furthermore, because "[t]here *is* an inheritance to divide," we suspect that "the parable depicts a wealthy family."[88] If so, given portrayals of the wealthy thus far in the Gospel (1:53; 6:24; 12:16–21), this only enhances the negative portrait of the younger son. J. York has argued that Luke's readers very quickly learn to expect the downfall of the wealthy and powerful coupled with a corresponding positive reversal for "those who are without honor, status, wealth, or religious appearance."[89] For those who see such "bi-polar reversal"[90] operative in Luke, one is inclined to expect the younger son's demise.

There is one final feature of this lexia not to be missed. The younger son defines the inheritance simply as "property" (οὐσίας), but the intradiegetic narrator offers a correction to the son's deficient perspec-

[85] *The Parables*, 138.
[86] Bailey, *Finding the Lost*, 114.
[87] For Fitzmyer, Ben Sira's counsel suggests that the practice of early distribution of the family estate "must have been common enough" (*The Gospel According to Luke X–XXIV*, 1087).
[88] Bailey, *Finding the Lost*, 120.
[89] *The Last Shall be First*, 160.
[90] Ibid., 92.

tive by substituting "means/resources for life" (βίον).[91] The younger son fails to see that the father's property is the substance that has enabled all of them to live well. The father's material possessions do not merely constitute "property"; they represent decades of hard labor, reflect where the family has been and who they are, and allow for the continuation of "life." That the younger son is willing to demand the family's "resources for life" before the father has approached his hour of death only increases our disdain for this character.

Two very different expectations, then, govern these opening lines. On the one hand, in view of the two-sons mytheme, we expect the younger son to be the family "favorite" and therefore ultimately succeed or triumph. A round, likable character, readers will likely sympathize or even identify with him. On the other hand, he insults his father by demanding a share of the inheritance prematurely, appears to be part of a wealthy family, and his request mirrors that of the man from the crowd in 12:13–15, whom Jesus indirectly characterized as greedy. Which of these expectations—if either—will be fulfilled?

[91] Long ago, Henry J. Cadbury analyzed some basic features of the Gospel's style and concluded that synonyms are often combined "in pairs," which reflects the author's Greek rhetorical training ("Four Features of Lukan Style," in *Studies in Luke-Acts* [ed. Leander Keck and J. Louis Martyn; Philadelphia: Fortress Press, 1980], 92). The two terms, οὐσία and βίος, are often treated as synonyms by commentators (see, e.g., H. Räisäsen, "The Prodigal Gentile and his Jewish Christian Brother [Lk 15, 11–32]," in *The Four Gospels 1992 Festschrift Frans Neirynck* Vol. II [ed. F. Van Segbroeck, C. M. Tuckett, G. Van Belle, and J. Verheyden; Leuven: Leuven University Press, 1992], 1630 n. 92; Hendrickx, *The Parables of Jesus*, 151). I would be inclined to agree if the same speaker had uttered both words in close proximity. Here, however, with a change in speaker (from the younger son to the narrator), a new word is introduced. Readers are to trust the intradiegetic narrator, but we do not yet know enough about the younger son to determine if his assessment of the family inheritance as οὐσία is appropriate or adequate. This change in terms is significant for other commentators as well (see, e.g., Mary Ann Tolbert, "The Prodigal Son: An Essay in Literary Criticism from a Psychoanalytic Perspective," *Semeia* 9 [1977], 8; Troost, "Reading for the Author's Signature: Genesis 21.1–21 and Luke 15:11–32 as Intertexts," 270–71; Bailey, *Finding the Lost*, 118–19). Bovon conflates the two terms and then offers the following interpretation: "The father therefore gives to his son possessions that will allow him to live" (*L'Évangile Selon Saint Luc 15,1–19,27*, 44). References for βίος as "resources for life" may be found in *BDAG* (176–77).

"And after not many days, the younger son gathered everything together[92] *and journeyed to a distant land and scattered his property there by living*[93] *wastefully. When he had spent everything, a severe famine occurred in that land, and he began to be in need."*

Viewed from one perspective, the two-sons mytheme appears to be playing out much as expected. The younger son cashes-in his inheritance as soon as possible and journeys to a distant land, where he spends it all. Impulsive and imprudent, he has presumably neither invested his money nor taken the time to acquire a trade by which he might support himself. Already destitute, a famine suddenly seizes the land and exacerbates the younger son's precarious position.[94] But according to the two-sons mytheme, the younger son has nothing to fear, for this tragic sub-plot will eventually give way to a comic macro-plot in which the protagonist moves upward toward well-being and inclusion within a new or renewed community.[95] Readers may be further encouraged to envision a comic macro-plot in view of the positive outcome of the two parables that form the pre-text (15:3–10). In both, what was once lost was recovered, and their recovery brought joy not only to the seeker but to the entire community ("friends and neighbors"; vv.6, 9). With the two-sons mytheme and the previous parables serving as backdrop, readers would not be in suspense about *what* will transpire, only about *how* the protagonist will arrive at well-being and wholeness.[96]

Viewed from another perspective, the younger son's actions resemble a genuine attempt at discipleship. Like Jesus' disciples, he leaves his family in haste (cf. 5:11, 28), embarks on a journey (cf. 9:57), faces a period of hardship and deprivation beyond his control (λιμὸς ἰσχυρὰ; v.14; cf. 12:11–12, 51–53), and eventually dispenses with all of his money and possessions (cf. 12:33; 14:33). Moreover, he does not appear to be overly

[92] Readers may either assume that the younger son sold his portion of the inheritance, in which case συναγαγὼν would refer quite literally to "gathering together" whatever he would need for his journey. However, *BDAG* states that συνάγω may also carry a "commercial connotation" of converting possessions and/or property into cash (962). Cf. Fitzmyer, *The Gospel According to Luke X–XXIV*, 1087.

[93] I read ζῶν as an instrumental participle.

[94] Scott suggests that the narrator's mention of a famine elicits readers' sympathy for the son: "A famine, a feared scourge of the ancient world, draws the audience's sympathy toward the son, for though he is responsible for his fate, he is not responsible for this downward turn" (*Hear Then the Parable*, 114).

[95] See Dan Via, Jr., *The Parables: Their Literary and Existential Dimension* (Philadelphia: Fortress Press, 1967), 96–97, 104.

[96] Bal, *Narratology*, 160–61.

concerned about what he will eat, drink, or wear (cf. 12:22–31), and if Kenneth Bailey, Brad Young, and others are correct in arguing that a premature demand for inheritance was tantamount to a death-wish for the father, then the younger son quite literally "hates" his father (see 14:26). Unlike the wealthy landowner in 12:16–21 who clings to material possessions and seeks to grow his wealth, he appears to have little if any regard for earthly possessions. Is he pursuing God's kingdom by exchanging items that are subject to theft and decay for an inexhaustible treasure in heaven (see 12:31, 33)?

There is one feature of the narrator's summary, however, that would prevent us from identifying him too closely with the disciples: wasteful living. "Scattering" (v.13) itself is certainly not problematic, as long as resources are "scattered" among those who really need it, but disciples are nowhere encouraged to live "wastefully" (ἀσώτως; v.13). While some commentators associate this adverb with a life of dissipation and debauchery,[97] the term actually carries "no necessary implications of immorality"[98] but refers first and foremost to careless, negligent squandering.[99] Because the narrator does not tell us precisely how the younger son wasted his resources, readers are frustrated in their attempt to further characterize the younger son. Has he sought out a life of pleasure, or is he simply negligent and careless? Jesus initially appeared to portray him in predominantly negative terms, but now, because some of his actions resemble those of his own disciples, we must suspend our negative evaluation and await what lies ahead.

"And he went and joined himself to one of the citizens of that land, who sent him into his fields to feed pigs. And he longed to be satisfied from the carob pods[100] *that the pigs were eating. And, no one was giving him [anything]."* Desperate and without further recourse, the younger son hires himself out to a local citizen, who assigns him a most humiliating task: feeding pigs. The verb ἐκολλήθη (v.15) is polyvalent and may refer generally

[97] This association is typically made in light of the elder son's later characterization of his brother's actions in the far country ("this son of yours who devoured you means for life with prostitutes"; v.30).

[98] Bailey, *Finding the Lost*, 124.

[99] See, e.g., Hendrickx, *The Parables of Jesus*, 152; Johnson, *The Gospel of Luke*, 236; Bovon, *L'Évangile Selon Saint Luc 15,1–19,27*, 45. See also *BDAG*, 148.

[100] κερατίων is the diminutive of κέρας and therefore literally means "little horns."

to close contact/association or more specifically to sexual union.[101] If the verb is taken to refer to sexual union, the son's wasteful spending is explicitly tied to immoral behavior. The younger son would not only have transgressed legislation in the Torah that forbids homosexual union (see Lev 18:22; 20:13) but abrogated his religion both by "attaching himself to a foreigner and feeding pigs."[102] As a Jew, the younger son would truly have reached a very low point. However, while ἐκολλήθη can indeed entail sexual union, the purpose behind the son's close association with this citizen seems to be mere survival and serves to highlight his state of utter deprivation (ἤρξατο ὑστερεῖσθαι; v.14). More likely, then, ἐκολλήθη suggests a kind of indentured labor whereby a free person binds him/herself to another "to do whatever was necessary or required" for a specified period of time.[103] Though this was nonslave labor, only truly desperate persons would enter into a contract in which all duties and obligations were "indeterminate."[104] The younger son would have had no choice but to go out and feed this citizen's pigs, and he probably did so unwillingly. His unfulfilled longing[105] for the pigs' carob pods enhances this portrait of deprivation further. Admittedly, it is a bit puzzling why he does not take some of the carob pods for himself. Perhaps, as Joseph Fitzmyer suggests, he was too disgusted to eat animal fodder,[106] or maybe for this herdsman preserving his pigs during the famine was of greater importance than providing sustenance for a foreigner. The narrator's brief comment, "And no one was giving him [anything]," reminds readers that because a famine has overtaken this region material resources are extremely scarce: alms will be nearly impossible to come by.

---

[101] *BDAG*, 555–56.

[102] Scott, *Hear Then the Parable*, 116. Scott, I should add, does not suggest the possibility of sexual union, only the two-fold sin included within the quotation marks.

[103] J. Albert Harrill, "The Indentured Labor of the Prodigal Son (Luke 15:15)," *JBL* 115 (1996), 715.

[104] Ibid., 714.

[105] The use of the imperfect tense here "expresses an unfulfilled or unattainable wish" (Fitzmyer, *The Gospel According to Luke X–XXIV*, 1088; See also *BDF* 359.2).

[106] *The Gospel According to Luke, X–XXIV*, 1088.

"And, when he came to himself, he said, 'How many of my father's hired laborers have an excess of bread, but I am perishing here in hunger! I will rise up and go to my father and say, "Father, I have sinned against Heaven[107] *and before you; no longer am I worthy to be called your son. Make me like one of your hired laborers."'"*

At his lowest point, the younger son wonders whether he may have made a big mistake in leaving home. After four verses of narration summarizing events that transpired over many months or even years (vv.13–16), Jesus offers us another glimpse of the younger son through direct discourse. While many commentators agree that the son's awakening in vv.17–18 is the story's pivot,[108] there are two issues about which there is still much debate: 1) Can the younger son's words be classified as interior monologue?; and 2) Does his proposed speech reflect genuine repentance?

In an article that explores the function of interior monologue in parables unique to Luke, Phillip Sellew lists the son's proposed speech in vv.17–18 alongside several examples of interior monologue in the Travel Narrative (see 12:16–20; 16:1–8a; 18:2–5).[109] If, as Sellew argues, the son's speech can be classified as interior monologue, then readers receive a glimpse into his true feelings and motives and can trust that what he says is an accurate reflection of his character. Jesus' introduction of his proposal (ἔφη; v.17), however, is not at all like Sellew's other examples: missing is the critical phrase ἐν ἑαυτῷ, which is present before each of the other speeches he examines (12:17; 16:3; 18:4). Here, the younger son does not speak to himself (ἐν ἑαυτῷ) but simply speaks (ἔφη). Thus, as George W. Ramsey has observed, "the confession of sin (v.18) is not what he said in candid reflection *to himself*, but what he proposes *in his mind* to say in direct speech *to his father*. In the narrator's skillful portrayal, then, the confession of sin is one step removed from the reliable candor of interior monologue."[110] Readers therefore cannot

[107] The capitalization indicates that this is a circumlocution for God.

[108] See, e.g., Anonyme, "La Parabole du Père et des ses deux Fils: Luc 15/11–32," *ETR* 55 (1980), 79; Bovon, *L'Évangile Selon Saint Luc 15,1–19,27*, 42. Contrast the position of M. J. J. Menken, who believes that the pivot occurs with Jesus' disclosure of the father's compassion in v.20 ("The Position of ΣΠΛΑΓΧΝΙΖΕΣΘΑΙ and ΣΠΛΑΓΧΝΑ in the Gospel of Luke," *Novum Testamentum* 30 [1988]: 107–14).

[109] "Interior Monologue as a Narrative Device in the Parables of Luke," *JBL* 111 (1992): 239–53.

[110] "Plots, Gaps, Repetitions, and Ambiguity in Luke 15," *PRS* 17 (1990), 40.

necessarily assume that the son's proposal accurately reflects his inner feelings and motivations.

While some commentator's argue that Jesus' introduction of the younger son's monologue with the phrase "he came to himself" (εἰς ἑαυτὸν... ἐλθὼν) is based on a relatively common Hebrew and Aramaic expression for repentance,[111] others are not so confident.[112] Generally speaking, when working with the Greek New Testament, arguments that hinge on an underlying Hebrew and/or Aramaic expression are not strong. Can we, for instance, be absolutely certain that this parable was not originally composed in Greek?[113] The phrase may in fact indicate nothing more than an "awakening" as to just how bad things had become. I would therefore propose that the embedded narrator's introduction to the son's discourse does not offer readers any sure guidance in adjudicating the son's motivations. We are much better off closely examining the monologue itself and then making inferences as to whether or not his proposal reflects authentic repentance.

Strikingly, based on the younger son's initial statement in v.17, the primary motivation behind the proposed speech appears to be relief from hunger: "How many of my father's hired laborers have an excess of bread, but I am perishing here in hunger!" Since he is penniless, apparently bereft of any skills that might allow him to practice a trade, and unable to find alms during this time of famine, returning home may be his only means for securing sustenance. Hunger pangs, it appears, ultimately drives the son's "confession," not remorse. If the son were to have acknowledged sin inwardly by means of interior monologue, readers could be relatively certain that he was penitent, but readers are nowhere given access to his true thoughts and feelings. Significantly, missing is any hint of a desire to reunite with his father, repair broken family relations, or earn back the money he lost.

---

[111] See, e.g. Jeremias, upon whom many have drawn in establishing this point (*Rediscovering the Parables*, 102). See also Roger D. Aus, "Luke 15:11–32 and R. Eliezer Hyrcanus's Rise to Fame," *JBL* 104 (1985), 457. Hendrickx goes so far as to say that "it has been established beyond any reasonable doubt that the expression 'he came to himself' is in Hebrew and Aramaic an expression of repentance" (*The Parables of Jesus*, 153). Young is equally confident: "Without a doubt, the expression 'he came to himself' is best understood as the Hebrew or Aramaic terminology for repentance" (*The Parables*, 147).

[112] See, e.g., Kilgallen, "Luke 15 and 16: a Connection," 372; Bailey, *Finding the Lost*, 130–33.

[113] Luise Schottroff, for instance, has ascribed the entire parable to the Gospel's author ("Das Gleichnis vom verlorenen Sohn," *ZTK* 68 [1971]: 27–52).

Moreover, the younger son's "confession" resembles a similar statement voiced by Pharoah during the plague cycle in Exodus: "I have sinned before the LORD your God and against you" (10:16).[114] For readers who foreground Pharoah's plea before Moses as an appropriate intertext (which stems not from contrition but a desire to put the plagues to an end as quickly as possible), further suspicion is cast upon the authenticity of the son's proposed speech. One may also point to the ambiguity of the comparative conjunction ὡς, which is found as part of the son's final request to be made "like/as (ὡς) one of your hired laborers" (v.19). Does he intend to be treated *exactly like* his father's laborers, or does he wish to assume a position on the estate that only *roughly approximates* theirs?[115] In sum, all readers really have at this point is a pre-prepared speech stemming from hunger pangs and an instinct for self-preservation. This lexia may in fact present us with nothing more than "a shrewd, calculating, self-seeking youngster"[116] in search of the sustenance that he so desperately needs.

There is yet further ambiguity in the son's planned "confession." Not only does the younger son's motivation for his return remain hidden, but it is not at all clear what he considers his sin to be. Some commentators believe that it constituted leaving home and separating himself from his father;[117] others propose that it was his squandering of the inheritance;[118] still others suggest that it included both his departure and lifestyle abroad.[119] In view of the fact that Jesus' disciples were asked

---

[114] See, e.g., Barbara Reid, *Parables for Preachers: The Gospel of Luke Year C* (Collegeville, MN: The Liturgical Press, 2000), 60–61.

[115] *BDAG* acknowledges that ὡς can mean either 'exactly like' or 'roughly similar to' (1103–6, esp. 1104). Bailey believes that the younger son wished to be trained as an independent craftsman so that he could, in time, return to his family the money he lost. Regarding the son's intentions, Bailey writes: "Once trained, he may work on the estate but as a paid craftsman. He will not live there. Years later he anticipates coming home with enough money to recover the lost inheritance. This will achieve reconciliation with the family and the village" (*Finding the Lost*, 142. See also 136–40).

[116] Ramsey, "Plots, Gaps, Repetition, and Ambiguity in Luke 15," 40.

[117] See, e.g., Anonyme, "La Parabole du Père et des ses deux Fils: Luc 15/11–32," 80.

[118] See, e.g., Bovon, *L'Évangile Selon Saint Luc 15,1–19,27*, 45.

[119] See, e.g., Via, *The Parables*: "It is difficult to believe that the parable places no judgment at all on the leave-taking as such though the emphasis may well be on the son's irresponsible squandering of his money with harlots" (170–71). Via believes the elder brother's characterization of the younger son is on the mark and therefore associates his squandering with immoral behavior. Cf. Hendrickx, who does not venture a firm decision on the matter: "It is not fully clear exactly what the prodigal referred to as his sin—his loose and wasteful living, his leaving home, or both—but he certainly

to leave their families behind (see 5:11, 28; 18:28), which entailed both "hating" one's parents (μισεῖ; 14:26) and "saying goodbye to everything" (ἀποτάσσεται πᾶσιν; 14:33), I have a very difficult time believing that his departure and separation from the family can be considered a "sin." His "scattering" (v.13) of the inheritance is not in itself problematic since Jesus essentially asks his disciples to do the same by selling possessions and giving alms (12:33). By process of elimination, then, "wasteful living" is the son's sin—or, more appropriately, what the son believes will constitute sin in his father's eyes. Finally, it is reasonable to assume that he overspent *on himself*, or possibly on others of his own social class who were not truly in need. If he had distributed resources to persons who really needed them, the intradiegetic narrator certainly would not have described his spending habits as "wasteful." On what, precisely, he chose to overspend is not stated. It remains to be seen whether readers are here presented with a temporary or permanent gap.[120]

"He rose up and went to his father. But while he was still far away, his father saw him and had compassion. Running, he fell on his neck and kissed him. And the son said to him, 'Father, I have sinned against Heaven[121] *and before you; no longer am I worthy to be called your son.'"*[122]

If in some ways the younger son's abandonment of his family, journey into the unknown, experience of hardship, and dispersal of resources may have looked like a genuine attempt at discipleship, the experiment is now at an end. Famished and with no other options before him, he returns home. He would be, as Jesus said, among those who put their hand on the plow, discovered the journey to be far too difficult, and glanced back at "the things behind" (τὰ ὀπίσω; 9:62). On his return and before he even has a chance to present his speech, he is greeted by his father with an embrace and a kiss, signs of forgiveness.[123] Such a reaction, argues Bailey, was completely unexpected. In fact, any "tradi-

---

believed that he had destroyed his relationship with his father and had thus lost the right of sonship" (*The Parables of Jesus*, 154).

[120] Rimmon-Kenan, *Narrative Fiction*, 128–30.

[121] The capitalization indicates that this is a circumlocution for God.

[122] A few early and important uncial manuscripts add "Make me like one of your hired laborers" (א B D), but the addition probably represents an attempt to harmonize the son's proposal with what he actually said to his father. The addition is missing in p^{75} A L W *Byz*, among others.

[123] Scott, *Hear Then the Parable*, 117; Fitzmyer, *The Gospel According to Luke X–XXIV*, 1089; Hendrickx, *The Parables of Jesus*, 155.

tional Middle Eastern patriarch" would have been expected to "exhibit indignation and anger" with his son and so "uphold the honor of the family."[124] In addition to breaking traditional mores by showing compassion and extending forgiveness, the father steps outside prescribed gender roles as well by running ("Middle Eastern gentlemen do not run in public",)[125] wrapping his arms around him, and kissing him. While mothers may "throw caution to the wind" with such a public display of love and compassion, men were supposed to concern themselves above all with maintaining the family's honor.[126] The younger son, it appears, is forgiven before he even has a chance to acknowledge his sin!

Forgiveness has been granted, but the son proceeds with his speech anyhow. With the exception of the final request to become like one of his father's laborers, he repeats verbatim what he planned to say. For George Ramsey, in spite of the expectation set by the two preceding parables for genuine repentance (15:7, 10), the verbatim repetition signals a pre-prepared, "canned" speech that lacks authenticity.[127] The younger son, suggests Ramsey, probably repeated his speech "over and over all the way back to the homestead" with the intent of making "a good impression on the 'old man.'"[128] Indeed, an expectation of authentic repentance based on 15:4–10 is frustrated. Moreover, one need not, as many commentators do, view the younger son's truncated version of the pre-prepared speech as a result of an interruption by his father[129] (v.22) or his willingness to "forgo pride and accept the gracious love of his father," who would not want him to become a laborer.[130] It is conceivable, I would argue, that he took advantage of his father's compassion and shrewdly omitted the request to be treated like a laborer in order to avoid unnecessary hardship. If so, his "confession" looks even more suspicious. The two previous parables may predispose readers to find genuine repentance here, but it certainly does not emerge with clarity. This is the last we will hear from the younger son. His

---

[124] *Finding the Lost*, 143.
[125] Ibid., 143–44.
[126] Ibid., 159. Scott also believes that the father "combines in himself maternal and paternal roles" (*Hear Then the Parable*, 122).
[127] "Plots, Gaps, Repetition, and Ambiguity in Luke 15," 40.
[128] Ibid.
[129] See Bovon, *L'Évangile Selon Saint Luc 15,1–19,27*, 47; Reid, *Parables for Preachers*, 61; Johnson, *The Gospel of Luke*, 237; Fitzmyer, *The Gospel According to Luke X–XXIV*, 1089.
[130] Hendrickx, *The Parables of Jesus*, 156. Cf. Bailey, who follows Ibn al-Tayyib and Ibn al-Salibi (*Finding the Lost*, 152–53).

true feelings and motivations—indeed, his very character—will remain "shrouded in ambiguity."[131]

"And the father said to his slaves, 'Quickly, bring out the best robe and put it around him, and provide a ring for his hand and sandals for [his] feet. And bring the grain-fed calf, kill it, and let us eat and celebrate. For this son of mine was dead and came back to life, was lost and found.' And they began to celebrate."

The narrator does not indicate how much time has elapsed between the son's altered "confession" and the father's orders to his slaves. The father may have mulled over his son's words for several minutes or even hours, perhaps removing himself from his presence while doing so. Interestingly, the father does not respond directly to the son's speech; rather, after an unspecified period of time, he turns to his *employees* and issues orders. Might the father's silence hint that he too is uncertain about the authenticity of his son's "confession"? Readers may have expected the son's pre-prepared monologue to at least initiate a genuine, mutual exchange, but his words fail to elicit a direct and personal rejoinder from his father. The son now recedes into the background and the father assumes center-stage.

At some point, the father decides that his son, in addition to being forgiven, should be fully reintegrated into the family and (re)invested with the status and power he once had as "son" on the estate. He commands his slaves to bring out three items, all of which his son is to put on before the festival begins: the best robe, a ring, and a pair of sandals. While the robe (literally, "the first robe") was reserved for honored guests, the sandals likely represent that he is free and the ring that he has (re)acquired[132] authority to give orders to employees on the estate.[133] Not only is the father's generosity truly surprising, but the level

[131] Ramsey, "Plots, Gaps, Repetition, and Ambiguity in Luke 15," 41.

[132] I will continue to place the prefix "(re)" in parentheses because the narrator does not tell us whether he is being reinvested with a level of authority he once had on his father's estate or acquiring it now for the first time.

[133] See Balembo, "Lecture Africaine de la Bible: Essai sur l'exégèse symbolique de Lc 15, 1–32," 236–37; Anonyme, "La Parabole du Père et des ses deux Fils: Luc 15/11–32," 80. Cf. Scott's very similar interpretation of these three items, although, following Plummer, he believes that the robe is the one worn by the father himself (*Hear Then the Parable*, 118). Bovon notes that στολὴν τὴν πρώτην may be translated either as "best robe," i.e., the one reserved for honored guests, or "first robe," i.e., the robe that the son used to wear before he departed on his journey (*L'Évangile Selon Saint Luc 15,1–19,27*, 47–48).

of (re)investiture borders on the absurd. What are readers to make of a father who hastily (re)invests a son with authority over matters of the estate who only recently squandered a large sum of money? Will his slaves agree with his decision? The father's competence as estate manager is already questionable. Against Ben Sira's advice not to distribute the family inheritance prematurely, the father nevertheless agreed to the son's request (v.11). More importantly, he even awarded his son the privilege of selling his share of the inheritance to do with as he pleased, thereby denying himself any usufruct rights on the property. Is the father compassionate and forgiving or foolish and incompetent? Readers have met one wealthy man already whom God called "fool" (12:20); do we have another here as well?

Readers have been given hints all along that this is a very wealthy family, but in this lexia it becomes clear. Early on, we learned that the father was able to give away one-third of his estate and still live well and that the portion with which he parted financed a journey into a distant land that sustained his younger son "for a fairly long time (*great* famines do not happen over night)."[134] Furthermore, while in the far country, it occurs to the younger son that even his father's hired laborers have more than enough bread (περισσεύονται ἄρτων; v.17). If even hired laborers live in abundance on this estate, how much more so the family itself! Now we discover that in addition to hired laborers the father commands slaves (plural!), owns animals, and may possess "a banquet hall large enough to accommodate the two hundred or more people required to eat a fatted calf."[135] The family also owns a special robe worn by honored guests and at least one ring. Finally, the family can, at a moment's notice, afford to throw an enormous party that, as readers soon discover, will include paid entertainers to provide music and dancing (v.25).[136]

On the one hand, in view of the overwhelmingly negative portrait of the rich in the Gospel thus far (e.g., 1:53; 6:24; 12:16–21), the family's extravagant wealth casts a shadow over *all* the characters. Perhaps we should have expected a foolish father and a self-serving, wasteful, devious son all along. On the other hand, the father's final remark in v.24 aligns this parable with the previous two, inviting readers to treat both

---

[134] Bailey, *Finding the Lost*, 121.

[135] Ibid., 120.

[136] Ibid. Cf. Aus's similar assessment of the family's socio-economic status ("Luke 15:11–32 and R. Eliezer ben Hyrcanus's Rise to Fame," 460–61).

father and son in a positive light. The father, like the shepherd and the woman before him, finds and restores what was lost; the son, once dead, has now come back to life (ἀνέζησεν; v.24). Consequently, there is joy—a joy that Jesus previously said mirrored heavenly joy (15:7, 10)—among many. In short, the father's statement in v.24 appears suddenly to revamp all of the characters' images, elicit readers' sympathy, and call forth joy at the son's return, reintegration, and (re)investiture. Might this encourage readers to disavow any critique of wealth that emerged thus far in the Gospel? Strangely and quite unexpectedly, a son who lives "wastefully" is welcomed back with open arms and given an elaborate, expensive party that in many ways replicates the kind of life for which he is judged. Has an emerging critique of both waste and wealth been suddenly overturned?

"Now, his elder son was in a field, and when he came and drew near to the house, he heard music and dancing. Calling to one of the young servants, he asked him what these things might be. And he said to him, 'Your brother has come, and your father has killed the grain-fed calf because he received him back healthy.'"

Jesus reintroduces the elder son, from whom readers have yet to hear anything. Based on the two-sons mytheme, which in some ways unfolded just as expected in the first section of the parable (vv.12–24), readers may anticipate a rather boorish, uninteresting character who is not favored by the father. That he is absent from the party and presumably at work in a field confirms this expectation. If he were in the father's good graces, would he not have been invited to the party? The celebration has already commenced (v.24b) and he has no clue what is going on. This peculiarity is sometimes overlooked or explained away by commentators. Bernard B. Scott, for instance, attributes it to the need to show readers that although the elder son has never left the estate he too is estranged (and therefore spatially separated) from his father: "How is it possible that the elder would be uninformed of the younger's return, the father's welcome, and the feast? Such a question ignores the art of fiction. The line is contrived, stage-managed, but in order to locate this character in his proper place in the story."[137] While I would not dispute that the elder's location in the field is a

[137] *Hear Then the Parable*, 119.

"spatial metaphor"[138] for estrangement, his location may also encourage readers to begin chipping away at the negative stereotype set up by the two-sons mytheme. Readers disenchanted by the younger son's squandering, his plan to deceive his father with a (possibly) contrived, canned "confession," and the seeming absurdity of his comprehensive (re)investiture find in the elder brother a positive, welcome contrast of dutifulness and prudence. The elder brother may indeed be estranged from his father as his brother was, but perhaps for good reason. The father, as we have seen, does not exactly model competence as estate manager or paterfamilias.

The young servant provides a fair, accurate account of the events, although his rationale for having the grain-fed calf slaughtered differs from that provided by the father. The father killed the calf because the son has come back to life and been found (v.24); the servant states that the calf was killed because the father "received him back healthy" (v.27). The father, in effect, appears more concerned with his son's psychic and spiritual well-being whereas the servant associates the father's joy primarily with the younger son's physical health. Significantly, neither character attributes the celebration to the son's repentance.[139]

"And he became angry and did not wish to come in..."

While, according to the two-sons mytheme, the elder son's anger may be viewed as a predictable confirmation of the stereotypical image of the elder, his reaction also seems fully justified. In fact, his reaction offers readers a necessary and welcome critique of both the younger son's wasteful manner of life and the father's willingness to so quickly (re)invest him with authority and throw a lavish, costly party. Not only has the younger son squandered his own inheritance but, within hours of his return, he is already beginning to deplete the elder son's portion by participating in the feast. As Garrison Keillor has observed, the elder son, who dutifully tended the fields and fed the animals in the younger son's absence, likely had a hand in "fatting" the calf, and it is the younger son who is now enjoying it![140] Thus, the elder brother,

---

[138] Ibid.

[139] Bailey translates ὑγιαίνοντα as "shalom," which he believes is further evidence of reconciliation between father and son (*Finding the Lost*, 167–71). His translation is a bit strained, however, since the primary meaning of ὑγιαίνω in the Gospels is "to be in good physical health" (*BDAG*, 1023).

[140] Mikeal C. Parsons, "The Prodigal's Elder Brother: The History and Ethics of Reading Luke 15:25–32," *PRS* 23 (1996), 167–68. Parsons is drawing upon a published version of the radio broadcast in *Antaeus* 66 (1991): 242–47.

while probably also estranged from his father, provides readers with a welcome voice of reason.

François Bovon has suggested that both positive and negative associations may be attributed to the elder son's anger (ὠργίσθη; v.28).[141] In the New Testament, anger as an interior disposition is generally "condemned" (see Matt 5:22; Jas 1:20) and deemed harmful to the human psyche and the Christian community.[142] In the Hebrew Bible, however, many of Israel's prophets exhibit a "righteous anger" in the face of injustice or oppression. The elder brother's anger, while traditionally used to characterize him as boorish and surly, may be read as a form of this second type of justifiable anger. Although the father has failed to exhibit an appropriate anger in the face of negligent squandering, the elder brother thankfully has, providing readers an outlet for *their* anger.

"... but his father, having come out, began to console him."
As with his younger son, the father also comes out to his elder son (cf. v.20). Readers are here provided with their first hint that the father does not favor one son over the other, as the two-sons mytheme dictates. While παρακαλέω is polyvalent and may mean "exhort," "implore," or "console/comfort,"[143] the father has yet to show any clear signs of anger, so it seems best at this point to assign the more positive connotation of "console" so as to render his character consistent with what readers have already seen in vv.11–24.

"But he answered and said to his father, 'Look, for so many years I have been slaving away for you and not once did I transgress your command, and not once did you give me a goat so that I might celebrate with my friends. And when this son of yours, who devoured your means for life with prostitutes, came, you killed the grain-fed calf for him.'"
The father's encouraging words (which the narrator chooses not to disclose) are immediately rejected by the elder brother, who proceeds to offer a rationale for his anger and for why he has chosen not to join

---

[141] *L'Évangile Selon Saint Luc 15,1–19,27*, 49.

[142] Ibid. Admittedly, Bovon's generalization is not entirely fair. Exceptions are numerous and would include, for instance, God's anger in Revelation with the Roman Empire and certain Christian congregations as well as Jesus' anger over the Temple and its guarantors.

[143] *BDAG*, 764–65.

in the celebration. While his brother was away in a distant land "living wastefully," he has been dutifully tending to the estate and fulfilling what he believed were his father's desires. His claim not to have transgressed his father's command even once (οὐδέποτε) does seem a bit unrealistic and suggests self-righteousness, but his concern for fiscally responsible celebration is laudable. While the father is eager to have the grain-fed calf killed soon after his son's return and without a clear apology, the elder son, who has been faithful, wishes for a modest celebration only among friends. Many translators render the phrase οὐδέποτε ἔδωκας ἔριφον (v.29) as "you never gave me *even* a goat,"[144] which implies that the elder son would gladly have accepted much more than a goat if the father had provided it. But the addition of "even" to the Greek text is unwarranted and changes the sense of his comment. Without it, the elder brother's defense loses much of its bitter tone,[145] demonstrates concern for fiscally responsible celebration, and offers a subtle critique of his father's excess. In contrast to a father who happily and impulsively kills *the* grain-fed calf (the presence of the definite article may indicate that this is the only one on the estate), the elder son would not ask for more than a goat, as the addition of "even" would imply, but simply *a* goat (an anarthrous construction that suggests more goats would have been available after the celebration).

While the elder son's criticism of waste and excess is welcome, readers admittedly may be wary of trusting the elder son's speech in its entirety. Because his use of the verb δουλεύω ("I am slaving away"; v.29) to describe life on the estate and his claim to have never transgressed his father's command seem exaggerated, it is difficult to trust his characterization of his brother as "one who devoured your means for life *with prostitutes*."[146] To be sure, the younger son has "devoured" the father's βίος, but the addition of μετὰ πορνῶν initially seems indefensible since there is no indication that he has received an account of his brother's journey. In fact, because the younger son seems unusually tight-lipped and unforthcoming upon his return, it is highly unlikely that any of the details of his journey would have come to light yet. Furthermore, during the first century it was not unusual for Jews to stereotype

[144] Fitzmyer, *The Gospel According to Luke X–XXIV*, 1091; cf. *NRSV*.

[145] See, e.g., Johnson, *The Gospel of Luke*, 238.

[146] See, e.g., Anonyme, "La Parabole du Père et des ses deux Fils: Luc 15/11–32," 81; Johnson, *The Gospel of Luke*, 238, 241.

Gentiles as sexually depraved, as Paul does in Romans 1:18–32.[147] Thus, in anger the elder brother may very well be calling upon a standard *topos*. However, even though he has not received an account of his brother's actual exploits abroad, might he be correct in assuming that his "wasteful" manner of life had personal gratification as its aim? Perhaps the addition of μετὰ πορνῶν, while hyperbolic, stereotypical, and as yet unsubstantiated, is his way of identifying the essential aim of his brother's consumptive habits. Beyond the elder brother's remarks here, readers will receive no further information on how the prodigal overspent his inheritance. Because the elder brother is, on the whole, portrayed positively and his justified anger, fiscal responsibility, and prudence do provide a welcome contrast to the younger son's waste and the father's foolishness and excess, I would propose trusting that he is at least correct to link his brother's spending habits with the pursuit of personal pleasure.[148] It is unfortunate, to be sure, that he has chosen relations with prostitutes as a paradigmatic form of personal gratification,[149] but such a selection was probably a natural one give the prevalence of the *topos*.[150]

[147] Although the younger son is not a Gentile, he nevertheless lived among them for some time and even engaged in the degrading task of feeding pigs, an activity appropriate only for Gentiles (v.15). Brendan Byrne lists several examples of similar stereotypical characterizations of Gentile behavior by Jewish writers during the first century (*Romans* [Sacra Pagina 6; Collegeville, MN: The Liturgical Press, 1996], esp. 65, 76–77).

[148] Interestingly, by referring to the inheritance as βίος and not simply οὐσία as the younger son did (see v.12), the elder son shares the embedded narrator's assessment of the true significance of the father's property and possessions. Might this also give readers some reason to trust his remarks?

[149] The elder brother's characterization indirectly portrays women as seductresses and willing participants and fails to account for any of the social and/or economic conditions that force so many into prostitution and keep them there. In the interest of accuracy, the charge ought to read: "You devoured our father's resources for life by financing (and thus perpetuating) an insidious institution that enslaves and degrades women."

[150] Very few commentators are willing to portray the elder son positively at this point in the narrative (For a very helpful account of how this character has traditionally been treated in the Christian tradition, see Parsons, "The Prodigal's Elder Brother: The History and Ethics of Reading Luke 15:25–32," 147–74). He has been called an "outwardly righteous sinner" (Young, *The Parables*, 157), "selfish" and "self-righteous" (Scott, *Hear Then the Parable*, 121), deemed greedy (Bailey, *Finding the Lost*, 182), and reprimanded for his failure both to act as mediator between his brother and father (Ibid., 122) and "to accept and celebrate his father's graciousness" (Reid, *Parables for Preachers*, 63). A few, however, do sympathize with this character and portray him in a more positive light (See especially Tolbert, "The Prodigal Son: An Essay in Literary

"But he said to him, 'Child, you are always with me, and everything that is mine is yours. But it was necessary to celebrate and rejoice, for this brother of yours was dead and came to life, was lost and found.'"
Addressing the elder son affectionately (τέκνον; v.31),[151] the father reminds him that he too has received part of the inheritance (see v.12). By no means has he been left out; in fact, as the elder son, he will be able to claim the largest share of the estate. Moreover, as Bernard Scott and Arie Troost point out, readers who have foregrounded the two-sons mytheme as part of this parable's repertoire and therefore expect the younger son to remain the favorite now discover that the father loves both sons equally.[152] Indeed, not only does the father go out to meet both sons while they are "still far away" (vv.20, 28),[153] but both receive clear confirmation that they are truly his "sons" and possess all the rights, privileges, and authority that accompany such status (vv.22, 31). Because "both are chosen" and neither one emerges as a favorite, the two-sons mytheme is subverted.[154]

With the phrase "this *brother* of yours" (v.31), the father offers a corrective to the elder brother's "this *son* of yours" (v.30), voiced only moments earlier. The rejoinder is a subtle reproach and critique of his elder son's insistence on shunning the prodigal for his behavior, but it is also stands as an invitation. He wishes that both of his sons would reconcile and that the dutiful, prudent elder would forgive the younger for his reckless waste. The initiative for reconciliation, it seems, lies with the elder brother. Will he, like his father, be able to show compassion and forgive, even without clear evidence of remorse or repentance from his brother? Should he even forgive until the prodigal shows clear signs of having altered his perspective and habits? Perhaps forgiveness is best left to the father for now. This family seems to need someone who is

---

Criticism from a Psychoanalytic Perspective," where the elder son represents Freud's super-ego, an essential part of any healthy human psyche [15–19]).

151 Bovon, *L'Évangile Selon Saint Luc 15,1–19,27*, 49; Hendrickx, *The Parables of Jesus*, 159.

152 Scott, *Hear Then the Parable*, 122–25; Troost, "Reading for the Author's Signature: Genesis 21.1–21 and Luke 15.11–32 as Intertexts," 264–67.

153 While this is literally true for the younger son upon his reunion with his father (αὐτοῦ μακρὰν ἀπέχοντος; v.20), the elder son's anger and spatial location outside the banquet hall (v.28) signify that he too is "far away" when his father comes out to console him.

154 Scott, *Hear Then the Parable*, 125. Parsons essentially replicates Scott's reading ("The Prodigal's Elder Brother: The History and Ethics of Reading Luke 15:25–32," 170–74).

cautious, dutiful, and prudent. Open and unresolved, the parable ends here. Ultimately, readers will have to decide whether its macro-plot is tragic or comic.

3. *Summary*

Neither the diegetic nor the intradiegetic narrator offers any concluding comments that might help readers integrate this parable into the surrounding narrative or identify points of comparison. While the introductory εἶπεν δέ (v.11) initially appeared to set this parable apart from the previous two in some way (15:4–10), the father's remarks in vv.24, 32 encourage readers to view it as part of the lost-found-joy schema and retain the audience of tax collectors, sinners, Pharisees, and scribes (15:1–2). As Luke Johnson has said, if we assume the parable was addressed specifically to the groups delineated in 15:1–2, "[t]he allegorical level of meaning is irresistible":[155] the younger brother represents tax collectors and sinners, who have been forgiven and reconciled, and the elder brother represents Jewish religious authorities who are reticent to include and associate with them. The parable, in short, would constitute both a defense of Jesus' ministry to the marginalized and an invitation to the religious authorities to embrace them as God's beloved. But the possibility of an allegorical interpretation only emerges with the father's remarks in vv.24, 32; prior to these allusions to the lost-found-joy schema introduced in 15:4–10, readers would not have received any guidance as to how to integrate this parable into its narrative context.

But the parable resists a neat, seamless integration into the larger narrative. In fact, in many places it stands in tension with its frame. While 15:7, 10 speak of "repentant sinners," it is not at all clear that the younger son in this parable repents. While the Gospel has thus far portrayed the rich negatively, the father's remarks in vv.24, 32 ask readers to momentarily set aside their suspicion of wealth and rejoice with this family. While the narrator's introductory remark may encourage readers to associate the father with Jesus,[156] it is very difficult to overlook the father's foolishness, imprudence, even incompetence—traits that do not fit well with Jesus' ethos elsewhere in the narrative. The

[155] *The Gospel of Luke*, 242.

[156] Because in Luke Jesus is God's faithful emissary and representative on earth, by implication these traits may be ascribed to God as well.

parable, in effect, fits the narrator's frame in 15:1–2 in some ways but also stands in tension with it. Readers attentive to issues of consumption and wealth will not so easily forget the many "alien" associations that emerged as part of the experience of this parable. Unfettered by concluding interpretive remarks that might restrict the parable's application, readers are free to ponder any and all of their prior intuitions and associations.

While all three main characters in this parable exhibit both positive and negative traits, it is the younger son who is the most deeply flawed. His bold, premature request for a share of the inheritance (v.12) demonstrated disdain for his father and encouraged readers to align him with the man from the crowd in 12:13–14, whom Jesus implicitly characterized as greedy (12:15, 21). Admittedly, his conversion of assets into cash, decision to abandon his family and journey to a distant land, encounter with adversity beyond his control, and rather cavalier treatment of money suggested a genuine attempt at discipleship. But this tentative association with Christian discipleship was soon called into question by the narrator's report that he squandered his father's means for life by "living wastefully," i.e., overspending and overconsuming, probably for the purpose of personal gratification. Furthermore, upon his return, he offers his father what appears to be a pre-prepared, canned "confession" that lacks the feel of authenticity and may have been altered to avoid unnecessary hardship (v.21).

The father and his eldest son are characterized more positively. The father, for instance, is willing to forgive and reconcile his younger son after he had "scattered" one-third of his estate and in spite of being presented with a highly dubious "confession." Furthermore, contrary to the two-sons mytheme, readers gradually discover that he favors neither son, going out to both while they were "still far away" (vv.20, 28). At times, however, he appears foolish and incompetent, recalling the rich landowner in 12:16–21. He is foolish to have distributed the inheritance before his death and awarded his younger son the right to sell his share so as to deprive himself of any usufruct rights, and his competence as estate manager and paterfamilias is seriously called into question when he hastily (re)invests the prodigal with authority and throws a lavish, very costly celebration. The elder brother is the one with whom readers attentive to issues of consumption and wealth can most easily sympathize. He is by no means perfect, for he offers his father a defense that is, in part, inaccurate and exaggerated (vv.29–30). Nevertheless, the elder son's dutifulness, prudence, fiscal responsibility, and justified anger provide readers with a welcome voice of reason and an outlet for *their* mounting frustration with characters who have not taken waste and overconsumption seriously enough.

The father's remarks in vv.24, 32 invite readers to align this parable with the previous two in 15:4–10 and rejoice with this family in having recovered a lost son, which would require readers to momentarily suspend the negative evaluation of wealth presented in the Gospel thus far. On the one hand, then, the parable threatens to undermine any emergent criticisms of wealth. On the other hand, the criticism of consumption that emerged in 12:13–21 remains and is in fact strengthened here through repetition. The only sin of which the younger son was guilty is "living wastefully." Though the father may have forgiven and (re)invested his son with authority too quickly, the elder son steps in and offers a welcome and valid criticism, which must be acknowledged before the family can reconcile fully. He may appear a bit unreasonable, stubborn, or aloof, but his reticence to join the celebration is entirely justified and now *required* since the father, instead of condemning his son's behavior, chooses to throw a lavish party that in part mimics his lifestyle abroad. In fact, in view of Jesus' mission to the poor and downtrodden (4:18–19) and since the other characters simply do not take consumption and waste seriously enough, his focalization of the events becomes determinative. The younger son's failure to offer a genuine and convincing apology or show clear signs of having changed his habits, his hasty (re)investiture coupled with a lavish celebration in which *the* grain-fed calf is slaughtered, and the father's apparent unwillingness to take seriously his son's wasteful lifestyle cannot be received by readers as "good news to the poor."

The elder brother's anger, aloofness, and reticence disrupt the image of a happy, wealthy family at play. He must speak; he must unsettle and unnerve. Without his voice, overconsumption and wealth go unchallenged. Given Jesus' mission as outlined in 4:18–19, the parable simply cannot end with a wealthy family at play—fully reconciled, perfectly content, and feasting sumptuously.

CHAPTER THREE

CRITICIZING WEALTH

A. The Parable of the Unjust Steward (Luke 16:1–13)

The diegetic narrator intrudes briefly after the father's final remark to his elder son (15:32) to inform us that Jesus' disciples will constitute the primary audience for his next parable (16:1). Nothing transpires in between the parables, and there is no indication that Jesus changes locale or that the tax collectors, sinners, Pharisees, and scribes have departed (see 15:1–2). In fact, in 16:14 readers are able to confirm that at least the Pharisees remain and (over)hear Jesus' words. At the conclusion of the first parable (12:16–21), readers encountered a similar transition in audience from curious onlookers to disciples (also without reference to any intervening events or dialogue) where Jesus further elaborated upon themes introduced in his speech to the crowd (διὰ τοῦτο λέγω ὑμῖν; v.22). Can readers expect Jesus to pick up on and further develop themes from 15:11–32 here as well?

1. *Reading the Parable: 16:1–13*

And he said to the disciples, "A certain rich man had a steward, and the latter was accused to him as one who was scattering his possessions."
Readers have met two wealthy men thus far (12:16–20; 15:11–32), and because neither was portrayed favorably it is not expected that this man will. The wealthy landowner in 12:16–20 was judged foolish by God (v.20) and avaricious by Jesus (vv.15, 21), and the father in 15:11–32 (who also appeared foolish, even incompetent, at times) failed to account for the seriousness of his younger son's wasteful, consumptive lifestyle abroad. One need not call upon the peasantry's supposed antipathy toward an "exploitative and predatory" wealthy elite in first century Palestine in order to frame this character in negative terms.[1] Jesus has already done so, though not in such a way that readers would loathe

[1] See William R. Herzog II, *Parables as Subversive Speech: Jesus as Pedagogue of the Oppressed* (Louisville: Westminster/John Knox Press, 1994), 240–41.

the rich. They are rather portrayed as tragic, pitiable characters whose actions are foolish, almost laughable. Thus, while readers certainly do not think of this man as a villain,[2] neither will they expect good things from him.

We do not have enough information yet to offer even a tentative evaluation of the steward. If he is a household slave[3] against whom a fabricated and slanderous accusation has been brought,[4] some may initially be inclined to sympathize with him. But he may just as well be a high-ranking retainer of the elite and therefore a well-educated, powerful estate manager entrusted with numerous responsibilities and a degree of autonomy.[5] Indeed, this would be a reasonable assumption especially if the master is viewed as an absentee landlord who only rarely visits the property. The steward may, of course, also be guilty of the charge. Because he could be a relatively powerful retainer and guilty of the accusation, sympathy is withheld for now; we will await his own actions and speech before offering a character evaluation.

The source of the allegation is not disclosed, but the charge itself of "scattering" (διασκορπίζων; v.1) recalls the wasteful, consumptive lifestyle of the younger son in the preceding parable (διεσκόρπισεν; 15:13). While the verb διασκορπίζω need not carry negative overtones and may simply mean "scatter,"[6] the reader will be inclined to impute the same connotation of waste and overconsumption ascribed to it by the fully trustworthy intradiegetic narrator in 15:13.[7] Moreover,

---

[2] See Scott, *Hear Then the Parable*, 260, 263.

[3] Mary Ann Beavis makes this case and therefore compares this story to ancient Greco-Roman trickster tales (such as those found in The *Life of Aesop*) in which slaves outwit their masters. Such tales ultimately function to dignify the role of slaves as moral agents who are "capable of making ethical choices over and above simple obedience to their masters" ("Ancient Slavery as an Interpretive Context for the New Testament Servant Parables with Special Reference to the Unjust Steward [Luke 16:1–8]," *JBL* 111 [1992], 54).

[4] According to *BDAG* (226), διαβάλλω may be translated neutrally (i.e., "charges were brought") or with strongly negative overtones (i.e., "charges were brought falsely/slanderously"). This is the verb's only occurrence in the New Testament. It is prudent at this point to employ the neutral sense unless it later becomes clear that the complaints were instigated with hostile, slanderous intent.

[5] Commentators who assume this position include, e.g., Hendrickx (*The Parables of Jesus*, 174), Herzog (*Parables as Subversive Speech*, 253), and Bailey (*Poet and Peasant*, 91–94).

[6] See *BDAG*, 236.

[7] Commentators vary widely on how to interpret the charge of διασκορπίζων. John Lygre argues that it only implies careless mismanagement, inefficiency, and probably general incompetence ("Of what charges? [Luke 16:1–2]," *BTB* 32 [2002], 27). Young

because διασκορπίζων is a present participle, we may infer that the steward had been in the habit of living wastefully for some time; this was not, at least according to his accusers, a one-time occurrence. If the charges are true, the steward is aligned with the brazen, self-centered, possibly devious and insincere younger son in the prior parable, and a negative portrait is already beginning to emerge. What remains to be seen, however, is whether he has been accused of habitually scattering his own possessions or those of his master. The pronoun "his" (ἀυτοῦ; v.1), a possessive genitive, is ambiguous: To whom do these possessions belong? If they belong to the steward, readers may wonder where and how he is acquiring enough money to live wastefully.

"He called him and said to him, 'What is this that I hear about you?'"
The rich man confronts the steward about the allegation, but surprisingly the steward is silent. While the reader may expect "a classic debate in which the steward loudly and insistently protests his innocence,"[8] he neither acknowledges the validity of the charge nor offers a defense on his behalf. Does his silence implicate him? Can we assume that he is guilty of the accusation? Some have argued that offering a defense would have proven futile since due process was "unavailable to persons holding subservient positions... in Roman-occupied rural areas,"[9] but the rich man does ask a good-faith question that goes completely unaddressed by the steward. His silence is telling; one would expect a truly innocent man to offer at least a sentence or two on his behalf.[10]

---

believes that it "most likely refers to dishonest business dealings rather than ineffectual management" (*The Parables*, 233). Herzog initially suggests that the "scattering" refers to "an alleged inefficient use of the master's property to make profits, because the failure to produce expected profits would constitute grounds for dismissal" (*Parables as Subversive Speech*, 244). Later in the same chapter, however, he appears to change his mind and concede that "the steward may have indulged in forms of status display and conspicuous consumption inappropriate to his social standing. If he had been accumulating too much and spending it in ways that caused a stir, he could have set himself up for his fall" (252). Many commentators who are attentive to the function of the parable within the narrative as a whole do draw an explicit connection to the younger son's wasteful lifestyle abroad in 15:11–32 (See, e.g., Donahue, *The Gospel in Parable*, 167; Fitzmyer, *The Gospel According to Luke X–XXIV*, 1100; Johnson, *The Gospel of Luke*, 244).

[8] Bailey, *Poet and Peasant*, 97.

[9] Lygre, "Of what charges? (Luke 16:1–2)," 26. Lygre is here drawing upon Joseph Fitzmyer's study *The Semitic Background of the New Testament* (Grand Rapids: Eerdmans, 1997), 175.

[10] John S. Kloppenborg, however, writes: "The fact that the steward is given a summary judgement *without* a hearing is not tantamount to an admission of guilt, but on the contrary confirms the listener's view of the rich man as capricious and unfair"

At any rate, it certainly could not hurt, especially given that the rich man so far is not portrayed as cruel or unreasonable.

"'Give back the record[11] *of your stewardship, for you are no longer able to serve as steward.'"*

Probably guilty of the charge, his employer immediately demands that the administrative records be returned and announces that he will be terminated.[12] In firing the steward, the rich man acts prudently, even if the steward has only been accused of scattering his own possessions. The rich man must retain his honor,[13] and a scattering either of his or the steward's own possessions would ultimately reflect poorly on him.[14] If his own estate manager (and primary broker and representative to the community) had acquired a reputation for wasteful, consumptive living, merchants and farmers may be hesitant to do business with him. Surely, good stewards would at least feign a public persona that conveys dependability, fiscal responsibility, and strong organizational skills. Most importantly, though, the rich man must protect his wealth. Even if the steward is scattering his own possessions and not those of

("The Dishonored Master [Luke 16, 1–8a]," *Biblica* 70 [1989], 488). Cf. Scott's similar position: "The steward gains sympathy and identification since he has no opportunity to explain his actions, to respond to his accusers, or even to know what the accusations are..." (*Hear Then the Parable*, 262).

[11] Admittedly, ἀπόδος τὸν λόγον may also be rendered more generally as "give an account" (*BDAG*, 109–10), but because the steward offers no such account and the rich man appears to subsequently fire him on the spot, I assume that the phrase refers to a return of the accounting books (Cf. Bailey, *Poet and Peasant*, 97).

[12] The phrase οὐ γὰρ δύνῃ ἔτι οἰκονομεῖν is ambiguous and may be rendered "for you are no longer capable of stewarding" or "for you can no longer serve as steward." The first translation would constitute a matter-of-fact commentary on the steward's lack of proficiency in administrative matters, but the second would imply immediate termination. Again, because the steward fails to respond, readers will likely assume that he is being fired. Several manuscripts (most notably A K L 33 *Byz*) preserve a future tense form of δύναμαι (δυνήσῃ), which would explicitly locate the steward's termination in the future, but the present tense form (δύνῃ) is much better attested and retained here. Moreover, as we will see, δύνῃ is in agreement with the steward's own assessment of what is taking place. In v.3, he too will make use of a present tense verb in order to describe the rich man's actions (ἀφαιρεῖται).

[13] On the importance of acquiring and maintaining honor in the ancient Mediterranean world generally and with respect to the rich man in this parable, see especially Kloppenborg ("The Dishonored Master [Luke 16, 1–8a]," 488–90) and David Landry and Ben May ("Honor Restored: New Light on the Parable of the Prudent Steward [Luke 16:1–8a]," *JBL* 119 [2000], 293–94, 298–305).

[14] Generally speaking, in antiquity "superiors were judged by the behavior of their subordinates" (Landry and May, "Honor Restored: New Light on the Parable of the Prudent Steward [Luke 16:1–8a]," 299).

his employer, the rich man would be wise to infer that such behavior cannot bode well for the management of his own resources. After all, if the steward is not prudent with what belongs to him, how can he be expected to treat with care what belongs to another? This rich man, therefore, acts prudently so far; he fires the steward both in the interest of retaining his honor and protecting his wealth.

"The steward said to himself, 'What shall I do?'"

Still, the steward is silent before his master. Having accepted his termination, he immediately begins to consider his options. Jesus discloses the steward's ensuing interior monologue (εἶπεν δὲ ἐν ἑαυτῷ; v.3),[15] which readers may employ confidently in constructing his character. While Jesus does not yet "tell" readers about the steward by attaching a descriptive label (as he did with the "rich" man in v.1), making transparent one's inner reflections is one of the most reliable ways of "showing" characters to readers.[16]

"'For my master is taking away the stewardship from me. I am not strong enough to dig; I am ashamed to beg.'"

By making use of the present tense verb ἀφαιρεῖται (v.3),[17] the steward believes his master is currently taking steps to formalize his termination. His internal ruminations therefore confirm our earlier interpretation of the rich man's ambiguous statement in v.2 (οὐ γὰρ δύνῃ ἔτι οἰκονομεῖν) as indicative of the steward's dismissal. However, not until the steward has turned over his records will the process be completed, so he does have a narrow window of opportunity to make preparations for his imminent departure.[18] We may infer that he does not

[15] Jesus' introduction of the steward's reflections parallels similar introductions to interior monologue in 12:17 and 18:4. Philip Sellew, in his article on the function of interior monologue in parables unique to Luke, does include 16:3 among his examples ("Interior Monologue as a Narrative Device in the Parables of Luke," 247). Contrast, however, Jesus' very different introduction to the younger son's proposal in 15:17 (ἔφη), which does not match the phrasing in 12:17, 16:3, or 18:4 and therefore should not be classified as interior speech.

[16] For a brief description of the two traditional classifications of "showing" and "telling," see Wayne Booth, *Rhetoric of Fiction*, 3–20; Malbon, "Narrative Criticism: How does the Story Mean?," 29; Powell, *What is Narrative Criticism?*, 52–53.

[17] Scott observes that the verb, which employs "the metaphor to cut off, to tear away," conveys "violence" (*Hear Then the Parable*, 262).

[18] See, e.g., Bailey, who argues that although the steward is fired on the spot, "because word of his dismissal is not out…he still has some room to maneuver until he turns in the account books" (*Poet and Peasant*, 97).

hold out much hope of finding a job as an estate manager since he considers digging and begging as legitimate employment options upon his release. Bernard Scott suggests that by "admitting that he lacks the strength to dig and is ashamed to beg, he distances himself from the hearer... [and] has taken on the airs of the rich."[19] However, the fact that he considers such options at all demonstrates both that he is aware of the severity of his offence (διασκορπίζων; v.1), which will forever damage his reputation in this region and probably prevent him from further service as a steward, and that he is willing to contemplate—if even for a moment—joining the expendable class[20] in order to make a living. After some reflection, he candidly acknowledges to himself that he is unable to engage in either task. Significantly, he does not say that he is ashamed to dig, only that he does not possess the strength. He is, therefore, a realist and a pragmatist: if his constitution will not bear hard physical labor, then he would be wise to steer clear of such an occupation, especially if he is counting on it for sustenance.[21] It is certainly no surprise to hear that he is ashamed to beg; most any Jew of the time would have agreed.[22]

The steward, then, having accepted his termination, briefly considers and then eliminates two options: digging and begging. While readers expect him to be fired soon, the steward still has a window of opportunity to tie up loose ends and prepare for his departure.

---

[19] *Hear Then the Parable*, 263.

[20] Assuming either position—digging or begging—would entail "a forfeiture of social status" and place the steward among society's "'unclean and degraded'" (Green, *The Gospel of Luke*, 590). Cf. Herzog's remarks: "To lose his stewardship and join the work force of day laborers is to drop out of the class of retainers into the class of expendables" (*Parables as Subversive Speech*, 242). Stanley Porter observes that in the ancient world the "thought of digging was universally and proverbially abhorred" ("The Parable of the Unjust Steward [Luke 16.1–13]: Irony *is* the Key," in *The Bible in Three Dimensions: Essays in celebration of forty years of Biblical Studies in the University of Sheffield* [ed. David J. A. Clines, Stephen E. Fowl, and Stanley E. Porter; JSOTSS 87; Sheffield: JSOT Press, 1990], 141).

[21] Both Kloppenborg ("The Dishonored Master [Luke 16, 1–8a]," 491) and Landry and May ("Honor Restored: New Light on the Parable of the Prudent Steward [Luke 16:1–8a]," 300) also interpret the steward's comment here as a frank, sober assessment of his (in)abilities, not as a sign of his unwillingness to mix with the lower classes.

[22] See Hendrickx, *The Parables of Jesus*, 176; Porter, "The Parable of the Unjust Steward (Luke 16.1–13): Irony *is* the Key," 141. In general, the Jewish wisdom tradition advocated a life characterized neither by poverty nor by riches (Proverbs 30:8), and because begging was a symbol of extreme poverty, it was to be avoided at all costs (see Sir 40:28).

"'I know[23] *what I will do, so that when I am removed from the stewardship they may welcome*[24] *me into their homes.'"*

After further reflection,[25] the steward decides on a course of action. While we learn that the motivation behind his scheme is to secure lodging upon his dismissal, we are not yet told precisely what the steward has planned.[26] Moreover, he does not identify from whom he will be seeking hospitality: neither the subject of the verb δέξωνται nor the referent of the possessive genitive ἀυτῶν (v.4) is revealed. Thus, by withholding the plan itself and refusing to disclose the identity of the steward's potential hosts, Jesus heightens suspense[27] and draws readers yet further into the story. Readers will be eager to see what transpires after the monologue and whom the steward calls upon for help.

Earlier, because Jesus' use of the personal pronoun "his" (αὐτοῦ), a possessive genitive modifying "possessions" (ὑπάρχοντα), was determined to be ambiguous (v.1), readers were not able to decide whether the steward was accused of scattering his master's or his own possessions. In view of the master's remarks in v.2 and the steward's self-assessment in vv.3–4, it is becoming increasingly difficult to view the steward as a household slave. The master does not indicate that the steward owes him any further service, nor is there any hint that the steward will have to purchase his freedom before his departure. Rather, without any further obligation to the master, he appears to be free to go wherever he wishes upon his termination. He is therefore probably a salaried employee[28] and highly-privileged, educated retainer of the elite.[29] If this portrait of the steward is assumed, one would expect that he would have saved enough money to purchase food and secure lodging (perhaps at a nearby inn) to last him at least a few weeks. It is very odd indeed that he is

---

[23] I read ἔγνων here as a dramatic aorist (lit. "I have come to know").

[24] As in 12:20 with ἀπαιτοῦσιν, Fitzmyer here argues that δέξωνται, an indefinite third plural form, is "a Semitic substitute for the pass. voice" (*The Gospel According to Luke X–XXIV*, 974, 1100). I much prefer to read it as a third plural verb with its subject as yet unidentified. The unidentified subject serves to draw the reader further into the story by heightening suspense.

[25] Based on his announcement of having devised a plan, readers will assume that the steward continued to deliberate (for an undisclosed span of time), even though his thoughts have not been introduced as part of the discourse. They remain hidden at the level of story.

[26] *L'Évangile Selon Saint Luc 15,1–19,27*, 70. Contrast 15:18–19, where readers were awarded access to the younger son's plan.

[27] On suspense, see Bal, *Narratology*, 160–61.

[28] See Via, *The Parables*, 157; Bailey, *Poet and Peasant*, 91–94.

[29] See especially Herzog, *Parables as Subversive Speech*, 241–44.

leaving the estate with nothing of his own and anxious about acquiring even the most basic provisions.[30] This suggests that he was in the habit of scattering *his own possessions*, not those of his master, which best accounts for why he—a free, salaried retainer of the elite—appears to have nothing at the time of his dismissal. More perplexing, perhaps, is that he does not appear to have any relatives or friends who would welcome him into their homes. Many facing a similar crisis undoubtedly had someone who would be willing and able to help for at least a short time, but his entire plan, curiously, is driven by the need to secure living arrangements.[31] One explanation for why the steward has no one to "welcome" him is that he, like the younger son in the previous parable, was in the habit of spending resources entirely *on himself*. Aware that he has done very little to endear himself to members of the community or his master's clients, he resolves that he must do something to win their gratitude—or, to frame the scenario in terms of patron-client relations, place others in his debt. At this point, then, the steward looks a lot like the younger son in the prior parable: spending all that he had on himself, he too embraced a life marked by overconsumption and waste.

The motivation for what the steward is about to do is clear, but readers are eager to see whom he calls upon for help and how he hopes to secure their hospitality once he is dismissed.

"And, having summoned each one of his master's debtors, he said to the first, 'How much do you owe my master?' And he said, '100 baths of oil.' And he said to him, 'Take your promissory notes;[32] *quickly, sit down and write "50."' Then, to another he said, 'And you, how much do you owe?' And he said, '100 cors of wheat.' He said to him, 'Take your promissory notes and write "80."'"* The steward first summons all of his master's debtors to one place.[33] He must act quickly before surrendering the records and before they

[30] Bailey also acknowledges that "[t]he steward is penniless" upon his release (*Poet and Peasant*, 111).

[31] Landry and May suggest that the steward hopes "to be welcomed into people's homes *as a steward*" ("Honor Restored: New Light on the Parable of the Prudent Steward [Luke 16:1–8a]," 301), but neither the steward nor the intradiegetic narrator provides any indication that this is his goal. Furthermore, as readers soon learn, it is highly unlikely that the debtors with whom he speaks would be able to fund the position of a fulltime steward.

[32] Some manuscripts (notably A K P W *Byz*) preserve the singular τὸ γράμμα. The plural (τὰ γράμματα) is the better attested reading.

[33] Some English translations render the phrase ἕνα ἕκαστον as "one by one" (e.g., the *NRSV*), which would imply that the steward met with each of the debtors privately.

discover that he is being terminated. While Jesus grants access to the steward's interactions with only two of his master's debtors, readers assume that these encounters are exemplary and that he interacted with others similarly.[34] Vv.5–7, then, give readers only a glimpse of what transpired in between the master's announcement of his dismissal and his departure.

Having tentatively identified the steward as a salaried retainer of the elite who was in the habit of squandering his possessions on himself in a manner similar to that of the younger son in 15:11–32 and whose plan is motivated entirely by the desire to secure living arrangements, readers probably will not expect an act of selfless benevolence from him. Our suspicions are confirmed when he asks both debtors to make adjustments to their promissory notes in their own handwriting. By doing so, the steward shifts final responsibility for the debt reductions to them.[35] The steward may facilitate the reductions by disbursing the promissory notes, but the debtors themselves actually enact (or record) the reduction. The steward is as little involved in the transaction as possible; indeed, his participation in the event will be difficult to trace or substantiate. Thus, the way in which he goes about this task only further enhances our negative portrait of him. The debtors, however, are by no means portrayed as innocent victims of a roguish scheme. Although they may not have been aware that the steward was in process of being terminated, they should have suspected mischief on his part. The steward, for instance, not only fails to provide a reason for the reductions (surely the debtors would have wondered what prompted such spontaneous generosity and whether the reductions had in fact

However, the steward phrases his question to the second debtor in such a way as to suggest that he merely turned to the next person in line: "And you, how much do you owe?" (v.7). Furthermore, when followed by a partitive genitive (as here), the most common rendering of ἕκαστος is "each/every" (see *BDAG*, 298). The master's debtors probably assembled in one place, and each knew just how much of the others' loans had been reduced.

[34] Readers may infer that other debtors beyond the two mentioned in vv.5–7 received reductions as well because: 1) the steward addresses the second debtor not with a substantive such as δεύτερος or ἔσχατος (as would be expected if only two debtors were present) but with ἑτέρῳ; 2) the steward summons "every/each one" of his master's debtors, not "both" or "two" (v.5). Both Kloppenborg ("The Dishonored Master [Luke 16, 1–8a]," 490 n. 55) and Fitzmyer (*The Gospel According to Luke X–XXIV*, 1100) view the exchanges in vv.5–7 as exemplary as well.

[35] William Loader suggests that this "is dubious practice, doubtless designed to cover the steward against a charge of fraudulence" ("Jesus and the Rogue in Luke 16,1–8A: The Parable of the Unjust Steward," *RB* 96 [1989], 526).

been administered with the master's approval), but he also asks them to act "quickly" (ταχέως; v.6), as if some devious, clandestine scheme were afoot.[36] The debtors, surprisingly, ask no questions; they receive their reductions gratefully and without any qualms.

The transactions present readers with many unknowns. Are we, for instance, to assume that the debtors are wholesale merchants or tenant farmers who have agreed to return part of the harvest as rent? Do the loan reductions constitute a cancellation of interest, the steward's commission, or possibly even part of the principal? Finally, will the reductions diminish the master's anticipated profit, or will the steward himself absorb the brunt of the loss?

The identity of the debtors—wholesale merchants or farmers—is difficult to establish, and many commentators are reticent to offer a firm decision.[37] Indeed, we may not need to make such a decision in order to offer a reading of the parable. It is important, however, to assess the amount each debtor owes both before and after the reductions. The first debtor owes 100 baths (a Hebrew liquid measure) of oil, which approximates 900 gallons,[38] or roughly "500–600 days of work for a laborer."[39] The second debtor owes 100 cors (a Hebrew dry measure) of grain, which is roughly equivalent to the yield of a plot of land "twenty to twenty-five times that of an ordinary family farm."[40] Moreover, although the steward deducts a greater percentage of oil (50%) than grain (20%), commentators generally agree that the net

[36] Cf. Porter's position, who writes that the debtors "should be a little suspicious of such a radical and hastily-conceived reduction" ("The Parable of the Unjust Steward [Luke 16.1–13]: Irony *is* the Key," 143). Contrast the position of Bailey, who believes that "the debtors assume the entire bill-changing event to be legitimate" (*Poet and Peasant*, 100).

[37] While a few commentators do assume that the debtors are tenant farmers (see, e.g., Hendrickx [*The Parables of Jesus*, 176] and Bailey [*Poet and Peasant*, 91]), most simply acknowledge that both are legitimate possibilities. See, e.g., Herzog, who variously refers to the debtors as "villagers," "merchants," and "peasants" (*Parables as Subversive Speech*, 253–58); Bovon, *L'Évangile Selon Saint Luc 15,1–19,27*, 71; Kloppenborg, "The Dishonored Master [Luke 16, 1–8a]," 482, 486.

[38] Fitzmyer, *The Gospel According to Luke X–XXIV*, 1100.

[39] Bovon, *L'Évangile Selon Saint Luc 15,1–19,27*, 71.

[40] See Green, *The Gospel of Luke*, 591–92. Cf. Kloppenborg's calculations, which he bases on Douglas E. Oakman's figures in *Jesus and the Economic Questions of His Day* ([Lewiston, N.Y.: The Edwin Mellen Press, 1986], 61–62): "One hundred cors of wheat (1,115 bushels) is far too large an amount to be seed grain and would represent a half-share rent for almost 200 acres, which is perhaps twenty times the size of an average family plot" ("The Dishonored Master [Luke 16, 1–8a]," 482).

reduction for each debtor is about equal: 500 denarii.[41] The steward is thus not favoring one debtor over another. In effect, because the reader is presented with such large sums, it is very difficult to identify these debtors as poor peasants or small scale merchants.[42] More likely, they are large scale renters or wholesale merchants[43] who, like the rich man in v.1, hope not only to pay rent and put food on the table but maximize their profit margin. Ronald A. Piper, who concedes that the large sums preclude identification with poor farmers or merchants, nevertheless argues that they would "have been compelled to pass on the reductions to the wider populace" so that "all who relied upon the foodstuffs" would benefit from the steward's act.[44] But there is no guarantee that the debtors will be inclined to pass on their savings to others. We know almost nothing about these ficelles (plot functionaries), other than they perhaps sense mischief afoot yet gladly accept their financial award without question. They may very well have a charitable disposition, but they may also be shrewd businessmen intent on securing a high profit. So, it appears that the steward is not offering much-needed relief to subsistence farmers plagued by debt (a widespread systemic problem in first century Palestine). By his own admission, he devises this scheme to ensure his own survival (v.4), not to alleviate the suffering of the poor.

While it seems clear that the steward is renegotiating contracts for persons of some means in order to procure a favor (which he hopes will be repaid soon), shall we assume that he is canceling interest on loans (usurious or otherwise), his own commission, or even part of the principal? A majority of commentators hold that the steward is canceling either interest or principal and therefore infringing upon the master's

[41] See, e.g., Bailey, *Poet and Peasant*, 101; Young, *The Parables*, 239. This conclusion is typically based on Jeremias's calculations (*The Parables*, 180–81). Contrast J. P. Molina's much higher figure, which totals 3,500 denarii for both debtors ("Luc 16/1 a 13: L'Injuste *Mamon*," *ETR* 53 [1978], 371).

[42] Jeremias attributes the high figures to exaggerated, hyperbolic language common in Jesus' parables (*The Parables*, 181).

[43] See Kloppenborg, "The Dishonored Master [Luke 16, 1–8a]," 482, 486.

[44] "Social Background and Thematic Structure in Luke 16," 1650–51. Commentators disagree on whether these reductions would have any substantial, lasting effect on the debtors. Green, for instance, argues that by "reducing their loan agreements so generously, the manager has done these debtors a significant favor" (*The Gospel of Luke*, 592), but Paul Trudinger describes the reductions as a "band-aid amelioration" that will bring no "real, lasting hope" ("Exposing the Depth of Oppression [Luke 16:1b–8a]: The Parable of the Unjust Steward," in *Jesus and His Parables*, 136).

anticipated profits.[45] However, those who hold that the steward is canceling interest have almost no reliable information from first century Palestinian sources upon which to draw in assessing whether a 100% mark-up on oil (v.6) or a 25% mark-up on grain (v.7) reflect typical interest rates. J. D. M. Derrett, for instance, is forced to turn to Mishnaic and Indian sources,[46] and John Kloppenborg offers a comparison based on Egyptian lending practices.[47] Neither offers clear and convincing evidence that the steward is canceling *interest*. We simply do not know what kinds of interest rates were widely accepted during the early part of the first century in rural Palestine. Rates undoubtedly fluctuated with the market and varied both by region and individual lender. Dan Via tentatively accepts Derrett's thesis that the steward cancels interest due to the master but prefaces his own reading of the parable with a telling (and most appropriate) phrase: "*Whatever* the exact socio-economic connections of the story. . . ."[48] Indeed, the socio-economic background of vv.5–7 is difficult to establish. Any reading of the steward's actions in vv.5–7 that stands or falls on a comparison with interest rates from sources outside rural Palestine (e.g., Egyptian or Indian) or that postdates the parable's story-world (e.g., Mishnaic) seems tenuous.

A minority of commentators believe that the steward cancels his commission,[49] a reduction that would not infringe upon the master's expected profits. If so, then the steward's commission is exorbitant, probably even higher than the interest attached to the loan. Such habitual overcharging on commissions would not go unnoticed. If the steward was in fact guilty of imposing preposterously high commissions, perhaps the *debtors* initially brought the charge of "scattering" against him (v.1) with the hope that the master, suspicious of how a retainer

---

[45] See, e.g., Herzog, *Parables as Subversive Speech*, 255; Scott, *Hear Then the Parable*, 263–65; Kloppenborg, "The Dishonored Master [Luke 16, 1–8a]," 486; Bailey, *Poet and Peasant*, 100–3; Via, *The Parables*, 158–61.

[46] *Law in the New Testament* (London: Darton, Longman & Todd, 1970), 67–70.

[47] "The Dishonored Master [Luke 16, 1–8a]," 482–84.

[48] *The Parables*, 159. The italics are mine.

[49] See Fitzmyer, *The Gospel According to Luke X–XXIV*, 1097–98, 1101; Bossuyt and Radermakers, *Jésus: Parole de la Grâce selon saint Luc 2. Lecture continue* (Institut d'Etudes Théologiques: Bruxelles, 1981), 352; Hendrickx, *The Parables of Jesus*, 177. Young also agrees that the steward "was canceling his own sizable commission," but he argues that because the deal was "negotiated in the master's name and would be designated for whoever served as his manager or for the landowner himself," any "loss of revenue would directly impact the wealthy master, regardless of whether it was the agent's commission or not" (*The Parables*, 240).

could acquire enough money to live wastefully, would "read between the lines" and fire him. The master's debtors, in other words, no longer able to tolerate the steward's grossly inflated commissions, would have informed the master of the steward's extravagant lifestyle and trusted that he would figure out what was really going on behind the scenes.

It is not yet possible to render a judgment on whether the steward was canceling interest/principal, which would diminish the master's profits, or his own exorbitant commissions, which would leave the master's anticipated profits intact. We must await the rich man's response.

"And the master praised the unjust steward because he acted wisely."
Readers will assume an ellipsis between the steward's interactions with the debtors and the master's response of "praise" in order to account for the master's discovery of the debt reductions. Its span, however, is unknown and may consist of just a few hours or even several days. All characters have exited the stage, and attention shifts to the intradigetic narrator, who simply summarizes the master's response. The master's praise, however, is specific to the steward's reducing of the debts and not an assessment of his overall character.[50] Jesus, in fact, labels him here as "unjust,"[51] which further encourages readers to judge only his previous interactions with the debtors as "wise."

With the master's reaction before us, we are now in a much better position to render a decision on whether the steward cancelled interest/principal or his own commissions. In a politically unstable and environmentally precarious region like first century Judea, the rich would have taken extra care to protect their wealth and not looked kindly upon employees who were careless with their money. As Kenneth Bailey observes, "[l]ife has always been precarious in the East," and anyone who manages to become rich would do most anything to preserve their wealth.[52] If the steward had in fact cancelled interest or principal due to the master, it is nearly impossible to explain the rich man's response of praise. The steward, in effect, would be stealing from the master, and one would expect him to be furious.[53] The best way

[50] See Daniel Lys, "Les Richesses Injustes (Luc 16/1–13)," *ETR* 76 (2001), 396; Hendrickx, *The Parables of Jesus*, 180; Bovon, *L'Évangile Selon Saint Luc 15,1–19,27*, 72; Piper, "Social Background and Thematic Structure in Luke 16," 1652.

[51] I am therefore reading τῆς ἀδικίας as a descriptive (or qualitative) genitive.

[52] *Poet and Peasant*, 94.

[53] See, e.g., the response of the wealthy nobleman in 19:11–27 who becomes irate when he learns that one of his slaves chose not to invest his money while he was in a distant land.

to account for the rich man's response is to assume that the steward cancelled his own exorbitant commissions. The master therefore offers his approval of the transactions in vv.5–7 only because his profits remain untouched.

In order to salvage the theory that the steward cancels interest/principal that ultimately belongs to the master, many commentators call upon a deeply embedded honor-shame code in ancient Mediterranean culture and suggest that the master willingly forgoes his own profit in lieu of the honor that will accrue to his name because of the steward's benevolence.[54] In short, honor trumps wealth, and the master seizes an opportunity to enhance his public image while agreeing to overlook the steward's dishonesty. However, is the master not setting a dangerous precedent in forgiving his debtors' interest/principal? Word of these reductions will spread, and others will undoubtedly expect similar generosity from him in the future. When he does not offer it, his debtors will appeal to this event as a precedent and demand to know why he cannot forgive part of their debt as well. Moreover, if the steward had depleted the master's anticipated profit, would not the master now be commending him for the very same actions for which he was terminated (vv.1–2)? Only, this time, instead of scattering his own resources he would be scattering his employer's. Finally, can we really assume that this character valued honor more than money? Surely, some rich people would have placed a premium on cultivating an honorable name, but others may have been far more concerned—perhaps exclusively so—with amassing and protecting their wealth. The two wealthy men readers have met thus far (12:16–20; 15:11–32) did *not* value how others perceived them. The landowner in 12:16–20 considers only himself and his own desires when planning for his future, and the father in 15:11–32 completely ignores cultural norms for a wealthy paterfamilias by running out to meet his son, embracing and kissing him. Because these wealthy men did not appear interested in how others perceived them, readers will not assume that this wealthy man is above all else preoccupied with his honor and would therefore gladly forego profits to enhance it. In effect, the master's response of praise makes the most sense if we assume that the steward is canceling his own commissions.

---

[54] See, e.g., Lygre, "Of what charges (Luke 16:1–2)," 26–27; Landry and May, "Honor Restored: New Light on the Parable of the Prudent Steward (Luke 16:1–8a)," 302, 309; Bailey, *Poet and Peasant*, 102, 107; Young, *The Parables*, 241.

When Jesus describes the steward with the qualitative genitive τῆς ἀδικίας, he would therefore not be drawing attention to "dishonest"[55] behavior in vv.5–7, since the steward has not cheated his master by reducing what the debtors owe. But the steward is certainly "unjust": by habitually overcharging his master's debtors, he has managed to fund an extravagant, wasteful lifestyle (v.1). In a limited good society where resources are perceived to exist in finite quantities and in short supply, if someone acquires and spends far more than is generally deemed appropriate, s/he does so *at others' expense*.[56] Such behavior is fittingly labeled "unjust" because it fails to take others' needs into account.[57] The steward, then, is an "unjust" character from beginning to end. He is praised not for selfless benevolence or responding to the needs of the poor but for having recognized the crisis posed by his imminent termination and reacted quickly to ensure his future.[58]

"For the sons of this age are wiser than the sons of light with respect to their own generation."

With the parable now at its (open-)end,[59] Jesus adds his own commentary, which is targeted primarily to disciples (16:1) but will be overheard

---

[55] Many commentators do render τῆς ἀδικίας as "of dishonesty" (= dishonest), but such is not the word's most common meaning (see *BDAG*, 20–21). ἀδικία typically carries much stronger overtones and describes unjust, often injurious behavior and practices.

[56] See Kloppenborg, "The Dishonored Master [Luke 16, 1–8a]," 487 n.44. For his understanding of a limited good society, Kloppenborg is drawing upon G. Foster ("Peasant Society and the Image of Limited Good," *American Anthropologist* 67 [1965]: 293–315).

[57] Significantly, the related verb ἀδικέω means to mistreat, injure, or wrong someone else (*BDAG*, 20).

[58] How can such self-interested behavior be called "wise" (φρονίμως ἐποίησεν; v.8)? By cleverly devising a scheme that will endear him to others without infringing on his master's profits, the steward manifested "an instinct for self-preservation" (Bailey, *Poet and Peasant*, 102), one of the many understandings of "wisdom" represented in the Hebrew Bible (see Proverbs 30:24–28).

[59] The majority of commentators today view v.8a as the parable's end and v.8b as the beginning of Jesus' interpretation. See, e.g., Bovon, *L'Évangile Selon Saint Luc 15,1–19,27*, 67–68; Fitzmyer, *The Gospel According to Luke X–XXIV*, 1096–99; Scott, *Hear Then the Parable*, 256–60; Hendrickx, *The Parables of Jesus*, 192; Kloppenborg, "The Dishonored Master [Luke 16, 1–8a]," 475–79; Landry and May, "Honor Restored: New Light on the Parable of the Prudent Steward (Luke 16:1–8a), 288–89; Loader, "Jesus and the Rogue in Luke 16,1–8A: The Parable of the Unjust Steward," 522; Douglas M. Parrott, "The Dishonest Steward (Luke 16.1–8a) and Luke's Special Parable Collection," *NTS* 37 (1991), 499–502. Contrast the position of Jeremias, who argues that ὁ κύριος in v.8a is not the master from vv.3, 5 but Jesus and that the parable ends with v.7 (*The Parables*, 45–47).

by Pharisees as well (16:14). Neither the steward's surrendering of the records nor his departure is narrated, and readers do not find out whether the steward's cancellations merited the hospitality he sought. However, surely at least one of the master's debtors would be impressed with the steward's decision to forgo all of his commissions and receive him. The two debtors introduced to readers by the intradiegetic narrator appear to be persons of some means and may have sufficient resources to support him temporarily (though not enough to hire him as a fulltime steward). Moreover, the debtors, who were not awarded access to the steward's true motivation for canceling the commissions (as readers were), may interpret his actions as a sign of repentance for habitual overcharging and overconsumption and thus be even more favorably disposed toward him.[60]

Jesus begins by aligning the characters in the parable with "the sons of this age," who are contrasted with "the sons of light." Because none of the characters was portrayed positively, it is no surprise that Jesus attaches such a label to them.[61] If the steward is to become exemplary in some way for disciples, only certain actions and/or motivations of his will become paradigmatic. His overall character is not laudatory and probably will not come into play. Given that Jesus' primary audience includes a group of itinerant followers who, by renouncing possessions and prioritizing mission over familial relationships and occupations, no longer ascribe to the dominant values of their age, it is reasonable to assume that they are numbered among "the sons of light."[62]

In his opening comment, Jesus does not recommend, exhort, or instruct. Rather, he offers an observation without value judgments: "the sons of this age" are wiser than "the sons of light" with respect to the affairs of this world. Are "the sons of light" deficient in some way? Could they stand to learn a lesson or two from "the sons of this age"? Or, is their lack of worldly wisdom perfectly acceptable?

---

[60] Readers were privy to the steward's interior monologue and therefore may not see such signs of repentance.

[61] While the steward overcharged his master's business partners in order to fund a life of overconsumption that deprives others of their fair share of the earth's resources, it was also suggested that the debtors may have suspected a clandestine, mischievous scheme but gladly received their reductions without qualms. The rich man was not portrayed negatively in the parable, but given earlier portrayals of rich men in 12:16–20 and 15:11–32, readers would immediately have framed him in a negative light.

[62] "Sons of light" designates Christians elsewhere in the New Testament (see John 12:36; 1 Thess 5:5; Eph 5:8). The Qumran Essenes also used the term as a self-designation (see 1QS 1:9; 2:16; 3:13, 24–25).

"And I tell you, make for yourselves friends from the mammon of injustice so that when it fails they may welcome you into eternal tents."

While the steward, whose overall character is not commendable, is numbered among "the sons of this age" (v.8b), Jesus nevertheless strongly encourages disciples to view his *actions in vv.5–7* as paradigmatic for discipleship. Like the steward, they too are to "make friends" for themselves in order to secure living arrangements, though not in earthly homes but in "eternal tents" (αἰωνίους σκηνάς). Friends are made by relinquishing all that one has (just as the steward did)[63] and trusting that the recipients of one's gifts will one day return the favor by providing a welcome reception.[64] Because Jesus' primary motivation for relinquishing possessions and embracing a rigorous, itinerant lifestyle is to improve conditions for the poor (4:18–19), readers may expect selfless altruism from his followers as well. Here, however, Jesus legitimizes and even encourages a renunciation based on hope for an eternal reward. That self-interest may ultimately drive dispossession does not come as

---

[63] Nearly all commentators suggest that the disciples are to emulate the steward's actions in vv.5–7 by *sharing* with the poor or *giving alms*, not necessarily by renouncing all that they have (See, e.g., Bovon, *L'Évangile Selon Saint Luc 15,1–19,27*, 73; L. John Topel, "On the Injustice of the Unjust Steward: Luke 16:1–13," *CBQ* 37 [1975], 226–27; Hendrickx, *The Parables of Jesus*, 190, 193–94; Young, *The Parables*, 244–45, 248; Johnson, *The Gospel of Luke*, 248; Fitzmyer, *The Gospel According to Luke X–XXIV*, 1107; Dennis J. Ireland, *Stewardship and the Kingdom of God: An Historical, Exegetical, and Contextual Study of the Parable of the Unjust Steward in Luke 16:1–13* [Supplements to Novum Testamentum 70; New York: E. J. Brill, 1992], 217–18). Piper, however, does acknowledge that divestiture is a possibility since the issue of "*how* one is to use μαμωνᾶς to make friends is left openended": "Whether this is to be accomplished by almsgiving, hospitality, cancellation of debts or more radical disposal of one's goods is left unspecified" ("Social Background and Thematic Structure in Luke 16," 1654). The steward, however, appears to leave the estate with nothing of his own, and divestiture fits well with the co-text, where Jesus' disciples are asked to abandon *everything* before joining the movement (e.g., 5:11, 28; 14:33).

[64] Joel Green suggests that although Jesus' recommendation would appear to foster patron-client relations between his followers and the poor (i.e., the poor would become indebted to disciples and must at some point reciprocate), "[s]uch an understanding is undercut... by Jesus' related insistence that giving be done freely, with no strings attached, without expectation of return" (*The Gospel of Luke*, 594). He is referring specifically to statements made by Jesus in his Sermon on the Plain (6:30, 32–25). There is undoubtedly a tension within the Gospel between giving without expectation of return (6:30, 32–35; 11:4) and giving with full expectation of a future reward (12:33), but in v.9 this tension is nowhere to be found: Jesus explicitly identifies reception into eternal tents as the primary motivation (ἵνα) for divestiture, and it is expected that the beneficiaries of the disciples' gifts are to "welcome" them at the appropriate time. While Jesus' own motivation for bringing good news is other-centered (4:18–19), he is not opposed to allowing for and even encouraging self-interest among his followers.

a complete surprise, however, since earlier in the Travel Narrative Jesus instructed his disciples to "sell [their] possessions and give alms" so that they may receive "an inexhaustible treasure in the heavens, where neither thief draws near nor moth destroys" (12:33).

Jesus therefore appears to be formulating an *a minori ad maius* application to the parable:[65] If even this unjust steward who overcharges and overconsumes can forgo all that he has and trust that the beneficiaries of his gifts will welcome him, how much more so you—you are *not* unjust? Moreover, because Jesus sets up an *a minori ad maius* argument rather than an allegorical reading, readers will not expect or seek to establish precise one-to-one correspondences between characters and events in the parable and characters and events in the co-text. For instance, readers will assume neither that the steward's unjust lifestyle mirrors that of the disciples nor that the steward's beneficiaries—wholesale merchants or large-scale farmers—would serve as suitable recipients for the disciples' gifts. Unlike the steward, the disciples have already relinquished possessions, occupations, and even familial relations, so habitual overcharging of business partners or squandering resources are no longer even options for them. And, in light of what we already know about Jesus' overall mission (4:18–19), it is reasonable to assume that disciples are asked to "make friends" not with persons of similar social or economic status but with the poor. After all, since it is the poor to whom the kingdom belongs (6:20), *they* are the ones who will be in a position to "welcome" Jesus' followers into "eternal tents."[66]

The term "mammon of injustice" is polyvalent and therefore ambiguous. "Mammon," a Hebrew or Aramaic loanword, while not found in the Hebrew Bible, occurs in Qumran literature, the Targums, and the Mishnah.[67] It may carry no negative overtones and refer simply to property, possessions, or "anything of value," or it may describe profit acquired through exploitation and injustice.[68] Because both the diegetic

[65] See Bovon, *L'Évangile Selon Saint Luc 15,1–19,27*, 72. Bailey agrees that Jesus formulates an *a minori ad maius* argument, but he places emphasis on the generosity and mercy of God (represented by the rich man): "If this dishonest steward solved his problem by relying on the mercy of his master to solve his crisis, how much more will God help you in your crisis when you trust his mercy?" (*Poet and Peasant*, 105).

[66] See Richard H. Hiers, "Friends by Unrighteous Mammon: The Eschatological Proletariat (Luke 16:9)," *JAAR* 38 (1970), 33–34, 36.

[67] See Hauck, "μαμωνᾶς," in *TDNT* IV, 388; Fitzmyer, *The Gospel According to Luke X–XXIV*, 1109.

[68] Hauck, "μαμωνᾶς," 388–89. Cf. Molina, "Luc 16/1 A 13: L'Injuste *Mamon*," 372–73.

and intradiegetic narrators have thus far employed τὰ ὑπάρχοντα as the generic designation for "possessions/property" (8:3; 11:21; 12:15, 33, 44; 14:33), rendering μαμωνᾶς in a similarly neutral sense would not help readers account for Jesus' introduction of this Semitic loanword here for the first time. In other words, treating ὑπάρχοντα and μαμωνᾶς as synonyms[69] does not help us explain why Jesus employs the word at all. Furthermore, readers know that Jesus does not view "possessions" themselves as "unjust" since they are used to fund his itinerant ministry (see 8:3). Disciples will require certain minimal provisions and are even encouraged to pray for them (11:3). If we were to ascribe its negative valence of "profit acquired unjustly and at the expense of others," then Jesus' qualifier τῆς ἀδικίας[70] would seem redundant, even though it would appropriately account for the origin of the steward's possessions through habitual overcharging. In neither of the preceding parables (12:16–20; 15:11–32) did Jesus seem concerned with how possessions were acquired (whether unjustly or justly), only that, when available *in abundance*, they encourage overconsumption and waste—which, in a limited good society, is perceived to be injurious to others. Possibly, then, in view of the parable's co-text, mammon refers not merely to ὑπάρχοντα but ὑπάρχοντα-in-excess, which Jesus believes in itself is "unjust" since it tends to arouse overconsumption, promote waste, and, consequently, deprive others of essential resources.[71] A suitable English translation for μαμωνᾶς might be "wealth," defined by *Webster's Ninth New Collegiate Dictionary* as an "abundance of ... material possessions or resources."[72]

---

[69] Hiers argues for equating the two terms ("Friends by Unrighteous Mammon: The Eschatological Proletariat [Luke 16:9]," 32).

[70] I view μαμωνᾶ τῆς ἀδικίας as parallel to Jesus' prior phrase τὸν οἰκονόμον τῆς ἀδικίας in v.8 and therefore read τῆς ἀδικίας here as a descriptive or qualitative genitive as well. Codex Bezae, anticipating Jesus rephrasing in v.11 (τῷ ἀδίκῳ μαμωνᾷ), makes explicit that τῆς ἀδικίας is a qualitative genitive by rewriting it to read τοῦ ἀδίκου μαμωνᾶ.

[71] The precise phrase μαμωνᾶ τῆς ἀδικίας is not paralleled anywhere in extent literature (in Greek, Hebrew, or Aramaic), which is why readers are encouraged to look to the parable's co-text for guidance. Marc Philonenko does highlight several related phrases (see especially Sir 40:13 LXX; Tob 12:8 א; 1 En. 97:8, 10; 63:10; 2 En. 10:5; Ps.-Phoc. 5), all of which seem to convey resources/money acquired *unjustly*, but none are exact equivalents ("De L'intérêt des Deutérocanoniques pour L'interprétation du Nouveau Testament: L'example de *Luc* 16,9," *Revue des Sciences Religieuses* 73 [1999], 179–82).

[72] (Springfield, Mass: Merriam-Webster, 1988), 1335.

Mammon, then, certainly would not preclude unjustly acquired profit but would refer more comprehensively to resources-in-excess.[73]

According to Jesus, wealth (which in itself is "unjust") will eventually fail[74] and be displaced by a fair, equitable distribution of resources.[75] In the meantime, disciples are strongly urged to renounce it now and so "make friends," who in time will "welcome" them into "eternal tents." Like the steward, they are to forgo all they have, yet as part of a larger network of his followers (see 8:3; 9:3–4; 10:4, 7) they can still expect to receive what they really *need* (11:3; 12:30–31). Moreover, it is not imperative that they be motivated entirely by concern for the poor, as he is (4:18–19). Jesus does acknowledge that self-interest (i.e., hope for an eternal reward) may play some role in motivating renunciation. Interestingly, however, Jesus' metaphor for this reward, "eternal tents," does not promise a substantial material return for their sacrifice. They will not be rewarded with a lavish, jewel-encrusted city containing a street of "pure gold" (Rev 21:10–27) or even with rooms in God's heavenly mansion (John 14:2). They can expect only "tents"—hardly an improvement over their current material existence. The metaphor, rather, suggests interdependence, community, permeability; it points toward a future when God is near,[76] people take only what they need and as God provides,[77] and walls are no longer required to keep others out and to guard against thievery and decay (12:33).

[73] Cf. Hendrickx's position: "'Unrighteous mammon' refers not only to clearly unjustly acquired wealth, but to wealth as such, inasmuch as it is usually connected with injustice... and often unjustly used" (*The Parables of Jesus*, 193).

[74] Several manuscripts (notably K M F Γ Δ U P f^{13} and several MSS from *Byz*) preserve a 2nd person plural form of ἐκλείπω (variously ἐκλείπητε; ἐκλείπετε; ἐκλίπητε), which would shift the emphasis from the dissolution of wealth to individual death. The 3rd person singular form is much better attested and retained here.

[75] Jesus draws upon jubilary language and themes in his programmatic announcement at the synagogue in Nazareth (4:18–19). Jubliary legislation in Lev 25 and Deut 15:1–11 sought (among other things) to repair a maldistribution of resources and award a second chance to those who had lost property, possessions, or even their freedom.

[76] Bovon (*L'Évangile Selon Saint Luc 15,1–19,27*, 74) suggests that σκηνάς may evoke the ancient tent of meeting, where God communicated with the Israelites during their 40 years in the wilderness (Exod 33:7–11; Num 11:16–17). Although Moses was the primary beneficiary of this divine communication, "*everyone* who sought the LORD would go out to the tent of meeting" (Exod 33:7; Italics mine).

[77] The Israelites lived in "tents" while they were in the wilderness, and God provided both manna and quail to all as needed (Exod 16:4–36). No one was supposed to gather or store more than would be required for daily sustenance (except on the day before the Sabbath).

"The one who is faithful with the smallest thing is also faithful in much, and the one who is unjust with the smallest thing is also unjust in much. So, if you are not[78] *faithful with unjust mammon, who will entrust to you what is true? And, if you are not*[78] *faithful with what is alien, who will give you what is [really] yours?"*

As with his initial comments on the parable (vv.8b–9), Jesus begins with a maxim-like observation (v.10) and then shifts immediately to second person plural direct address (vv.11–12). Initially, Jesus does not identify what "the smallest thing" (v.10) is, but because he adds two parallel statements, readers are soon able to infer that it is "unjust mammon" (v.11). He appears to be reminding disciples that although many believe material wealth (itself "unjust") is one of the most significant and highly esteemed things, it is in fact but "the smallest thing." Indeed, one day it will fail (v.9). Disciples also learn that mammon is "alien," "strange," or "unsuitable," even a hostile "enemy" (τῷ ἀλλοτρίῳ; v.12).[79] It is so because it deprives others of essential resources and arouses overconsumption and waste. In exchange for material abundance, disciples should seek both for "what is true" (τὸ ἀληθινὸν) and "what is [really theirs]" (τὸ ὑμέτερον). Material possessions do not really belong to them anyhow. As creator, God ultimately owns all of the land and its resources, and human beings are but stewards—who, one day, will also have their stewardship taken away (v.3). Disciples are reminded to be trustworthy with mammon now, and for them such faithfulness involves complete divestiture, in part a confession that God owns all.

Although disciples are the primary addressees (v.1), because εἰ ... οὐκ ἐγένεσθε (vv.11–12) may also be rendered "if ... you do not *become*," readers may overhear an exhortation to the parable's secondary audience, consisting of tax collectors, sinners, Pharisees, and scribes (15:1–2), none of whom have apparently departed yet.

---

[78] Or: "you do not become" (οὐκ ἐγένεσθε).

[79] See *BDAG*, 47–48. Although most commentators render the substantive adjective as "what belongs to another" (Johnson, *The Gospel of Luke*, 246; Fitzmyer, *The Gospel According to Luke X–XXIV*, 1105), I much prefer Bovon's translation, "strange/foreign" ("étranger"), which is not only consistent with how the adjective is most commonly rendered when it appears as a substantive but also with the overall tenor of Jesus' polarizing "either/or" rhetoric in vv.10–13 (*L'Évangile Selon Saint Luc 15,1–19,27*, 86; *BDAG*, 47–48).

"No servant can serve two masters. For either s/he will hate the one and love the other or s/he will cling to one and treat the other with contempt. You cannot serve God and mammon."

As with his two prior comments (vv.8b–9, 10–12), Jesus again begins with a proverb and only after shifting to second person plural direct address (οὐ δύνασθε) does he identify the two masters as God and mammon. Because it is clear by now that mammon is "unjust," Jesus is able to drop qualifiers employed earlier (τῆς ἀδικίας and ἀδίκῳ). While many undoubtedly try to serve God and mammon simultaneously,[80] in no uncertain terms does Jesus declare this impossible. The mere existence of mammon means that the earth's resources are unfairly distributed, and in order to testify publicly that God owns all, he strongly encourages his disciples to "hate" (μισήσει) or "treat with contempt" (καταφρονήσει) personal excess by divesting completely. God and mammon are totally incompatible. Indeed, as many commentators have observed, Jesus for the first time appears to personify mammon as an evil, powerful, cosmic force[81] diametrically opposed to God's plan of release for captives and freedom for the oppressed (4:18).

2. *Summary*

Debtors fed up with a steward who has been exacting exorbitant commissions in order to fund a lifestyle marked by reckless overconsumption and waste leak information about his extravagant existence to the landowner with the hope that he will "read between the lines" and fire him. Their plan succeeds, but because the steward has been in the habit of squandering money on himself, he faces the prospect of leaving the estate with nothing of his own and having no one who is willing to welcome him into their home. So, in order to secure basic provisions upon his release, the steward cancels all of his commissions with the confidence that someone will be impressed with his generosity and gladly receive him. His master, a wealthy man (v.1) who would not take theft lightly, is able to praise the steward's actions only because he has left his profits untouched. Jesus does not tell us whether the steward's plan achieved its desired effect, though one may assume that at least

---

[80] Readers soon learn that, according to Jesus, one group within the secondary audience (the Pharisees) is trying to serve both God and mammon (16:14).

[81] See, e.g., Green, *The Gospel of Luke*, 596; Hendrickx, *The Parables of Jesus*, 192; Bovon, *L'Évangile Selon Saint Luc 15,1–19,27*, 87–88; Johnson, *The Gospel of Luke*, 246. Many consequently capitalize mammon in their translations.

one of the debtors responded favorably and elected to support him for a short time.[82]

In his commentary, Jesus sets up an *a minori ad maius* argument for his disciples: If this unjust steward who overcharged and overconsumed can forgo all he has and trust that he will receive what he needs, how much more so you—you who are neither unjust nor have been constrained by external forces to give up everything? Disciples are encouraged to emulate the steward's *actions* (not his character) by relinquishing all and trusting that they too will be cared for and receive necessary provisions (see 11:3; 12:29–32). In fact, Jesus even allows for divestiture based, at least in part, on self-interest (i.e., hope for an eternal reward; v.9), even though he himself is motivated by concern for improving conditions for the poor (4:18–19). Although many may see wealth (resources-in-excess) as one of the most honorable and significant things, Jesus urges his followers to view it as but "the smallest thing" (ἐλαχίστῳ) and "alien" or "unsuitable" (ἀλλοτρίῳ) for those who are "on the way." Furthermore, says Jesus, wealth in itself is "unjust" (μαμωνᾶ τῆς ἀδικίας; ἀδίκῳ μαμωνᾷ),[83] because it tends to arouse overconsumption and deprive others of what they need. As a symbolic gesture and confession of their belief that *God* owns all, disciples are to not merely to share or give alms but to give up everything. The mere existence of mammon means that the earth's resources are unfairly distributed, and disciples, through their radical, itinerant lifestyle, offer a clear critique of current economic arrangements and testify to a vision of just distribution heralded in jubilary legislation (Lev 25 and Deut 15:1–15). Mammon, in fact, has become so destructive that Jesus concludes his address by framing it as an evil force that opposes God's plan of release for captives and freedom for the oppressed (4:18).

Overconsumption and waste have been criticized consistently in each of the three parables, but with Jesus' final statement, "You cannot serve God and mammon" (v.13), readers find their first clear, uncompromising critique of wealth itself. Hints of such a critique have, to be sure, already emerged (see 1:53; 6:24), but Jesus' prior parable in 15:11–32

[82] Based on the sizeable quantities of oil and grain listed in the promissory notes (vv.6–7), both debtors introduced by Jesus appear not to be poor peasants but persons of some means who may have had sufficient resources to support the steward for a short time.

[83] Jesus' attributive use of the adjective ἀδίκῳ in the second phrase confirms our reading of τῆς ἀδικίας as a descriptive (or qualitative) genitive.

momentarily threatened to overturn these negative assessments. Jesus' comments in vv.10–13 therefore not only confirm earlier hints of a critique of wealth in the Gospel but strengthen them: God or mammon! For disciples, there is simply no middle ground, and Jesus strongly urges them to demonstrate their loyalty to God as well as their commitment to their neighbor through an act of complete divestiture.

B. The Parable of the Rich Man and Lazarus (16:19–31)

1. *Exploring the Pre-Text: 16:14–18*

Although readers are given no indication that any group mentioned in 15:1–2—tax collectors, sinners, Pharisees, and scribes—has departed, the narrator highlights only the Pharisees' response to Jesus' words (v.14). Having (over)heard everything Jesus has said from 15:4–16:13 (ἤκουσον δὲ ταῦτα πάντα; v.14), their grumbling (διεγόγγυζον; 15:2) intensifies to open ridicule (ἐξεμυκτήριζον; v.14). But the reason behind this shift is not entirely clear. Are the Pharisees perturbed, for instance, at Jesus' earlier remarks about joy in heaven over the repentance of even one "sinner" (15:7, 10) or his most recent comments on mammon (16:9–13), particularly his rather outrageous claim that God and personal wealth are totally incompatible (16:13)? In an aside to readers, the narrator draws attention specifically to the Pharisees' love for money (φιλάργυροι ὑπάρχοντες; v.14),[84] so readers may reasonably infer that Jesus' nimshalim on mammon provoked this shift from murmuring to mockery.

Jesus builds upon the narrator's negative characterization of the Pharisees by accusing them of justifying themselves (δικαιοῦντες ἑαυτοὺς) and adhering to values that, while lauded by many (τὸ ἐν ἀνθρώποις ὑψηλὸν), are a polluting abomination (Βδέλυγμα)[85] before

---

[84] It is important to mention that Luke's characterization of the Pharisees as "lovers of money" may have very little to do with the historical Pharisees. At the time Jesus was preaching, the group, composed largely of laypersons, did not have much political power, and there is certainly no historical evidence to substantiate the narrator's claim that they were especially greedy (or greedier than any other group). As Luke T. Johnson points out, φιλαργυρία (love of money) "was one of the standard vices in Greek moral teaching" and often attributed to one's opponents in polemical discourse (*The Gospel of Luke*, 249–50).

[85] While βδέλυγμα generally refers to something that is disgusting or loathsome, the word occasionally carries connotations of pollution or defilement as well (*BDAG*, 172).

God (v.15). He further announces that a new era has dawned with the inauguration of a radically inclusive kingdom (v.16)[86] that calls these widely cherished values into question and offers good news to the poor, release to captives, and freedom to the oppressed (4:18–19). To some, it may appear as if his teaching is undermining the Law and the Prophets, but he is quick to emphasize that the ethical demands of the kingdom are firmly rooted in Jewish scripture (vv.16–17).[87] Jesus, in fact, assures them that it is easier for heaven and earth to pass away than for even one stroke of a letter in the Law to fall away (v.17). In order to demonstrate his commitment to the Law, he offers the Pharisees a reading of one prohibition in the Decalogue: "You shall not commit adultery" (Exod 20:14; Deut 5:18). Precisely what constitutes adultery was, of course, hotly debated in the first century, and Jesus weighs in by arguing that anyone who either divorces and remarries[88] or marries

[86] The phrase "radically inclusive kingdom" is based on rendering Jesus' statement in v.16 πᾶς εἰς αὐτὴν βιάζεται as "everyone is being invited/urged into [the kingdom of God]." The verb βιάζεται may, of course, be translated in a number of ways. One must, for instance, decide whether to opt for the middle or passive voice and whether to ascribe a connotation of violence/force or earnest invitation (see *BDAG*, 175–76). Juan Cortes and Florence Gatti have recently argued for rendering the verb in the passive voice (which has the advantage of aligning it with the adjacent passive voice verb εὐαγγελίζεται) while ascribing to it the weakened sense of "being earnestly invited/urged" ("On the Meaning of Luke 16:16," *JBL* 106 [1987], 247–59). Not only is this use of βιάζω found in other literature of the time (see POxy 2.294.16–18) but Jesus elsewhere in Luke urges his disciples to "compel [people] to come into" the kingdom (14:23) and hopes that "repentance for forgiveness of sins" will be proclaimed to "*all* nations" (24:47). A case can therefore be made for rendering βιάζεται here in the passive voice and with the connotation of urgent invitation, much like the warm, "'genteel constraint imposed on a reluctant guest'" (*BDAG*, 176).

[87] Many commentators have persuasively argued that in Luke Jesus' preaching of the kingdom does not entail abandoning or abrogating the Law but is, in fact, fully continuous with Jewish scripture. See, e.g., Piper, "Social Background and Thematic Structure in Luke 16," 1656–57; Green, *The Gospel of Luke*, 600, 603.

[88] J. Fitzmyer's claim that Jesus "presents marriage as indissoluble" and "forbids divorce absolutely, i.e. without any exceptions" in v.18 is a bit perplexing (*The Gospel According to Luke X–XXIV*, 1120–21. Cf. L. T. Johnson's similar statement that Jesus here presents an "absolute and unequivocal prohibition of divorce" [*The Gospel of Luke*, 255]). Divorce itself is not prohibited, only divorce *and* remarriage. Elsewhere, Jesus commands his disciples to "hate (μισεῖ)...wives and children" (14:26). While Jesus may be speaking hyperbolically, it nevertheless seems clear that he is asking his followers to prioritize their new fictive kin relationships over their real (or biological) familial relationships. Such prioritization of mission over family probably did not go over well with spouses who did not join the movement and may have led to divorce in some cases. Given the all-consuming nature of discipleship under Jesus and his repeated invitations to leave behind everything and everyone for the kingdom, it is not at all surprising that divorce itself would be permitted.

a divorcee is guilty of breaking this commandment (v.18). While his opinion on this issue successfully demonstrates a fair hearing of (or faithful engagement with) Mosaic legislation on divorce and remarriage,[89] it is clear that Jesus is nevertheless out of step with mainstream Jewish thought.[90] Strikingly similar to the Qumran Essenes' understanding of divorce,[91] his interpretation is unusually stringent and foreshadows similar sectarian rigor on the themes of consumption and wealth in the subsequent parable (vv.19–31). Of course, having denied any compatibility between personal wealth and service to God in 16:13 and therefore sharply criticizing any religious tradition that would tie material prosperity to divine favor, Jesus has already placed himself outside the mainstream. Readers will not expect back-peddling or compromise in the parable that follows.[92]

2. *Reading the Parable: 16:19–31*

"A certain man was rich, and he used to dress himself in purple and fine linen and celebrate splendidly every day."

In Jesus' preceding three parables, overconsumption was either inferred (12:16–21; 16:1–8a) or mentioned only briefly and without an accompanying description of precisely how resources were spent (15:11–32). Here, however, the intradiegetic narrator offers a vivid portrayal of

---

[89] Deuteronomy 24:1–4 is the only place in the Torah where divorce and remarriage is addressed directly. The text presents a hypothetical case ("*Suppose* a man enters into marriage with a woman..."; v.1) in which the practice of divorce appears to be assumed. The issue is not treated extensively, and no general principles are supplied. For anyone in search of such principles, they must be deduced or inferred from this single example. Here, a man who divorces his wife is prohibited from remarrying her if, during their separation, she chose to marry another man. The Torah has therefore offered only one circumstance under which remarriage is prohibited. Later rabbis, of course, would add other circumstances to this one. Instead of entertaining such circumstances, Jesus elects to prohibit remarriage altogether, a hermeneutical move that does not necessarily contradict the hypothetical scenario in Deut 24:1–4. His second injunction not to marry a divorcee, while similarly categorical and dismissive of specific circumstances, may be unusually rigorous but also does not contradict Deut 24:1–4.

[90] Both the Schools of Hillel and Shammai, for instance, were much more lenient and willing to identify specific "cases" or circumstances under which divorce and remarriage were permissible.

[91] See, e.g., 11QTemple 57:17–19; J. Fitzmyer, *The Gospel According to Luke X–XXIV*, 1121. See also J. Fitzmyer, "The Matthean Divorce Texts and Some New Palestinian Evidence," *TS* 37 (1976): 197–226.

[92] Readers, however, will expect Jesus' teaching to reflect faithful engagement with the Law and the Prophets, even if his reading of Jewish scripture appears unreasonably rigorous and "out of touch" with mainstream voices.

daily opulence and habitual overconsumption. The use of the imperfect tense (ἐνεδιδύσκετο) coupled with a present participle (εὐφραινόμενος)[93] suggests that decadence and lavish celebration had become a customary way of life extending back many years. While the rich man's habit of dressing in purple fabrics may suggest an association with or a comparison to royalty,[94] the combination of fine, imported linen undergarments (βύσσον)[95] with purple outer garments (πορφύραν) certainly places him among the region's most wealthy and powerful elite.[96] Of course, daily opulence of this magnitude is only possible because of this man's extraordinary wealth (πλούσιος). As in Jesus' preceding parables, it is excess or superabundance that enables (even entices one into) a life of overconsumption.

It has been suggested that first century Judeans distinguished between the honorable and the dishonorable rich.[97] While the honorable rich refrain from accumulating land, capital, and possessions at the expense of others and work only to sustain the resources they have, the dishonorable rich use their power to seize resources that rightfully belong to others.[98] In a limited good society, it is argued, any accumulation must come only at the expense of someone else and is therefore condemned. In his portrayal of the rich man, Jesus at no point indicates that he acquired his wealth unjustly or sought to increase his capital by, for instance, acquiring other properties or issuing loans with exorbitant interest rates. Rather, this man takes what is already his and spends it on his own pleasures. Tentatively, readers may classify this character among the "honorable" rich.

---

93 It is here rendered as a participle of attendant circumstance.

94 See, e.g., Judg 8:26; 1 Macc 8:14. Several commentators mention the royal overtones associated with costly purple dye and fabrics (See, e.g., Bovon, *L'Évangile Selon Saint Luc 15,1–19,27*, 106; Hultgren, *The Parables of Jesus*, 112; Johnson, *The Gospel of Luke*, 251; Fitzmyer, *The Gospel According to Luke X–XXIV*, 1130). Cf. Jesus' earlier remark in 7:25, where those who wear fine clothing and live in luxury are said to dwell in royal palaces (βασιλείοις).

95 Reputedly worn by India's elite and certain Egyptian priests, this imported linen was rare and very expensive (See Pierre Batiffol, "Trois Notes Exégétiques. Sur Luc XVI, 19," *RB* 9 [1912], 541. Cf. Bovon, *L'Évangile Selon Saint Luc 15,1–19,27*, 106).

96 See especially Herzog, *Parables as Subversive Speech*, 117–18. Herzog claims that the use of purple dye was "severely limited even among elites" (117).

97 See D. H. Reinstorf, "The rich, the poor, and the law," *Hervormde Teologiese Studies* 60 (2004), 330–32. For this distinction, Reinstorf is drawing especially upon B. J. Malina, *The New Testament World: Insights from Cultural Anthropology* (Louisville: Westminster John Knox Press, 1993) and B. J. Malina and R. L. Rohrbaugh, *Social-science Commentary on the Synoptic Gospels* (Minneapolis: Fortress Press, 1992).

98 Ibid., 332.

Does this tentative classification suggest that readers will view the rich man favorably? While no explicit mention is made of unjust acquisition, Luke's readers have already internalized a negative assessment of wealth (1:53; 6:24; 16:9–13) and overconsumption (12:13–21; 15:11–32; 16:1–13) and therefore will not expect good things from him. In all three of Jesus' previous parables, those with access to excess resources overspent on themselves, and no change in behavior is anticipated here. Furthermore, as a wealthy man who has been enjoying only the finest clothing and foods for many years, he stands in stark contrast to Jesus' disciples, who have been asked not only to leave behind all of their possessions (14:33) but to seek and consume only what is "essential" (ἐπιούσιον; 11:3). While first century Judeans may have distinguished between honorable and dishonorable wealth, in these four parables from Luke's Travel Narrative, that distinction has not been made. In his nimshalim following the parable of the unjust steward (16:9–13), Jesus for the first time condemned wealth itself—whether acquired unjustly or not—in unambiguous fashion. Wealth and service to God, he concluded, are totally incompatible (16:13). At this point, therefore, readers can only expect a tragic plot to unfold in which this anonymous rich man moves ever closer toward "catastrophe and...isolation."[99]

"A certain poor man named Lazarus had been laid at his gate. Covered with sores, he was longing to be satisfied from what was falling[100] *from the rich man's table. But dogs also used to come and lick his sores."*

A mere stone's throw from the banquet hall where the rich man and his guests routinely gather to celebrate and feast, opulence and festivity are displaced by chronic hunger and physical pain, for readers learn that "a poor man named Lazarus"—famished, covered with open wounds, and plagued by frequent visitations from unclean street dogs—resides just beyond the mansion's magnificent gate. The imperfect verbs and present participles upon which this portrait is constructed (ἐπιθυμῶν; πιπτόντων; ἐρχόμενοι; ἐπέλειχον) suggest that this is no momentary, fleeting affair: Lazarus has been here for many years. Probably for as long as the rich man has been dressing extravagantly and feasting sumptuously, Lazarus has been aching for relief. The stark contrast between such

[99] Via, *The Parables*, 96.

[100] A few manuscripts (ℵ[2] A W Θ Δ Ψ 33 *f*[13]*Byz* among others) add "*little crumbs* (τῶν ψιχιῶν) that were falling," but the addition appears to be based on Matt 15:17.

opulence and dire poverty is jolting and deeply troubling. Indeed, it is almost inconceivable that abundance and poverty can coexist in such close proximity for so long without any alteration. Lazarus' very name, "God helps,"[101] seems to foreshadow an intervention—and therefore a change—of some sort, but through whom will it arrive? Will the rich man eventually come to his side? Will the abundance behind the gate find its way out into the city streets?[102]

Bernard B. Scott argues that the gate is a metaphor for relational possibility and suggests the rich man "will become the patron of the poor man."[103] Jesus, after all, places not a wall between them but a traversable passageway—a gate that can be swung open wide at a moment's notice. But this is no ordinary gate: comparable to the "large, impressive gateways" that lead into "temples and palaces,"[104] this enormous structure (πυλῶνα) suggests impermeability and demarcates clearly defined, generally untraversable social boundaries. Furthermore, from Jesus' previous three parables, readers have learned that excess does not engender beneficence or almsgiving but entices its recipients to overspend on themselves. To be sure, an intervention of some kind is expected, but readers will not expect the rich man behind the gate to initiate it.

While the rich man inside appears to exert full control over his environment, dressing in the finest garments and preparing lavish celebrations whenever it suits him,[105] Lazarus is subject to whatever

---

[101] Lazarus (לעזר) is an abbreviated from of Eleazar/Eliezer (אלעזר), meaning "God has helped" or "God helps."

[102] While the narrator does not specify whether readers are to imagine a large country estate or a magnificent home in the city, an urban residence would be the most likely candidate since the wealthy generally spent most of their time in cities. Through the remainder of this section (vv. 19–22), I will assume an urban dwelling as backdrop for Jesus' portrait. Cf. Herzog's position: "With these deft strokes, Jesus has sketched the life of the *urban elite* whose 'houses' (*oikoi*) control the political and economic life of the preindustrial city and its surrounding countryside" (italics mine; *Parables as Subversive Speech*, 118).

[103] *Hear Then the Parable*, 151.

[104] *BDAG*, 897. In contrast to the smaller and more common πύλη, πυλών is used, for instance, of "the entrances of the heavenly Jerusalem," "the magnificent city gates of Babylon," and even of the passageways into King Herod's Temple (Ibid.). Contrast the position of V. Tanghe, who argues that πυλῶνα in this case refers not to the gate itself but a portal or vestibule to which the gate provides access ("Abraham, Son Fils et Son Envoyé [Luc 16, 19–31]," 566–67). The rich man and Lazarus, according to Tanghe, would therefore reside on the same side of gate.

[105] Both ἐνεδιδύσκετο and εὐφραινόμενος are in the middle voice and show that he is fully capable of acting by and for himself (or in his own interest).

circumstances develop about him. He is placed at the gate by others (ἐβέβλητο), entirely dependent upon others' generosity for sustenance, and unable to fend off roaming wild dogs. In fact, at no point does he act of his own volition. He "longs" (ἐπιθυμῶν), that is all.[106] Moreover, Jesus provides no indication that he was ever able to acquire the object of his desire:[107] those small pieces of bread used by celebrants as napkins and tossed under the table as refuse.[108] Gradually realizing that it would be too much to ask for a full loaf of bread, Lazarus was forced long ago to lower his expectations.

Astonishingly, however, it is the poor man whom Jesus elects to name and the rich man who remains anonymous, a "Nobody."[109] Would not all of the townspeople have known the rich man's name but scratched their heads and shrugged if asked this poor beggar's name? But Jesus reverses readers' expectations by naming the nameless and so dignifying him. The town's somebody is forgotten; its nobody is remembered.[110]

---

[106] Some commentators have suggested that Lazarus must be "pious," which would not only help explain the etymology of his name but also the coming reversal in his favor (For a recent defense of this position, see, e.g., Hultgren, *The Parables of Jesus*, 112. Richard Bauckham documents earlier examples ["The Rich Man and Lazarus: The Parable and the Parallels," *NTS* 37 (1991), 232 n. 20]). Jesus, however, neither glorifies poverty nor equates it with piety. In sharp contrast to the protagonist in the *Testament of Job*, for instance, who actually seeks to *increase* his suffering and thereby enhance his piety, Lazarus, who "was longing to be [fully] satisfied from what was falling from the rich man's table," sought to eradicate his perpetual hunger but was unable to do so because of his illness. On one occasion, Job even reports that he replaced worms that jumped off his body (T. Job 20:8–9)! Lazarus, by contrast, never seeks to enhance or prolong his suffering; he earnestly "longs" for a change in his condition.

[107] A few commentators argue that Lazarus actually did eat the rich man's leftovers (see, e.g., Hultgren, *The Parables of Jesus*, 116; Duane Warden, "The Rich Man and Lazarus: Poverty, Wealth, and Human Worth," in *SCJ* 6 [2003], 81), but the embedded narrator nowhere provides any indication of this. It is more likely, in fact, that he was dependent upon the generosity of other townspeople or passersby, whose gifts sustained him year after year. A few manuscripts (f^{13} 1071 it^{1} vg^{cl} among others) insert, "but no one was giving [anything] to him," but the addition seems to be a scribal expansion based on the embedded narrator's earlier remark in 15:16.

[108] See Herzog, *Parables as Subversive Speech*, 118; Green, *The Gospel of Luke*, 606; Jeremias, *Rediscovering the Parables*, 146. Of this practice, which some later rabbinic traditions require for "reasons of purity and hygiene," Herzog writes: "It was another form of conspicuous consumption that turned the necessities of life into disposables" (118).

[109] An early Sahidic manuscript names the rich man "Nineve(h)," which K. Grobel suggests may appropriately be rendered "Nobody" ("'...Whose Name was Neves,'" *NTS* 10 [1964], 381–82). The earliest Greek manuscript of this Gospel (p^{75}; Bodmer Papyrus) also attaches a name to the rich man, "Neues," which appears to reflect a shortened form of the name found in the Sahidic version (Ibid., 382; Cf. Metzger, *A Textual Commentary on the Greek New Testament*, 140).

[110] The naming of Lazarus is all the more striking (and significant) given that this is the only one of Jesus' parables in which a character is named.

It is not at all clear why or how Lazarus came to reside here. Chronically ill with a skin condition[111] that would likely render him unclean, he should have been ordered far away from this man's mansion and outside the city gates. Conceivably, Lazarus' friends or family members long ago decided to place him directly in front of the rich man's estate because they believed that here he would have his best chance of receiving the resources he so desperately needed.[112] Frequent celebrations must be accompanied by excess food, they may have reasoned, and the estate's owner would certainly offer what was left over to Lazarus. Indeed, given widespread expectations during the first century that the wealthy should regularly give alms, how could he refuse to come to his aid? It appears, however, that even those who initially placed Lazarus here forgot about him, for this is now his permanent home.[113] So far as we know, street dogs[114] are his only companions.

While Jewish tradition generally expected almsgiving from persons endowed with excess and Greco-Roman tradition similarly expected beneficence, in all four of Jesus' parables examined thus far characters with access to wealth have elected to spend it on themselves. With his opening portrait (a durative summary describing a situation that remained unchanged over many years), might Jesus be suggesting that Judea's economic system, which depended almost exclusively upon almsgiving and/or beneficence to redistribute resources to the poor, is failing miserably to address the enormous gap between haves and have-nots, elites and non-elites? To be sure, exhortations to almsgiving and beneficence, if routinely and widely heeded, may help alleviate some inequity, but Jesus' wealthy characters either are not aware of such exhortations or deliberately ignore them and choose rather to

[111] ἕλκος denotes an abscess or ulcer (*BDAG*, 317–18), and the perfect participle εἱλκωμένος suggests that they had overtaken his entire body.

[112] Many commentators have noted that the passive form of βάλλω (here ἐβέβλητο) is elsewhere used with reference to persons who are crippled or bedridden due to chronic illness (e.g., Matt 8:6, 14; 9:2; Rev 2:22. See Hultgren, *The Parables of Jesus*, 112; Fitzmyer, *The Gospel According to Luke X–XXIV*, 1131; Green, *The Gospel of Luke*, 606; Jeremias, *Rediscovering the Parables*, 145).

[113] The pluperfect passive ἐβέβλητο suggests an ongoing past state of affairs resulting from a previous, singular act. Thus, Lazarus is not laid at the rich man's gate each morning and then taken back home in the evening; rather, having been laid there (once) long ago, this is now his permanent home.

[114] Street dogs (κύνες) were generally viewed as unclean animals (*BDAG*, 579. See also Bovon, *L'Évangile Selon Saint Luc 15,1–19,27*, 108; Herzog, *Parables as Subversive Speech*, 118; Johnson, *The Gospel of Luke*, 252). Lazarus' only companions are, like himself, unclean.

hoard and overspend on their own desires. If Jesus is indeed codifying a failure in Judea's economic system (specifically its dependence upon almsgiving and/or beneficence to alleviate gross inequity), may readers expect him to suggest an alternative?

"And it happened that the poor man died and was carried away by angels to Abraham's bosom. But, the rich man also died, and he was buried."
Shifting from durative summary to singulative narration, Jesus punctuates the opening portrait with the deaths of Lazarus and the rich man, the story's first true events. Appropriately, the poor man—chronically ill, bedridden, and likely malnourished—dies first, and the rich man, whose good personal hygiene, fine foods, and medical care enabled him to reach full maturity, dies second. Tragically, though not entirely unexpectedly, readers are now able to confirm that the rich man never initiated a relationship with Lazarus or sought to relieve his hunger or the physical pain associated with his abscesses. While the rich man continued to celebrate and live decadently, Lazarus, perhaps only yards away from the banquet hall, lay hungry and in agony. But it is Lazarus who, at death, enters the communion of others (ἀγγέλων; Ἀβραάμ) and the rich man who finds himself alone and, finally, no longer able to act or "do" for himself (ἐτάφη).[115] While it is difficult to discern the precise nature of their respective fates, it is nevertheless clear that Lazarus is in a much better place. The expression "Abraham's bosom" (κόλπον Ἀβραάμ) is unknown "elsewhere in pre-Christian Jewish literature,"[116] but it seems to suggest either that Lazarus has been awarded a place of honor next to Abraham at the heavenly banquet[117] or, more generally, a close relational bond between Lazarus and Israel's chief patriarch.[118] Having been forgotten by friends or family and repeatedly ignored by the rich man, God has finally intervened, and the event foreshadowed by Lazarus' very name ("God helps") has now come to pass. On the

[115] The middle voice from the opening portrait (ἐνεδιδύσκετο; εὐφραινόμενος) is here supplanted by the passive voice (ἐτάφη).

[116] Fitzmyer, *The Gospel According to Luke X–XXIV*, 1132.

[117] See, e.g., John 13:23. Commentators who opt for this association include Outi Lehtipuu, "Characterization and Persuasion: The Rich Man and the Poor Man in Luke 16.19–31," in *Characterization in the Gospels* (Sheffield: Sheffield Academic Press, 1999), 92; Hendrickx, *The Parables of Jesus*, 202; Herzog, *Parables as Subversive Speech*, 121; Jeremias, *Rediscovering the Parables*, 146.

[118] See, e.g., John 1:18. Commentators who prefer this association include Bovon, *L'Évangile Selon Saint Luc 15,1–19,27*, 109; Johnson, *The Gospel of Luke*, 252.

other hand, Jesus' description of the rich man's fate—"and he was buried"—is terse and leaves readers guessing what will become of him and his fortune.

"And in Hades, when [the rich man], who was enduring severe torments, raised his eyes, he saw Abraham from afar and Lazarus in his bosom(s)[119].[120] *He called out and said, 'Father Abraham, have mercy on me and send Lazarus so that he might dip the tip of his finger in water and cool my tongue, for I am in agony in this flame.'"*

After a highly accelerated summary (vv.19–22), the story now decelerates rapidly as the embedded narrator details the rich man's initial response to his new setting in Hades: he raises his eyes (ἐπάρας), spots Abraham in the distance (ὁρᾷ), and shouts a request (φωνήσας εἶπεν). The sudden slow-down requires readers to shift their attention from an enduring state persisting over several years to a singular event that transpires over the span of a few seconds. The narrator, moreover, for the first time loosens his grip on the story by allowing one of the characters to speak for himself, thereby transferring the burden of character construction to readers. Jesus previously informed us that this man, while on earth, was wealthy and chose to spend his resources on his own pleasures (v.19): What may readers now infer about him through his own speech and actions?

Astonishingly, although the rich man wastes no time in asking for relief from the intense heat, he already seems to have accepted his fate. He offers no protest of the judgment rendered on him.[121] Did he, perhaps, know all along that such an end awaited him? Not only has he reconciled himself to this new form of existence in flame and torment, but in asking for so little—a mere drop of water—he tacitly acknowledges that he is now utterly powerless to alter his situation for the better and completely dependent upon the generosity of others for relief. Just as Lazarus, only moments ago confined within a similar prison of powerlessness, dependence, and pain, was forced to lower

[119] Curiously, Jesus switches from the singular "bosom" (κόλπον) to the plural "bosoms" (κόλποις). *BDAG* notes that the plural form is elsewhere used figuratively for close association or intimacy (556–57). While the shift may seem a bit strange, even inexplicable, it does complement the equally odd plural form βασάνοις ("severe torments") in the same verse (v.23).

[120] A few manuscripts (D Θ) actually describe what Lazarus is doing at Abraham's bosom: "resting/relaxing" (ἀναπαυόμενον).

[121] See Bovon, *L'Évangile Selon Saint Luc 15,1–19,27*, 110.

his expectations for relief because of his unsympathetic neighbors, so now can the rich man hope only for the minutest of concessions to ease his pain. The two men have effectively exchanged places: the one who drenched his palate with the finest wines is parched, and the one who longed for table scraps is preparing to partake of the heavenly banquet.

It is unclear why the rich man chooses not to address Lazarus directly but rather issues his request through Abraham. It has been suggested that the rich man appealed to Abraham because of his reputation for hospitality (see Gen 18:1–15; T. Ab. 1:1–5 Recension A),[122] but he may still feel as if communication with a member of the expendable class is beneath him and so directs his attention to someone of similar socio-economic status.[123] Indeed, it appears as if the rich man views Lazarus as no more than a servant who exists to do his bidding (πέμψον Λάζαρον).[124] While the rich man has come to terms with his fate and his new state of powerlessness and dependence, he is not yet able to acknowledge Lazarus' elevated status at Abraham's bosom.

Initially, it is puzzling why the rich man does not ask someone other than Lazarus to offer him the relief for which he longs. He must surely be desperate if willing to tolerate physical contact (on his tongue, no less!) from an "untouchable" who was covered with open wounds. Implied, perhaps, is the complete absence of other members of his social class (whether family or friends) at Abraham's bosom. In other words, because none of his family or friends had received an invitation to dine with Abraham at the heavenly feast, he has no choice but to receive assistance from the poor beggar who lay at his gate.

Because Abraham shared a similar socio-economic background with the rich man and was widely known for his hospitality, readers may very well expect him to respond favorably to his appeal and send Lazarus to offer him some respite from heat and thirst. After all, the rich man is not asking for a jug of wine and a full meal but a tiny drop of water. Will Abraham show compassion and assent to—or perhaps

---

[122] See, e.g., Scott, *Hear Then the Parable*, 153.

[123] The tradition of Abraham's wealth was widely known in the first century (see, e.g., Jub. 13:14; T. Ab. 1:1–5 Recension A) and based on his portrayal in Genesis (see 13:2: "Now Abram was very rich in livestock, in silver, and in gold" [*NRSV*]).

[124] See Herzog, *Parables as Subversive Speech*, 123.

even exceed—this man's modest request, or are readers being mislead and encouraged to develop false expectations?[125]

"But Abraham said, 'Child, remember that you received your good things in your life, and Lazarus likewise [received] bad things. But now, he is being consoled here, and you are suffering pain.[126] *And, in addition,*[127] *between us and you a great chasm has been established*[128] *so that those who wish either to cross over from here to you or to cross over from there to us may not be able.'"*

In spite of the great chasm that now separates the men, Abraham acknowledges a kinship bond with the rich man by addressing him affectionately as "Child" (τέκνον).[129] Moreover, while Abraham's response is firm, his tone is neither harsh nor accusatory but paternal, even sympathetic. In fact, because Abraham at this point appears to be serving as God's spokesperson in the afterlife,[130] readers too will have a very difficult time condemning or detesting this man. His character is tragic,[131] not malevolent or wicked. While Abraham surprisingly denies the rich man his very modest request for a drop of water, he nevertheless graciously takes time to explain: 1) why he is now enduring immense pain (v.25) and; 2) why his request cannot be granted (v.26). Abraham does not berate him for having behaved immorally or unjustly but asks him first to recall and reflect on (μνήσθητι)[132] the kind of life he enjoyed on earth. His immense suffering now, explains Abraham, is due to the fact that he received and enjoyed "good things" (ἀγαθά) while Lazarus received "bad things" (κακά). Furthermore, continues Abraham, the reason why Lazarus may not bring him a drop of water to cool his

[125] Drawing on the work of Roland Barthes, Rimmon-Kenan lists the "snare" or "misleading cue" among one of several possible "retardatory devices" (*Narrative Fiction*, 127).

[126] On translating ὀδυνᾶσαι like a present tense verb, see *BDF* 87.

[127] Fitzmyer suggests that the phrase ἐν πᾶσι τούτοις is used to express addition in the LXX (Sir 48:15; Job 12:9; *The Gospel According to Luke X–XXIV*, 1133).

[128] The narrator employs the same verb (στηρίζω) at the start of the Travel Narrative with reference to Jesus' unwavering commitment to proceed to Jerusalem (9:51).

[129] Cf. Luke 15:31.

[130] This position of authority is likely derived from his role as "father" of the Jewish people (1:73; cf. 13:16; 19:9). Readers are therefore encouraged to align themselves with Abraham's focalization of the rich man's character (ethos) and chosen lifestyle. It is in his words that readers may discern an overall evaluative point of view for Jesus' parable (see especially O. Lehtipuu, who also suggests that Abraham's primary role in this parable is "to explain God's point of view" ["Characterization and Persuasion: The Rich Man and the Poor Man in Luke 16.19–31," 100]).

[131] See M. Gourgues, *TheParaboles de Luc*, 199.

[132] According to *BDAG*, μιμνησκομαι may occasionally carry the added nuance of "give careful attention to" (652).

tongue is that God has fixed[133] between them a vast, impassible chasm. Even if Abraham or Lazarus had wanted to relieve the rich man's suffering, they simply could not because of Hades' topography.[134] Sadly, the rich man's gate, which he could have opened at a moment's notice, has become an unbridgeable chasm.[135]

Abraham's rationale for why the rich man is suffering and Lazarus is at his bosom—the rich man received "good things" on earth while Lazarus received "bad things" (v.25)—is generally seen by commentators as insufficient and therefore in need of further explanation. Are we really to believe, for instance, that mere reception of "good things" in this life warrants suffering and deprivation in the next? Can poverty and/or illness unaccompanied by good deeds really merit eternal bliss? Many therefore assume in Abraham's statement the presence of a gap, one which is sometimes filled by accessing parallel accounts from the

---

[133] Although the agent of ἐστήρικται is not explicitly identified, it is reasonable to infer that God has created this chasm (traditionally known as a "theological/divine passive").

[134] Commentators have debated precisely where these three characters are located. A minority believe that Abraham and Lazarus are already in paradise or heaven and therefore in a different locale from the rich man altogether (see, e.g., Ferdinand O. Regalado, "The Jewish Background of the Parable of the Rich Man and Lazarus," *Asia Journal of Theology* 16 [2002], 343; Hultgren, *The Parables of Jesus*, 113–14). Others, however, suggest that all three men are in Hades (the Greek equivalent to Sheol) and that a final judgment upon their "shades" is still expected. Of these commentators, a few look to Egyptian conceptions of the netherworld as an appropriate backdrop (see Grobel, "'...Whose Name was Neves,'" 379–80; J. Gwyn Griffiths, "Cross-cultural Eschatology with Dives and Lazarus," *ET* 105 [1993], 11), while others call primarily upon descriptions of holding chambers for the righteous and wicked in 1 Enoch and 4 Ezra (see Larry Kreitzer, "Luke 16:19–31 and 1 Enoch 22," *ET* 103 [1992], esp. 141; Bovon, *L'Évangile Selon Saint Luc 15,1–19,27*, 109; Herzog, *Parables as Subversive Speech*, 122; Green, *The Gospel of Luke*, 607). Indeed, it seems as if all three men are being held *temporarily* in a netherworld whose topography very closely resembles descriptions found in 1 Enoch and 4 Ezra. According to 1 En. 22, human beings are held in "corners" within a "great and high mountain of hard rock" (vv.1–2) until the final judgment. While the righteous have access to a "spring of water" (v.9), those who were not punished or judged during their stay on earth must endure "great pain, until the great day of judgment" (v.11). Likewise, in 4 Ezra 7, all persons at death are held in "chambers" (v.37) until the final judgment arrives. While the wicked "immediately wander about in torments," the righteous are "gathered into their chambers and guarded by angels in profound quiet" (vv.80, 95). While the parallels between the postmortem setting in the parable and descriptions found in these two pseudepigraphical works are striking, there is one very significant difference: in 1 Enoch and 4 Ezra, persons are assigned their respective temporary abodes based on whether they were "righteous" or "wicked" on earth, but in Jesus' parable each man is assigned his place in view of good or bad things received.

[135] See Walter Vogels, "Having or Longing: A Semiotic Analysis of Luke 16:19–31," *Église et Théologie* 20 (1989), 39–40.

ancient Mediterranean world. Since the publication of H. Gressmann 's landmark study *Vom reichen Mann und armen Lazarus: eine literargeschichtliche Studie* in 1918,[136] commentators have regularly called upon a similar story from Egypt (Setme and Si-Osiris) and seven later Jewish versions derived from it[137] in search of a more tenable, satisfactory rationale.[138] In each of these parallels, a rich man and a poor man experience reversal at death. The rich man, once able to acquire anything he needed and much more, suffers deprivation in the next world while the poor man is awarded abundance and bliss. However, in *each* account, their respective postmortem fates are ultimately determined by weighing their goods deeds relative to their bad deeds. The rich man finds himself in the netherworld because his bad deeds exceeded his good deeds, and the poor man now enjoys bliss because his good deeds exceeded his bad deeds. Consequently, the rich man is retrospectively characterized as unjust or immoral, and the poor man is deemed pious.

Although many commentators import into Jesus' story (whether consciously or not) some form of the rationale present in these parallels,[139] there are difficulties with such a solution. First, and most importantly, missing from Abraham's statement is any indication that the two men have been judged according to good and bad deeds. Second, Jesus portrays neither the rich man as unjust nor Lazarus as pious. Richard Bauckham argues that one misuses the Egyptian and later Jewish parallels when importing their rationale for the men's postmortem

[136] (Abhandlungen der königlich preussischen Akademie der Wissenschaften: Philosophisch-historische Klasse, 1918 no. 7; Berlin: Verlag der königlich Akademie der Wissenschaft).

[137] The earliest of these versions may be found in the Palestinian Talmud (y. Sanh. 6.23c; y. Hag. 2.77d) and involves a wealthy taxcollector and a poor Torah scholar. For a helpful summary and analysis, see Bauckham, "The Rich Man and Lazarus: The Parable and the Parallels," esp. 227–30.

[138] See, e.g., Griffiths, "Cross-cultural Eschatology with Dives and Lazarus," 12; Jeremias, *Rediscovering the Parables*, 146. Ronald Hock, in an effort to "cast the comparative net wider," appeals rather to "two literary gems of imperial Cynicism" by Lucian of Samosata, the *Gallus* and the *Cataplus* ("Lazarus and Micyllus: Greco-Roman Backgrounds to Luke 16:19–31," *JBL* 106 [1987], 456–57). These works, he argues, help readers further specify both the nature of the rich man's wrongdoing (hedonism) and Lazarus' piety (self-control) (Ibid., esp. 460–62).

[139] While the parallel Egyptian and Palestinian accounts are not always explicitly foregrounded, many nevertheless assume that the rich man was punished because of his wickedness (e.g., J. Duncan M. Derrett, "Fresh Light on St Luke XVI. II. Dives and Lazarus and the Preceding Sayings," *NTS* 7 [1961], 373) and that Lazarus was rewarded for his piety (e.g., Hultgren, *The Parables of Jesus*, 112).

fates into Jesus' story.[140] Such a hermeneutical move, he argues, fails to take *Abraham's* explanation of the reversal in v.25 seriously. Following Bauckham, I would argue that Abraham's explanation for why the rich man is suffering is entirely comprehensible and sufficient and that there is therefore no need to posit and fill a gap by appealing to parallel accounts. If we focus exclusively on Abraham's unique formulation of the rationale in v.25, the rich man is not punished for failing to give alms to Lazarus or acquiring or sustaining his wealth unjustly but for being wealthy.[141] Abraham could have offered the rich man any number of reasons for his present suffering, such as "You failed to aid Lazarus in his time of need" or "You extorted and maintained your wealth through unjust means," but he offered precisely (and only) this rationale: "You received your good things" (ἀπέλαβες τὰ ἀγαθά σου). Thus, had the rich man opened the gate and given alms to Lazarus *yet remained wealthy*, he would not have improved his chances of joining Abraham and Lazarus on the other side of the chasm. Relinquishing his wealth (so that he could no longer be classified as "rich" [πλούσιος; v.19]) would have been the first and most important step in attaining a position of honor at the patriarch's side.[142]

One of the harshest tirades against the rich that emerged from within the Jewish apocalyptic tradition may be found in the Epistle of Enoch (1 En. 91–107).[143] The Epistle contains numerous woes directed against a powerful, wealthy elite accused of persecuting the righteous and acquiring and sustaining wealth through oppression and injustice. The persecuted righteous, from whose perspective the Epistle is written, state that the rich have obtained "silver and gold by unjust means" (97:8) and constructed their homes "with sin" (94:7) and "through the hard toil of others" (99:13). Although the criticism of the ruling elite is relentless and severe, the righteous themselves hope for wealth one day

[140] Bauckham, "The Rich Man and Lazarus: The Parable and the Parallels," 231.

[141] Bauckham is therefore one of the very few to argue that "the rich man suffers in the next life just because he was rich in this life, while the poor man is blessed in the next life just because he was poor in this life" (Ibid., 232–33). However, he does not go on to say that Jesus is here criticizing wealth itself but rather highlighting "the intolerable injustice of the situation where one enjoys luxury and another suffers want" (Ibid., 233).

[142] Such an interpretation of Abraham's statement in v.25 is consistent with Jesus' recent, uncompromising critique of wealth in 16:9–13.

[143] E. Isaac dates the Epistle to the early second century BCE ("1 [Ethiopic Apocalypse of] Enoch: A New Translation and Introduction," in *OTP* 1, 7). Cf. the position of George Nickelsburg, who also places the Epistle in the second century BCE ("Revisiting the Rich and the Poor in 1 Enoch 92–105 and the Gospel of Luke," 579).

too, though they will acquire it by just means. As George Nickelsburg observes, because God will "grant wealth and prosperity to the righteous" after the earth is purified of sin, the Epistle does not necessarily offer a critique of wealth itself.[144] Indeed, only wealth that is obtained unjustly is criticized consistently throughout the Epistle. Here, however, neither the intradiegetic narrator nor Abraham (who appears to serve as spokesperson for the divine point of view) shows any concern for how the rich man acquired or sustained his wealth. Rather, wealth *per se* is condemned without regard for its origin or its use. Jesus' parable therefore advances a critique far more severe and uncompromising than what is found even in the Epistle of Enoch! Not surprisingly, Jesus' sectarian rigor, already evident in his treatment of divorce and remarriage in 16:18, reemerges yet again, though now with respect to the theme of wealth and possessions. Personal wealth is not permissible under any circumstances, even if accompanied by generous almsgiving. It is, quite simply, incompatible with service to God (16:13).

The rich man has accepted his fate, but will he also accept Abraham's explanations for why he is suffering (v.25) and why Lazarus cannot relieve him from heat and thirst (v.26)?

"But he said, 'I therefore request of you, father, that you send him to my father's house—for I have five brothers—so that he might continue testifying to them, in order that they might not come into this place of torment as well.' "

The rich man does not contest Abraham's remarks but instead acknowledges his position of authority as God's spokesperson. Fully convinced that his situation cannot be altered, he now shifts his attention to his five brothers, all of whom are still alive and presumably in grave danger of entering flame and torment as well. Lazarus may not be able to cross the chasm, reasons the rich man, but perhaps he can reenter the earthly sphere and warn his brothers of what lies on the other side.

The rich man's respect for Abraham's authority and concern for the welfare of his family may momentarily endear some readers to him, but other aspects of his request are disconcerting and serve to further distance readers from him. First, he will not address Lazarus directly; the request is issued only through another person of his own socioeconomic class. Second, because διαμαρτύρηται is in the present tense,

---

[144] "Revisiting the Rich and the Poor in 1 Enoch 92–105 and the Gospel of Luke," 589, 592.

it appears as if the rich man wants Lazarus to return not for a brief conversation one afternoon but for an extended stay, until his brothers are fully persuaded that radical lifestyle changes will be necessary to avoid suffering in Hades. Lazarus suffered immensely for many years while on earth, and to ask that he return almost as soon as he had arrived at Abraham's side and remain there until his brothers change their ways is insensitive and cruel. The rich man still refuses to acknowledge both Lazarus' humanity and his position of honor at Abraham's side. Lazarus continues to be perceived as "a servant, a domestic, an errand boy,"[145] an instrument to further his own desires.

It is unclear what the rich man hopes Lazarus will convey to his brothers. Is Lazarus merely supposed to inform them of the various fates that await persons at death and trust that they will figure out how to avoid holding chambers with flame and torment, or does the rich man wish that Lazarus tell them precisely how to join the patriarch at his side? It is also unclear *how* Lazarus is to testify. He may be expected to initiate a conversation with the brothers in hope of changing their minds through rhetorical persuasion. However, the chances that they will respond to an overture from a member of the expendable class are slim to none. Because Lazarus has yet to speak at all in this story, one wonders if the rich man expects Lazarus to be sent back in his original condition to his former residence at the gate to testify not with speech but with his very life—and remain there until the five brothers see their error![146] If so, the rich man has learned absolutely nothing since his arrival, and readers are quickly loosing any sympathy they may have garnered for this character through Abraham's patient paternalism.

---

[145] Herzog, *Parables as Subversive Speech*, 123.

[146] Many commentators suggest that Lazarus is to return only briefly either in a vision or a dream (see, e.g., Bovon, *L'Évangile Selon Saint Luc 15,1–19,27*, 112; Fitzmyer, *The Gospel According to Luke X–XXIV*, 1134; Jeremias, *Rediscovering the Parables*, 147; Herzog, *Parables as Subversive Speech*, 126), but because διαμαρτύρηται is in the present rather than the aorist tense and neither the rich man nor Lazarus has given up his body at death (e.g., the rich man feels immense physical pain, has a tongue, and requires water to alleviate heat and thirst, and Lazarus presumably still has fingers [with which he is asked to transmit water to the rich man's tongue]), readers may envision an extended stay in corporeal form.

"But Abraham said, 'They have Moses and the Prophets; let [your brothers] listen to them.'"

Abraham once again denies the rich man's request, though he does not say that Lazarus cannot reenter the earthly sphere. Such a visit is simply unnecessary since the information his brothers need is already found in the Law and Prophets.[147] In view of Jesus' words in 16:16–18, which underscore the continuity between the Jewish scriptures and his proclamation about God's kingdom, it comes as no surprise that a special revelation would be superfluous. Moreover, it is unreasonable and insensitive to ask Lazarus to return to earth now, especially when he, a member of the expendable class, would most likely either be ignored (as before) or rebuffed. He has suffered enough.

Abraham does not specify which portions of the Law and Prophets are especially relevant to the brothers' situation and would require their immediate attention. Will Abraham offer further clarification, or have readers been presented with a permanent gap that must be filled by appealing to Jesus' teaching elsewhere? Minimally, readers may look to Jesus' programmatic address in the synagogue at Nazareth (4:16–21), in which he sketches the primary objectives of his ministry. There, he draws attention specifically to the Torah's jubilee traditions (see Lev 25), which anticipate a redistribution of resources and repairing of unequal social and economic relations.[148] Among the ruling elite, these traditions may have been neglected in favor of, for instance, almsgiving traditions that permitted limitless wealth accumulation if accompanied by periodic donations to Temple or synagogue or purity traditions that drew sharp boundaries often falling along class lines.[149] In any case, it is not "Moses and the Prophets" generally to which Abraham refers but to the Jewish scriptures as focalized through the eyes of the Gospel's protagonist, a Galilean peasant from the tiny hamlet of Nazareth whose heart is with the poor.

---

[147] V. Tanghe argues that Abraham's injunction to listen to the Law and Prophets does not reflect the Gospel's point of view, which is rather to be found in God's announcement from the cloud during Jesus' transfiguration: "Listen to [Jesus]!" ("Abraham, Son Fils et Son Envoyé [Luc 16, 19–31]," 572–73). Abraham's focalization of events, then, would be at odds with Luke's overall evaluative point of view.

[148] For further discussion, see Chapter 1, Section B.2.

[149] D. H. Reinstorf, for instance, argues that Judea's first century elite prioritized the Torah's "purity code," which demarcated clean from unclean, insiders from outsiders, at the expense of its "debt code," which instructed Israelites, all of whom were "indebted to God" for having been rescued from slavery in Egypt, to share wealth produced by the land ("The rich, the poor, and the law," 341–45). The elite elected to promote the purity code because it served to further guarantee their power and privilege.

Interestingly, Abraham enjoins the rich man's five brothers to "listen" (ἀκουσάτωσαν)[150] to a body of literature to which he himself never had access, a peculiarity that may offer a clue as to why Jesus has enlisted a figure known for his wealth to serve as an authoritative spokesperson against wealth.[151] In addition to being wealthy (Gen 13:2; 24:35; Jub. 13:14), Abraham was widely known for his generosity and hospitality (see Gen 18:1–15; T. Ab. 1:1–5 Recension A) as well and likely served as a model of faithful obedience for many persons of means. This popular portrait of Abraham, however, ultimately benefited Judea's elite. The practice of almsgiving need not undermine or even impinge upon the extravagant lifestyles of the rich, for as long as they divest a portion of their excess on occasion, they are permitted to remain wealthy. Almsgiving, moreover, while requiring no significant modifications to existing social or economic structures, offers the added benefit of forestalling unrest by cultivating an "image" of resource redistribution. By casting Abraham, exemplar of generous almsgiving, in this role, Jesus may be redefining the patriarch's eschatological function.[152] In this parable, instead of simply showing hospitality or giving alms, acts that offer temporary relief without the lasting structural changes that would most benefit the poor, Abraham condemns wealth per se (v.25), without regard for how it was acquired or sustained, and even invites unclean beggars like Lazarus to assume a position of honor at the heavenly banquet (vv.22–23). No longer a model of generosity for the elite and guarantor of a bourgeois ethic, Abraham is now an intimate companion of the poor and a critic of personal wealth and existing economic and social relations. Jesus may enlist him for this new role because he predates "Moses and the Prophets" and therefore was not held to the same rigorous standards applicable in the rich man's day. Presumably, generous giving sufficed during Abraham's lifetime. Abraham, however, does appear to recognize just how fortunate he is to reside on this side of the chasm, for at no point does he embrace an accusatory, judgmental, or self-righteous tone with the rich man.

[150] F. Bovon notes that in the Jewish tradition hearing often implies obedience (*L'Évangile Selon Saint Luc 15,1–19,27*, 112–13), and *BDAG* states that this implication is occasionally present with ἀκούω in the NT (38).

[151] It has been argued that wealth itself cannot be condemned in this parable since Abraham himself was rich (see, e.g., Scott, *Hear Then the Parable*, 153).

[152] See especially Herzog, *Parables as Subversive Speech*, 130.

Tellingly, he remains sympathetic and paternal, saddened by the rich man's fate rather than gleeful.

"But he said, 'No, father Abraham, but if someone from the dead should go[153] *to them, they will repent.'"*

Although the rich man continues to address his interlocutor with respect ("Father" [πάτερ]), for the first time he resists Abraham and refuses to accept his counsel.[154] The Jewish scriptures, he believes, are impotent to effect the change that will be required to save his brothers from flame and torment,[155] yet he is firmly convinced that a visitation by Lazarus would inspire repentance.[156] Both the intradiegetic narrator (16:17–18) and Abraham (v.29), however, clearly believe that the scriptures are sufficient and contain the guidance they need. A special revelation from beyond the grave would add nothing to the information they currently possess. How are readers to account for their differing opinions on the adequacy of the Jewish scriptures to effect repentance (which, in this case, would require ceasing to be wealthy)? The intradiegetic narrator and the rich man refract "Moses and the Prophets" through very different lenses and therefore work with vastly different constructions of the scriptures. Undoubtedly, Judea's elite manufactured a "canon within the canon" that had very little in common with constructions embraced by poor Galileans like Jesus. Given the rich man's social location, it would not at all be surprising if his construction of the canon emphasized wealth as divine blessing (e.g., Gen 24:35; Job 42:10–15) and either omitted or marginalized references to fair and equal distribution of the land or God's special concern for the poor (e.g., Deut 15:1–11; 24:19–22). Given the social location of intradiegetic narrator among

---

[153] While the majority of manuscripts read πορευθῇ ("proceed"), p^{75} reads ἐγερθῇ ("be raised up") and ℵ 579 read ἀναστῇ ("rise"). The first option, πορευθῇ, is much better attested and therefore retained.

[154] The rich man prefaces his response with οὐχί, "a strengthened form of οὐ" that conveys emphatic negation (*BDAG*, 742). Cf. similar emphatic uses of οὐχί in Luke 1:60; 12:51; 13:3, 5.

[155] See Hendrickx, *The Parables of Jesus*, 208; Herzog, *Parables as Subversive Speech*, 125.

[156] The rich man's response in v.30 is structured as a third class conditional sentence of the future more probable type. In such constructions, if the condition holds true (i.e., if Lazarus does in fact return), the apodosis will very likely be fulfilled (i.e., the brothers will repent). Some manuscripts (Ψ M Γ 28 157 565 1346 1424) include an aorist subjunctive form of μετανοέω (μετανοήσωσιν) rather than the future indicative form (μετανοήσουσιν), which would weaken the force of the conditional sentence. The majority of early manuscripts, however, do include the future indicative form, which has been retained here.

the *am ha aretz* (see Luke 1:48; 2:7, 24), it would not be unexpected if his version focused heavily on God's interest in and provisions for the poor. His inaugural speech in Nazareth confirms that this was indeed the case (4:16–21). Both men readily accept "Moses and the Prophets" as an authority, but each has refracted these texts through very different lenses.

Abraham has shown sympathy for the rich man, to be sure, but he has also been firm and unwillingly to negotiate, so readers will not expect him to change his mind on the issue of sending Lazarus back to testify.

"But he said to him, 'If they are not listening to Moses and the Prophets, neither will they be persuaded[157] *if someone should rise*[158] *from the dead.'"*
Abraham reiterates that a visitation from beyond the grave would be superfluous and add nothing to the instruction that the brothers may already access in the Law and Prophets. To be sure, acknowledges Abraham, because the rich man's five brothers are firmly entrenched in elite social patterns and behaviors and have grown accustomed to a luxurious lifestyle, radical reorientation will require some persuasion (πεισθήσονται), but Lazarus[159] will not be able to offer anything beyond what is already available. The Jewish scriptures are a sufficient

[157] While the majority of manuscripts read πεισθήσονται, a few include a form of πιστεύω (e.g., D: πιστεύσουσιν; W: πιστεύουσιν).

[158] The majority of manuscripts read ἀναστῇ (B A Ψ f[13] ℵ *Byz* K L M N among others), but p[75] reads ἐγερθῇ (cf. p[75] in v.30), W reads ἀπελθῇ, and D conflates W's variant with the majority to read ἀναστῇ καὶ ἀπελθῇ. V. Tanghe argues in favor of W's ἀπελθῇ over ἀναστῇ since it better complements πορευθῇ in v.30. Moreover, argues Tanghe, the notion of a literal resurrection from the dead is simply unnecessary here (Lazarus may testify in a vision or a dream) and seems like a later development based on Jesus' resurrection in 24:1–12 ("Abraham, Son Fils et Son Envoyé [Luc 16, 19–31]," 575–76).

[159] Some commentators see an explicit allusion to Jesus' resurrection here (*L'Évangile Selon Saint Luc 15,1–19,27*, 113; Fitzmyer, *The Gospel According to Luke X–XXIV*, 1128, 1134). Indeed, the verb used by Abraham (ἀναστῇ) is also used of Jesus' resurrection in 18:33 and 24:46. Within the thought-world of the parable itself, however, the "someone" (τις) to whom Abraham refers must either be Lazarus or someone else currently in residence in this chamber of Hades. Certainly, readers like Theophilus who are already familiar with the outcome of the story may "overhear" a reference to Jesus' resurrection, in which case one would identify the phrase τις ἐκ νεκρῶν ἀναστῇ as a double entendre (cf. Bauckham, "The Rich Man and Lazarus: The Parable and the Parallels," 243), but the primary referent remains Lazarus or another at Abraham's bosom. I much prefer conceiving of the phrase in these terms, which has the advantage of prioritizing the thought-world of the parable, rather than as a direct, unmistakable allusion to Jesus' resurrection.

guide,[160] and, if consulted with a commitment to listening attentively to all of its parts, they would be able to save the brothers from flame and torment.

Abraham is here concerned not with whether the brothers have heard the scriptures at all but with *how* they are hearing them. It is almost inconceivable that the brothers would not have heard portions of the Jewish scriptures read aloud and discussed. In fact, because they are among Judea's elite, it is likely that they both know how to read and have access to certain scrolls from the Torah and/or Prophets. Jesus himself expresses a concern similar to Abraham's at the conclusion of his interpretation of the Parable of the Sower, where he exhorts his disciples: "Watch how (πῶς) you hear!" (8:18). Merely hearing the parables is simple enough, but cultivating "ears to hear" (8:8) is another matter altogether. The rich man's five brothers have undoubtedly heard Moses and the Prophets, but as persons profoundly shaped by elite ways of reading, their hermeneutical lens may filter out, overwrite, or hastily bypass traditions that might undermine their status and lifestyle. In effect, the brothers may be engaged in a highly selective "hearing" of the scriptures that conveniently edits out portions unfavorable to their preferred way of life. According to Abraham, then, the brothers are failing to acknowledge and grapple with traditions in "Moses and the Prophets" that might challenge their position of privilege in society and the economic and social structures that continue to ensure their status as Judea's elite.[161]

---

[160] Because Abraham functions as God's spokesperson, it is no surprise that his statement on the sufficiency of the Jewish scriptures is consistent with the position taken by the Gospel's protagonist moments earlier in 16:17–18, where Jesus expresses his conviction that the preaching of God's kingdom is faithful to the Torah's central claims.

[161] Abraham's final remark is structured as a simple conditional sentence in which the protasis is assumed to be true. Because Abraham represents the divine viewpoint, readers will therefore assume that the brothers are, in fact, not "hearing" Moses and the Prophets as they should. Several commentators have argued that Abraham's concluding statement contributes to an anti-Jewish rhetoric in Luke (see Frank H. Hughes, "The Parable of the Rich Man and Lazarus [Luke 16.19–31] and Graeco-Roman Rhetoric," 39–40; Tanghe, "Abraham, Son Fils et Son Envoyé [Luc 16, 19–31]," 577), but it need not be taken this way. Abraham's comment, for instance, is *not* directed toward Jews in general but to a few wealthy men who have elected to spend extravagantly on themselves. There is no clear indication either in the parable itself or its co-text that these five brothers stand for all Jews. Moreover, both the intradiegetic narrator (16:17–18) and Abraham (vv. 29, 31) reaffirm the sufficiency of the Jewish scriptures to guide human beings into appropriate relations with others and God. A special "Christian" disclosure that either supersedes or is discontinuous with the Law and Prophets is entirely absent here.

Admittedly, Abraham's final remark does have a fatalistic, hopeless tone and may give readers little if any reason to believe that the five brothers will repent. However, the parable is open-ended: the brothers still have time to engage the Jewish scriptures in their entirety, and they still have time to encounter and appropriate new ways of reading them. Desire for wealth and the decadence it may afford (τὸ ἐν ἀνθρώποις ὑψηλὸν; 16:15) may be deeply embedded and difficult to root out, but voices offering alternatives to dominant cultural values may be found in many corners of the Empire (one of which is presented here in this Gospel). The brothers need only open the gate, establish relations beyond their socio-economic class, and listen attentively to the rich dialogue all around them. If they do, who knows what they may find and what changes they may make in their own lives? As with all four parables examined in this study, the true end of the story remains to be told.[162]

3. *Summary*

Neither Jesus nor the narrator comments on this parable, so readers are left to grapple with its significance on their own. How might readers who live in the midst of extraordinary wealth and rampant overconsumption receive this parable?

Jesus does not portray the rich man in such a way that readers will detest or loathe him. To be sure, because Jesus labels him as "rich" (πλούσιος) and discloses that he has been in the habit of spending extravagantly on his own desires for years (v.19), readers will not expect good things from him. Yet, neither Jesus nor Abraham hints that he acquired or sustained his wealth unjustly, treated his servants

[162] See Wright, "Parables on Poverty and Riches (Luke 12:13–21; 16:1–13; 16:19–31)," 219; Lehtipuu, "Characterization and Persuasion: The Rich Man and the Poor Man in Luke 16.19–31," 101. Certainly, the brothers' fate is not sealed, but because the final judgment has not yet occurred, is it possible that even the rich man himself may, once he has sufficiently atoned in Hades for his chosen lifestyle, be given a second chance? Drawing on Oesterly, Herzog writes: "According to rabbinic belief, even 'the wicked in Hell are capable of repentance,' and when they do repent and atone for their previously unacknowledged sin, then Abraham 'descends into Hell' and leads them 'into Paradise'" (*Parables as Subversive Speech*, 123). Consequently, Herzog rather humorously recommends: "Keep the heat on; perhaps it will lead to recognition, and recognition to repentance" (Ibid.). Contrast the positions of Hendrickx (*The Parables of Jesus*, 205) and Hultgren (*The Parables of Jesus*, 113–14), both of whom argue that the rich man's fate is irrevocably fixed for eternity and that redemption is out of reach.

and seasonal employees with contempt, neglected to participate in traditional religious observances, or failed to offer appropriate tithes and sacrifices. In fact, though enduring great physical pain in Hades, he even manages to show concern for his brothers by issuing a special request to Abraham on their behalf (vv.27–28). Admittedly, throughout his conversation with the patriarch, he continues to regard Lazarus as an expendable "nobody" and servant to do his bidding, but such an attitude was probably quite common among the elite, even expected, and would not have qualified him as impious or wicked, at least not among persons of his own class. If the rich man was not unusually cruel, immoral, or impious, what accounts for his current suffering in Hades?

Many have argued that if the rich man had given generously to Lazarus and sought to improve his condition, he probably would have avoided Hades' torments. For these commentators, the parable consequently exhorts possessors to generous almsgiving and to caring for one's neighbor in need.[163] Others have suggested that the rich man's chief fault lay in refusing to open the gate and establish a relationship with Lazarus.[164] In this case, the parable would encourage transgressing social barriers coupled with a willingness to develop meaningful relations outside one's social and/or economic class. Giving alms and establishing relations outside one's class are indeed laudable, but Abraham offers neither of the above rationales for the rich man's current state of deprivation and physical pain. Rather, it was mere reception and enjoyment of "good things" (τὰ ἀγαθά) on earth that merited his present location opposite Abraham and Lazarus across the great chasm (v.25). As noted above, the elite may give alms without ever ceasing to be rich or altering their consumption patterns in any significant way. Had the rich man given alms to Lazarus, he still would have possessed and enjoyed "good things," in which case his fate, according to Abraham's

[163] This position is taken by a majority of commentators. See, e.g., Bovon, *L'Évangile Selon Saint Luc 15,1–19,27*, 111; Hultgren, *The Parables of Jesus*, 116; Bossuyt and Radermakers, *Jésus: Parole de la Grâce selon saint Luc 2. Lecture continue*, 359; Johnson, *The Gospel of Luke*, 256; Piper, "Social Background and Thematic Structure in Luke 16," 1661; Green, *The Gospel of Luke*, 610; Gourgues, *The Paraboles de Luc*, 204; Derrett, "Fresh Light on St Luke XVI II. Dives and Lazarus and the Preceding Sayings," 373; Kreitzer, "Luke 16:19–31 and 1 Enoch 22," 141–42; Regalado, "The Jewish Background of the Parable of the Rich Man and Lazarus," 346; Jeremias, *Rediscovering the Parables*, 146–47.

[164] See, e.g., Scott, *Hear Then the Parable*, 158–59; Hendrickx, *The Parables of Jesus*, 205, 213; Eugene S. Wehrli, "Luke 16:19–31," *Interpretation* 31 (1977), 279.

rationale in v.25, would not have been altered in the least. Instead of recommending almsgiving or beneficence, the parable codifies the breakdown of these redistributive systems in meeting the needs of society's most vulnerable. These systems fail because the rich, at least according to the intradiegetic narrator, too often choose to spend their excess on themselves rather than redistribute it to those in need. In all four parables, in fact, each character with access to abundance elected to spend on his own desires. Even when almsgiving is practiced widely and with regularity, it cannot really be received by the poor as good news (4:18), for it offers only a mirage of resource redistribution and fails to provide any lasting, structural changes. Almsgiving, in effect, does not challenge the existing social order: the rich retain their wealth, power, and privilege while the poor struggle to subsist.[165] For the rich man, then, the first (and most important) step to meriting entrance into Abraham's chamber would have been disposal of excess resources so that he could no longer be called "rich" (v.19). According to Abraham (who in this parable mediates the divine viewpoint), anything short of this would result in suffering in the opposing chamber.

As in the preceding parable and nimshalim (16:1–13), wealth itself is here dealt a firm blow. If wealth as such is criticized, implied also is a critique of any religious tradition that links prosperity to divine favor[166] as well as any attempt to distinguish between the honorable and dishonorable rich.[167] Neither Jesus nor Abraham cares how the rich man acquired or sustained his wealth. The mere fact that he possessed excess and used it to fund a life of decadence and overconsumption accounts for his present locale opposite Abraham. This parable therefore confirms and reinforces Jesus' final statement in his nimshalim on the preceding parable: personal wealth, however it may be obtained or sustained, is totally incompatible with service to God (16:13). Not surprisingly, readers have learned that Jesus' position on wealth and

---

[165] Cf. Hendrickx's comment: "Aid does not express a real solidarity; it is not a real sharing; it does not establish real justice in relationship; it does not make the rich see" (*The Parables of Jesus*, 213).

[166] See C. M. Amjad-Ali, "No Name for the Rich: The Parable of Lazarus," 32 (1990), 26; Herzog, *Parables as Subversive Speech*, 129.

[167] For a discussion of this distinction, see comments on the parable's first lexia as well as Reinstorf, "The rich, the poor, and the law," 330–32.

possessions, like his position on divorce and remarriage in 16:17–18, is unusually rigorous, sectarian in nature, and therefore out of step with mainstream voices. However, if asked to offer a defense of this position, Jesus would undoubtedly argue that it is solidly grounded in a reading of "Moses and the Prophets."

CHAPTER FOUR

ELIMINATING WEALTH

Introduction

The purpose of this chapter is to explore whether or not the construction of Jesus' teaching on consumption and wealth offered in the prior two chapters may be substantiated in the remainder of the Travel Narrative (17:1–19:27). Since each of the protagonists in the previous four parables was either explicitly identified as rich by the intradiegetic narrator (12:16–21; 16:19–31) or, in the course of the reading, determined to have access to wealth (15:11–32; 16:1–8a), I have chosen to focus on Jesus' subsequent encounters with other wealthy characters. The diegetic narrator describes two of Jesus' ensuing interlocutors as "rich" (πλούσιος), an unnamed ruler (18:23) and a tax collector named Zacchaeus (19:2), and so it is to Jesus' dialogue with these men in 18:18–23 and 19:1–10 that I now turn. Will readers be able to confirm the uncompromising critique of consumption and wealth that emerged in conversation with Jesus' four previous parables, or will the present construction be challenged or even undermined?

While the overall composite literary approach employed in the previous two chapters will be retained, neither episode will be broken into individual lexias and analyzed with the same level of detail as before. The reading, however, will still proceed sequentially and cumulatively and give special attention to whether expectations are confirmed or shattered, how characters take shape and whether they elicit approval or disapproval, surprising plot developments that may take the reader off-guard, and ambiguous constructions that simultaneously unsettle and draw the reader yet further in. Moreover, narratology and narrative criticism will once again furnish the conceptual framework and terminology for describing how both encounters are processed and structured, and the reader will prioritize the literary and socio-cultural repertoire available to persons of the first century Mediterranean world.

A. Jesus' Encounter with the Rich Ruler

1. *Exploring the Pre-text: 17:1–18:17*

Although Jesus does not address the theme of wealth and possessions directly in this section, the overall portrait of discipleship that has emerged thus far in the Travel Narrative is reconfirmed. Anyone who wishes to follow Jesus "on the way" must be willing to endure privation in the present (17:7–10) and forgo his or her own life (17:33) for the sake of God's kingdom. In fact, those who refuse to break with their prior way of life and continue "eating, drinking, buying, selling, planting, [and] building" much as before cannot expect forbearance when "the Son of Humanity is revealed" (17:26–30). While following Jesus now may be accompanied by hardship and assumed only at the greatest personal cost, disciples can also be confident that God will not delay in granting justice to those who persevere (18:7–8a). But they must be willing to assume the lowly, vulnerable position of a child—unable to claim honor, status, power, economic independence, or private ownership of land or possessions—in order to enter God's kingdom (18:15–17).[1]

2. *Reading Jesus' Encounter with the Ruler: 18:18–23*

An unnamed ruler (τις...ἄρχων)[2] accosts Jesus and poses a question: "Good teacher, what must I do to inherit eternal life?" With the exception of the initial adjective (ἀγαθέ), his inquiry is identical to one posed by a lawyer at the very beginning of the journey into Jerusalem (10:25). Are readers, then, to align him with the lawyer who "stood up to test [Jesus]" and later sought "to justify himself" with a follow-up question (10:25, 29)?[3] Or, is the ruler genuinely intrigued yet perplexed by Jesus'

---

[1] Jesus' language here is strong and emphatic: "Truly I tell you, whoever does not receive / take the kingdom of God like a child shall never (οὐ μὴ) enter into it!" On the requirement of assuming this lowly and vulnerable position, Jesus will *not* negotiate.

[2] While some commentators assume that this man is a Jewish religious leader (e.g., Robert C. Tannehill, *The Narrative Unity of Luke-Acts: A Literary Interpretation* [Facets and Foundations; Philadelphia: Fortress Press, 1986], 1: 187), possibly "a member of the Sanhedrin" or "one of the leaders of the Pharisaic movement" (Bovon, *L'Évangile Selon Saint Luc 15,1–19,27*, 206), the narrator does not identify him as such. At this point, it is prudent to assume only that he holds a position of power, the nature and extent of which is unknown.

[3] L.T. Johnson evaluates the ruler negatively in part because he poses the same question as the lawyer: "Rather than a sincere request to learn about discipleship...we

prior statement on the necessity of receiving the kingdom like a child and earnestly searching for further illumination?[4] While readers were unable to construct a favorable portrait of the lawyer, here the narrator neither specifies a motivation for the ruler's inquiry nor positions readers against him with pejorative labels or descriptive tags.[5] The ruler is characterized only indirectly through his speech, so the burden of constructing his portrait will rest squarely on readers' shoulders.

On the one hand, the ruler's position of power contrasts sharply with the powerlessness and vulnerability of the infants nearby, whom Jesus just identified as models for those who wish to enter God's kingdom (18:15–17).[6] According to Jesus, then, there are few further from the kingdom than he. Moreover, his self-interested question reflects a preoccupation with securing his own eternal destiny and is therefore out of step with Jesus' other-centered mission to improve conditions for the poor (4:18–19). Jesus' disciples are rather to seek first the kingdom and leave their "inexhaustible treasure in heaven" to God (12:31, 33). Admittedly, the inquiry itself may articulate a desire shared by many to live forever,[7] but he asks not on behalf of all in the crowd or for their benefit but for himself alone. To be sure, then, there are several reasons why one might judge the ruler negatively.

On the other hand, the ruler shows greater respect for Jesus than the lawyer by prefacing his initial address with the adjective "good" (ἀγαθέ) and, as stated above, is not characterized negatively by the

---

recognize the sort of testing question posed by the lawyer in 10:25" (*The Gospel of Luke*, 280).

[4] Jesus fails to specify which qualities of a child his followers should emulate, so many, including the ruler, may be confused and hoping for further explanation (cf. Matt 19:13–15, where these qualities *are* delineated). At the end of the preceding paragraph, I identified a few possibilities based on the proximate narrative context, but it is not at all clear how familiar the ruler is with Jesus' teaching or which aspects of the most recent discourse he has heard. If the ruler is seeking further illumination on Jesus' statements in vv.16–17, then he has (unwittingly?) equated entrance into the kingdom with reception of eternal life—an equation that may not hold up.

[5] Many commentators therefore view the ruler's inquiry as sincere and initially evaluate him favorably (Tannehill, *The Narrative Unity of Luke-Acts: A Literary Interpretation*, 1: 187; Fitzmyer, *The Gospel According to Luke X–XXIV*, 1197–98; Seccombe, *Possessions and the Poor in Luke-Acts*, 121; Marshall, *The Gospel of Luke: A Commentary on the Greek Text* [The New International Greek Testament Commentary; Grand Rapids: Eerdmans, 1983], 684).

[6] Although the narrator tells us that only the very smallest and most vulnerable of children were present (τὰ βρέφη; v.15), Jesus employs the more inclusive term παῖς (any child "below the age of puberty" [*BDAG*, 750–51]) in his analogy.

[7] See Bovon, *L'Évangile Selon Saint Luc 15,1–19,27*, 212.

narrator. Furthermore, his question pointedly expresses a tension in Jesus' teaching between meriting an eternal reward and receiving it as a gift, which may momentarily elicit readers' approval. Disciples certainly "do" (ποιήσας; v.18) something by selling their possessions (12:33) and leaving everything behind for the sake of the kingdom (5:11, 28; 14:33); indeed, by leaving family, possessions, and occupations they "make (ποιήσατε) purses for [them]selves that do not grow old" (12:33). Yet, because God is ultimately the one who prepares and distributes their reward (12:42–48; 16:11–12), it is also true that they will "inherit" (κληρονομήσω; v.18) eternal life. This man, therefore, does a fine job of articulating a paradox in Jesus' own teaching. Our initial portrait of the ruler, therefore, is mixed; we must await further comments from him and from Jesus[8] to develop his character further.

Jesus' response to the ruler's address is unexpected: "Why do you call me 'good'? No one is 'good' except one, God" (v.19). While readers may have anticipated that he would attend immediately to the inquiry (as was the case following the lawyer's identical question in 10:26), Jesus becomes angry and abruptly dismisses the flattering appellation. Kenneth Bailey attributes Jesus' perplexing retort to his impatience with social conventions of the elite: "[The ruler] is trying to impress with a compliment and perhaps hopes to be greeted with some lofty title in return. In the Oriental world, one compliment requires a second. The ruler starts with 'Good Teacher' and may expect 'Noble Ruler' in response."[9] In addition to disassociating himself from such conventions, Jesus disallows the ruler an opportunity to set him apart from the ordinary people gathered around him. In rejecting this title, he expresses solidarity both with those of humble origin from whom he came (1:48; 2:7, 24) and with the poor to whom he was sent (4:18).[10]

Jesus' perturbed tone persists when turning to the inquiry itself (v.20). Instead of offering a thoughtful, original response, Jesus hastily refers the ruler to the ten commandments and then recites five concerning human

[8] Without the assistance of the narrator, Jesus' focalization of persons and events becomes determinative since his perspective contributes to the Gospel's overall evaluative point of view as well.

[9] *Through Peasant Eyes: More Lucan Parables, Their Culture and Style* (Grand Rapids: Eerdmans, 1980), 162.

[10] For a brief but excellent summary of the variety of explanations given for Jesus' retort, see Fitzmyer, *The Gospel According to Luke X–XXIV*, 1199. Both Fitzmyer (Ibid.) and Johnson (*The Gospel of Luke*, 276) argue that Jesus is simply attributing all goodness to its rightful source (i.e., in God).

beings' relations with one another.[11] Most any Jew could have offered such an answer,[12] and the reply betrays Jesus' reticence to engage this man seriously on the matter of eternal life. Is he simply uninterested in the topic, or is there a certain quality or feature about him that Jesus finds irksome? Moments earlier, Jesus was eager to receive infants in spite of his disciples' strong opposition (ἐπετίμων αὐτοῖς; 18:15), but it appears that he wants nothing at all to do with this ruler. If Jesus is aware (as readers are) that he is a member of the ruling elite, he likely assumes that he is wealthy too. Although the man did not introduce himself as such, perhaps his apparel, demeanor, and manner of speech gave him away. Since Jesus has already pronounced a woe upon the rich (6:24) and none of the protagonists with access to wealth in the prior four parables was portrayed positively, Jesus may be dismissing him out-of-hand simply because he is rich. Indeed, not only has Jesus stated in unambiguous terms that wealth and service to God are incompatible (16:13), but the final parable in the series (16:19–31) concludes on a very pessimistic note and offers readers little hope that the rich can or will participate in God's kingdom. The wealthy are opposed both to God (16:13) and to his mission of bringing good news to the poor (4:18), and he may not wish to waste what little time remains before his arrest and crucifixion (see 9:21–22, 43b–45) with them.

Understandably dissatisfied with Jesus' banal reply and perhaps eager for something truly novel or esoteric, the ruler quickly affirms that he has kept all of the commandments since his youth (v.21). Because Jesus was satisfied with the lawyer's recitation from the Torah at the beginning of the journey to Jerusalem ("You answered correctly; continue doing this and you will live" [10:28]), readers may very well expect him to acknowledge the ruler's laudable conduct and conclude the conversation

[11] See Green, *The Gospel of Luke*, 655; Marshall, *The Gospel of Luke*, 685. Jesus' ordering of the commandments follows Deut 5:17–20 LXX (B), with the exception that the fifth commandment ("Honor your father and mother") is placed last. Bailey observes: "To our knowledge the placing of the commandment on honor to parents at the end of a selection of the Decalogue is without precedent" (*Through Peasant Eyes*, 159). Is Jesus deemphasizing this commandment in view of the rigorous requirements placed upon his disciples? Children who suddenly decided to sell their belongings and leave town would undoubtedly be perceived by a great majority as dishonorable and negligent. In many traditional societies, children are expected to care for their parents in old age; mass liquidation of possessions coupled with a sudden departure would hardly qualify as honoring one's parents.

[12] Cf. Fitzmyer's comment: "Jesus responds with a generic answer which any teacher of the Law in his day would have given" (*The Gospel According to Luke X–XXIV*, 1197).

here. Instead of dismissing the ruler and moving on, however, Jesus finally decides to give serious consideration to his inquiry.[13] This time, his reply is hardly commonplace; the ruler, it seems, will receive the original response for which he hoped.

Jesus neither contests the ruler's claim that he has kept the commandments nor invalidates obedience to them as an appropriate path to eternal life but informs him that there is yet one more thing he must do: sell absolutely everything he has (πάντα ὅσα ἔχεις)[14] and redistribute (διάδος)[15] the proceeds to the poor. Only then will he acquire "treasure in heaven" (v.22).[16] Has Jesus introduced a requirement that is inconsistent with the Jewish scriptures? Does the radical directive take the ruler far beyond the scope of the ten commandments to a truly novel teaching? Iain Provan suggests that the ten commandments are not "an exhaustive summation" of divine expectations but "only selected examples of the kinds of things that loving God and one's neighbor involves."[17] When Jesus, in his initial response to the ruler's inquiry, recites five that focus exclusively on human beings' relations with one another, he therefore may be evoking a whole stream of related values and legislation from the Law and Prophets. While divestiture and redistribution are not explicitly mandated in the Jewish scriptures, it is difficult to imagine a more powerful demonstration of love for one's neighbor (Lev 19:18) or a more concrete expression of one's commitment to a fair, equitable distribution of resources (Lev 25). Divestiture and redistribution may be extraordinary acts, but they are scarcely inconsistent with the overall ethical orientation of the Law and Prophets.[18] If, according to Jesus, the ruler wishes to move beyond

---

[13] The narrator, who remains covert until the very end of the episode (v.23), does not provide an explanation for Jesus' sudden change of heart (cf. Mark 10:21).

[14] Neither Mark (10:21) nor Matthew (19:21) presents Jesus' demand with such (overstated) clarity.

[15] Jesus' use of διαδίδωμι here is critical and not to be missed; this is the language of (re)distribution (*BDAG*, 227–28), not almsgiving (δὸς; cf. Mark 10:21 and Matt 19:21).

[16] While Jesus does promise "treasure in heaven" to the ruler if he should choose to liquidate everything he owns, is Jesus' primary goal in issuing the directive to bring salvation to the ruler? In view of Jesus' programmatic address in 4:18–19, his most immediate and pressing concern throughout his ministry is to improve conditions here and now for the poor, not open avenues to eternal life for the rich. Moreover, Jesus explicitly identifies the purpose of divestiture to be a redistribution of resources for the benefit of the poor (διάδος πτωχοῖς [where πτωχοῖς is taken to be a dative of advantage]).

[17] "'All these I have kept since I was a boy' (Luke 18:21): Creation, Covenant, and the Commandments of God," *Ex auditu* 17 (2001), 38.

[18] Jesus, in fact, believes that his *entire* mission (preaching, teaching, and healing)

the narrow purview of the ten commandments—which are exemplary rather than exhaustive—and offer an outward demonstration of full commitment to core values underlying *all* of God's commands, divestiture and distribution to the poor will be required.[19]

It has been argued that Jesus here presents the ruler with "a unique... directive" that is "uncharacteristic of the third gospel" and therefore does not constitute "a normative ethic" suitable for Jesus' followers or for Luke's readers.[20] The requirement, however, is entirely consistent with his teaching elsewhere in the Travel Narrative (e.g., 12:33; 14:33)[21] as well as with his disciples' early response in Galilee (e.g., 5:11, 28). The mandate is rigorously uncompromising and sectarian in nature, to be sure, but it is not exceptional. For the ruler—indeed, for *anyone* persuaded by Jesus' reading of the Jewish scriptures and eager to reorient her life accordingly—renunciation and distribution are prerequisites for joining Jesus "on the way."

Although absent throughout the exchange,[22] the narrator now steps in to describe the ruler's reaction: "When he heard these things, he became deeply grieved (περίλυπος)" (v.23). Included also is a rationale for the ruler's response ("for [γὰρ] he was extremely wealthy") as well as confirmation of his economic status (πλούσιος), suggested initially by his position as "ruler" (v.18). The dialogue between the two men concludes here; readers do not learn whether the ruler opted to maintain his current lifestyle or to divest and distribute.[23] Significantly, the ruler

---

is faithful to and solidly grounded in a reading of the Jewish scriptures (see 4:18–19; 16:16–18, 29–31). See also Joel Green's comment: "[Jesus'] charge concerning the disposition of material goods on behalf of the poor must be understood... as an interpretative expansion of the Ten Commandments" (*The Gospel of Luke*, 656).

[19] As argued in the prior chapter, only such radical redistributive measures can truly be received by the poor as good news. Almsgiving and beneficence are inadequate because they leave present social and economic structures fully in tact: the rich retain their wealth and power while the poor continue to struggle for basic provisions.

[20] Phillips, *Reading Issues of Wealth and Poverty in Luke-Acts*, 163–64. Seccombe similarly argues that the injunction, offered primarily with the intent of exposing the ruler's "love for the things of this world," is "meant specifically for this man" and no one else (*Possessions and the Poor in Luke-Acts*, 126–27).

[21] See Cassidy, *Jesus, Politics, and Society*, 27; Tannehill, *The Narrative Unity of Luke-Acts: A Literary Interpretation*, 1: 121.

[22] The narrator withdraws after introducing Jesus' interlocutor as a "ruler" (v.18) and intrudes during the dialogue only to aid readers in identifying a change of speakers.

[23] Most commentators assume that the ruler fails to follow through with divestiture and returns to his former way of life (see, e.g., Tannehill, *The Narrative Unity of Luke-Acts: A Literary Interpretation*, 1:122; Green, *The Gospel of Luke*, 658; Bovon, *L'Évangile Selon Saint Luc 15,1–19,27*, 204, 212; D'Sa, "The Salvation of the Rich in the Gospel of Luke,"

is not angered, perturbed, or offended by Jesus' reply, which disinclines readers from aligning him with the religious authorities, whose hostility toward him is escalating (15:2; 16:14). As F. Bovon observes, in Luke "sadness" rarely constitutes "the final word of the story" but often signifies "the first act of conversion."[24] While this is the only occurrence of περίλυπος in the Gospel, it is used once in Matthew to describe Jesus' state of mind in the Garden of Gethsemane just before his arrest and trial (26:38) and once in Mark to express Herod's reaction to Herodias's request for John the Baptist's immediate execution (6:26). In both cases, a sudden realization that some difficult or unpleasant course of action must be taken triggers the response of "deep grief." Although neither Jesus nor Herod wishes to carry through with his obligation, both ultimately do (Matt 27:35a; Mark 6:27–28). While the Lukan narrator does not report the ruler's final decision, it at least seems clear that he took Jesus' proposition very seriously and that the potential consequences of following through upset him deeply.

At the conclusion of the episode, then, readers are unable to portray the ruler in entirely negative terms. To be sure, the narrator confirms his membership among Judea's elite (πλούσιος σφόδρα; v.23), but, unlike the lawyer whom Jesus met at the beginning of the journey to Jerusalem, he has sought neither to test Jesus nor to justify himself (10:25, 29). His inquiry, on the contrary, appears to be earnest and sincere. Moreover, he has yet to make a final decision for or against Jesus' proposition, and his response of grief suggests that he has accepted Jesus' injunction as a valid requirement for obtaining eternal life and already even begun considering its cost. Will the encounter awaken resolve within the ruler to follow through with this most difficult task, or will he return to what is safe and familiar?[25]

178.) Contrast the position of J. Fitzmyer, who acknowledges the open-endedness of the encounter (*The Gospel According to Luke X–XXIV*, 1197).

[24] *L'Évangile Selon Saint Luc 15,1–19,27*, 208. As an example of grief foreshadowing both conversion and rededication, Bovon points to Peter's sadness over having denied Jesus three times (22:62). Readers familiar with the macro-plot of Luke-Acts know that Peter eventually becomes a leader of the Christian community in Jerusalem.

[25] David May identifies likely consequences of divestiture for this man ("Leaving and Receiving: A Social-Scientific Exegesis of Mark 10:29–31," *PRS* 17 [1990], 144–46). In addition to forfeiting his esteemed position within the community, he would probably bring dishonor upon his immediate and extended family. Consequently, he would be ousted from his natural kinship structure and required to establish a new identity within a fictive kinship structure (i.e., among Jesus' followers).

3. *Exploring the Post-text: 18:24–30*

Aware of the ruler's grief, Jesus elects not to pursue the conversation further. Rather, he turns to those around him and acknowledges how exceedingly difficult it is for the rich to divest and so participate in God's kingdom: "How with great difficulty are those who have possessions (οἱ τὰ χρήματα ἔχοντες) entering into (εἰσπορεύονται) God's kingdom! For it is easier for a camel to enter into a needle's eye than for a rich person (πλούσιον) to enter into the kingdom of God" (vv.24–25).[26] Astonishingly, while vividly expressing through hyperbole how unlikely it would be for any rich person to obtain a place in the kingdom (v.25),[27] Jesus nevertheless seems to suggest that some are even now entering in (v.24)! Up to this point, neither Jesus nor the narrator has provided readers with any indication that wealthy individuals are divesting and distributing proceeds to the poor—preliminary requirements for any who wish to follow Jesus "on the way." But because Jesus employs the present tense verb εἰσπορεύονται,[28] readers will infer that some are now doing so, even though no such events have been narrated.[29] Our prognosis for the rich is suddenly not quite so grim. They

[26] Because Jesus links these two statements with the postpositive particle γάρ, I assume that the proverb in v.25 further expands upon his general observation in v.24 and therefore that both οἱ τὰ χρήματα ἔχοντες (v.24) and πλούσιον (v.25) refer to the rich (i.e., rather than two separate groups consisting of any who can claim private ownership and the truly wealthy).

[27] Although it is impossible for a camel to pass through a needle's eye, Jesus' statement may be taken as an example of hyperbole (see, e.g., D'Sa, "The Salvation of the Rich in the Gospel of Luke," 179; Pilgrim, *Good News to the Poor*, 120; Marshall, *The Gospel of Luke*, 687; Fitzmyer, *The Gospel According to Luke X–XXIV*, 1204). If it is taken literally, then Jesus contradicts himself by first acknowledging that some rich persons are now entering the kingdom (albeit with great difficulty) and then claiming that such an event is impossible. Some scribes apparently sought to soften the hyperbole by substituting κάμιλον (a rope or ship's cable) for κάμηλον (*f*[13] 180 579 1010 1424 as well as several lectionaries). See, e.g., Bailey, *Through Peasant Eyes*, 165; Fitzmyer, *The Gospel According to Luke X–XXIV*, 1204. Contrast the positions taken by Bovon, who argues that the scribal alteration does nothing to soften Jesus' proverb since a ship's cable, like a camel, simply cannot pass through a needle's eye [*L'Évangile Selon Saint Luc 15,1–19,27*, 208], and Metzger, who suggests that the variant arose because the "two Greek words had come to be pronounced alike" [*A Textual Commentary on the Greek New Testament*, 40]).

[28] This present tense form of the verb is found in only three manuscripts (B L 892), yet N.-A.[27], UBS[4], and Westcott-Hort all place it in the text. Although εἰσπορεύονται is found in only one early Greek manuscript (L dates to the 8th century; 892 dates to the 9th century), the very well-attested variant εἰσελεύσονται is perhaps best explained as an early harmonization to Jesus' similar statement in Mark 10:23 (cf. εἰσελεύσεται in Matt 19:23).

[29] Narratologists would refer to this missing information (i.e., missing in Luke's discourse but present at the level of story) as an ellipsis.

undoubtedly face a monumental challenge in divesting, yet some presently are selling all they own and thereby obtaining a place in God's kingdom. Will readers be introduced to one or several such persons who are fulfilling this requirement, or must we be satisfied with this single inference?

An unidentified group nearby (οἱ ἀκούσαντες; v.26), perplexed by Jesus' observation and accompanying proverb (vv.24–25), queries: "Then, who can be saved (v.26)?" The source of their confusion, it seems, is the popular notion that material abundance is a sign of divine favor,[30] an assumption that this itinerant Jewish teacher clearly does not share. Although they wish to know from him precisely upon whom, alternatively, God's favor now rests, Jesus responds with a frustratingly vague maxim: "Things that are impossible with human beings are possible with God" (v.27). Although evasive and unforthcoming, Jesus' statement nevertheless seems to confirm readers' recent inference that while the wealthy face a nearly insurmountable hurdle in divesting, *with God's assistance* some are managing to do so.

Peter, perhaps puzzled as to why Jesus did not at least identify his closest traveling companions among those who have met the requirements for salvation, interjects: "Look! We have left everything that belongs to us (τὰ ἴδια) and followed you!" (v.28). Jesus' failure to identify the disciples is understandably disconcerting to someone who long ago left everything behind (5:11), and Peter wants to be sure that he and his companions' sacrifice will be rewarded. In addition to offering Peter the assurance he is seeking, Jesus finally addresses the inquiry posed earlier on the matter of who—if not the rich—can be saved: "There is not one who has left home or spouse or siblings or parents or children on account of God's kingdom who shall not receive many times as much in this time and, in the coming age, eternal life" (vv.29–30). Because the disciples have renounced anything they might call their own (v.28; cf. 14:33), not only do they already possess the eternal reward sought by the wealthy ruler (ζωὴν αἰώνιον; vv.18, 30) but they are promised "many times as much (πολλαπλασίονα)[31] in this time" as well. Interestingly,

[30] See, e.g., Pilgrim, *Good News to the Poor*, 121; Green, *The Gospel of Luke*, 657; Marshall, *The Gospel of Luke*, 688.

[31] While the vast majority of manuscripts read "many times as much" (πολλαπλασίονα), some read "seven times as much" (D it sa^{ms}) and few others read "one-hundred times as much" (1241 sy$^{s.c}$).

Jesus leaves unspecified the nature or content of the "many times as much." Might it broadly constitute social, material, and psychological benefits derived from living in a community in which persons renounce private property (v.28), distribute God's resources justly and equitably so that rich and poor are nonexistent (v.22), and then consume only what is needed (11:3)?

4. *Summary*

When accosted by a rich ruler on the matter of inheriting eternal life, Jesus initially appears perturbed and disengaged, perhaps because of this man's association with Judea's wealthy ruling elite. Unwilling to seriously entertain the ruler's self-interested inquiry, he hastily refers him to the ten commandments, quoting five that focus exclusively on human beings' relations with one another. Understandably dissatisfied with Jesus' commonplace reply and eager for a truly original response, the ruler affirms that he has faithfully kept them all. Electing, finally, to give thoughtful consideration to the man's inquiry, Jesus informs him that there is yet one more thing he must do in order to acquire "treasure in heaven": divest and redistribute the proceeds to the poor (v.22). The ruler, we learn, is not angered, offended, or amused by Jesus' reply but deeply saddened (περίλυπος), which suggests that he has accepted Jesus' injunction as a valid requirement for obtaining eternal life and even begun considering its cost. The encounter is open-ended and concludes here; the narrator does not tell us whether he opted to return to his familiar lifestyle or to sell all that he owned and redistribute the proceeds to the poor.

Significantly, Jesus does not portray the "one thing that remains" (v.22) as a unique, exceptional requirement that is demanded only of this man. Indeed, *anyone* who wishes to follow Jesus "on the way" must "say goodbye to all of his/her possessions" (14:33). Furthermore, according to Jesus the injunction is based on a faithful reading of the Law and Prophets and entirely consistent with its overall ethical orientation. As argued above, while divestiture and distribution may not be mandated in the Jewish scriptures, it is difficult to imagine a more powerful demonstration of love for one's neighbor (Lev 19:18) or a more concrete expression of one's commitment to an equitable, just distribution of resources (Lev 25). Finally, Jesus' primary rationale for issuing the requirement is neither to teach this man how to rely on God,[32] to expose his love for worldly, material things,[33] nor to elicit his unwavering loyalty.[34] Rather, in keeping with his programmatic sermon in Nazareth at the inception of his ministry (4:18–19), Jesus is seeking first an equitable redistribution of essential resources for the benefit of the poor (v.22). The rich ruler may participate in God's kingdom—indeed, with God's assistance some wealthy persons already are (vv.24, 27)!—but only if he first ceases to be rich.

Although overconsumption is not directly addressed in this episode, the critique of personal wealth that emerged in the final two parables (16:1–13; 16:19–31) is sustained. In demanding the elimination of personal wealth, however, Jesus is also undermining the *material* source of overconsumption. As argued in the prior chapter, for Jesus generous almsgiving will not suffice since it fails to offer any structural or systemic changes that would provide real, lasting relief for society's most vulnerable. Only the elimination of personal wealth itself coupled with a fair distribution of the earth's resources can be received as good news by the poor. Anything short of this allows the elite to retain control of capital and essential resources while continuing to spend extravagantly on their own desires. The poor, meanwhile, although finding occasional, temporary relief through almsgiving and/or beneficence, continue to struggle for even the most basic provisions.

B. Jesus' Encounter with Zacchaeus

1. Exploring the Pre-text: 18:31–43

In this section, Jesus reiterates for his disciples the inevitable outcome of their journey into Jerusalem (vv.31–34) and continues his ministry to the poor (vv.35–43). Although the issue of wealth and possessions is not addressed directly, Jesus' encounter with the blind beggar (τυφλὸς...ἐπαιτῶν; v.35) on the road into Jericho reminds readers why, in part, Jesus has advanced such a strong critique of overconsumption and wealth: the region's resources are distributed so inequitably at present that many must beg for basic provisions. Jesus assists this man

[32] Schmidt, *Hostility to Wealth in the Synoptic Gospels*, 161–62.
[33] Seccombe, *Possessions and the Poor in Luke-Acts*, 127.
[34] Bailey, *Through Peasant Eyes*, 164.

in regaining the capacity to see,[35] a central component of his ministry to the poor (4:18), yet, as one without even a place to lay his head (9:58), is not able to alleviate his poverty. For this aspect of the good news, Jesus trusts that many who embrace his message and mission (including those who are wealthy and in positions of authority) will assume the initiative in restructuring institutions, rewriting policies, and re-imagining patterns of consumption that award greater access to the land's resources for all.

2. *Reading Jesus' Encounter with Zacchaeus: 19:1–10*

Moving ever closer "along the way" toward Jerusalem, Jesus finally enters Jericho (19:1; cf. 18:35). Having informed readers that the protagonist is making his way through town (διήρχετο), the narrator rather abruptly (καὶ ἰδοὺ) directs our attention to one resident in particular: Zacchaeus, a "chief tax collector" (ἀρχιτελώνης)[36] who is also "wealthy" (πλούσιος; 19:1–2). His name may hold special significance since it is disclosed prior to his occupation and socio-economic status and prefaced by an unusual pleonastic construction (ὀνόματι καλούμενος; v.2). The redundancy[37] encourages readers to pause here and consider the name's meaning and what bearing it may have upon the episode's plot.[38] In the last of the four parables analyzed (16:19–31), readers sensed similar significance in Lazarus's name, since it represented the first time Jesus had assigned a name to a character in his parables.[39] It was determined that the poor man's name, meaning "God helps," did not reflect a present condition but foreshadowed a future event: God's placing of Lazarus at Abraham's bosom upon his death (16:22). Readers likewise will expect Zacchaeus's name, meaning "righteous/clean one,"[40] to foreshadow a coming event or change in status rather

[35] The verb ἀναβλέπω (vv.41–43) may also indicate acquiring sight for the first time (*BDAG*, 59).

[36] In one manuscript, the narrator introduces Zacchaeus as a "ruler of the synagogue" (Ψ) rather than as a "chief tax collector."

[37] The duplication is grammatically unnecessary and perhaps accounts for why a few manuscripts omit καλούμενος (D G 892 1241 among others).

[38] See D. A. S. Ravens, "Zacchaeus: Final Part of a Lucan Triptych?," *JSNT* 41 (1991), 29; John O'Hanlon, "The Story of Zacchaeus and the Lukan Ethic," *JSNT* 12 (1981), 12.

[39] This is, in fact, the only instance in all of Jesus' parables in which a character is named.

[40] See Fitzmyer, *The Gospel According to Luke X–XXIV*, 1223; Marshall, *The Gospel of Luke*, 696; Ravens, "Zacchaeus: Final Part of a Lucan Triptych?," 29; O'Hanlon, "The Story of Zacchaeus and the Lukan Ethic," 12.

than signify a current condition. Thus, while the tax collector may not qualify as "righteous" or "clean" now, readers expect him to acquire such status soon, perhaps as a result of an encounter with the man who is currently proceeding through town with his disciples.

The narrator's initial sketch of the tax collector is highly ambivalent. On the one hand, his occupation and socio-economic status place him in an unfavorable light. Although it is unclear whether the term ἀρχιτελώνης constitutes an official title or simply reflects Zacchaeus's authority over other tax gatherers in the region,[41] he nevertheless "would have belonged to a circle of persons almost universally despised."[42] Moreover, given Jesus' recent and uncompromising critique of wealth in the final two parables (16:1–13; 16:19–31), his membership among Judea's wealthy elite (πλούσιος; v.2) can only elicit a negative response from readers. Finally, in "seeking to see Jesus (καὶ ἐζήτει ἰδεῖν τὸν Ἰησοῦν)" (v.3), readers may momentarily align him with Herod, the region's wealthy and powerful man *par excellence*, who also "sought to see him" (καὶ ἐζήτει ἰδεῖν αὐτόν; 9:9). On the other hand, Zacchaeus's small stature (ἡλικίᾳ μικρὸς; v.3) coupled with his willingness to run ahead of the crowd and scramble up a sycamore tree (v.4)[43] encourage readers to align him with the children whom Jesus recently called to himself and likened to those who shall enter God's kingdom (18:15–17).[44] Furthermore, while Zacchaeus, like Herod, wishes "to see [Jesus]" (v.3), he also hopes to learn something about the man himself and perhaps even his mission (καὶ ἐζήτει ἰδεῖν... *τίς ἐστιν*; v.3). The tax collector's sincere interest in another contrasts both with the king's bare curiosity and with the ruler's self-interested preoccupation over securing his own future (18:18). As with the rich ruler in 18:18–23, then, readers are

[41] This is due to the term's absence in Greek literature both preceding and contemporaneous with the Gospel of Luke (see Fitzmyer, *The Gospel According to Luke X–XXIV*, 1223; Green, *The Gospel of Luke*, 668; Pilgrim, *Good News to the Poor*, 131).

[42] Green, *The Gospel of Luke*, 669.

[43] Such behavior likely would have been deemed unbecoming for an adult male (see, e.g., Green, *The Gospel of Luke*, 669; Robert C. Tannehill, "The Story of Zacchaeus as Rhetoric: Luke 19:1–10," *Semeia* 64 (1994), 203. Cf. the similarly inappropriate response of the father to his youngest son's return in 15:20.).

[44] Contrast the position taken by Mikeal C. Parsons, who argues that Zacchaeus's small stature would rather connote a "small-mindedness" indicative of poor character for the Gospel's earliest audiences ("'Short in Stature': Luke's Physical Description of Zacchaeus," *NTS* 47 (2001), 52–55, 57).

once again presented with a highly ambivalent portrait and must await Jesus' response and any further comments from the narrator.[45]

Surprisingly, after the narrator's detailed report of the initiative taken by Zacchaeus in positioning himself advantageously along the road in order to catch a glimpse of the itinerant teacher (v.4), readers discover that Jesus is the one who actually initiates the encounter (v.5). Jesus spots Zacchaeus in the tree, commands him to come down, and informs him that he "must" (δεῖ) stay in his home today (v.5). According to Jesus, this is no chance encounter; it is part of God's plan of redemption.[46] Zacchaeus descends immediately and welcomes (ὑπεδέξετο) him into his home with joy (χαίρων; v.6). The tax collector's spontaneous, joyful reception of Jesus, which contrasts with the ruler's silence and indecision (18:23), suggests receptivity to his message and mission. But what, precisely, will Zacchaeus learn about Jesus during his stay, and in what way will he respond?

After the two men enter Zacchaeus's home,[47] the narrator informs us that the townspeople begin to grumble (διεγόγγυζον), for they are astonished that someone like Jesus would choose "to lodge" (καταλῦσαι) with a "sinner" (ἁμαρτωλῷ ἀνδρί; v.7). It is unclear at this point whether the crowd is correct in its assessment of Zacchaeus or what qualities or past actions may account for the label, but readers are reluctant to trust its estimation without explicit confirmation either from Jesus or the narrator, two voices that contribute to the Gospel's evaluative point of view. Indeed, readers began to distrust judgments rendered by crowds at the very inception of Jesus' ministry, when the townspeople of Nazareth attempted to cast Jesus off a nearby precipice after his haphtarah reading and subsequent sermon (4:29). Will readers be able to confirm the crowd's evaluation of one of its resident tax collectors?

At some point during Jesus' stay,[48] Zacchaeus stands up and announces: "Look! My half (τὰ ἡμίσιά μου) of the possessions, Lord, to the poor

---

[45] Tannehill constructs a conflicted portrait of the tax collector as well ("The Story of Zacchaeus as Rhetoric: Luke 19:1–10," 202–3).

[46] William P. Loewe, "Towards an Interpretation of Lk 19:1–10," *CBQ* 36 (1974), 326; Pilgrim, *Good News for the Poor*, 131; O'Hanlon, "The Story of Zacchaeus and the Lukan Ethic," 15; Marshall, *The Gospel of Luke*, 697; Johnson, *The Gospel of Luke*, 285; Fitzmyer, *The Gospel According to Luke X–XXIV*, 1224.

[47] The crowd's use of the aorist tense verb εἰσῆλθεν suggests that the two men have departed and that Jesus has already "entered into" Zacchaeus's house (v.7).

[48] Together, the verbs μεῖναι ("to stay"), ὑπεδέξετο ("he welcomed"), and καταλῦσαι ("to lodge") in vv.5–7 seem to suggest a hospitable reception that would include meals and at least one night's lodging (see, e.g., Dennis Hamm, "Zacchaeus Revisited Once

I shall give (πτωχοῖς δίδωμι). Moreover, if I brought any false charges against anyone,[49] I shall restore (ἀποδίδωμι) four times as much [to that person]" (v.8). Zacchaeus's announcement consists of two parts: 1) a vow to relinquish all he owns and distribute (the proceeds?) to the poor; and 2) a promise to make abundant recompense if it is discovered that he mistakenly accused anyone of either underpaying or altogether neglecting his or her tax obligations. The narrator does not inform readers what transpired during the early hours of Jesus' visit in his home, including what prompted Zacchaeus's response or at what point during their meeting the tax collector elected to make his announcement. There is, therefore, a significant ellipsis here in Luke's discourse to which we do not have access, and readers are left to infer both its seminal events and its duration. Zacchaeus, however, probably would have declared his intention to divest and distribute only after learning something about Jesus, which is initially why he ran ahead of the crowd and climbed the sycamore tree (ἐζήτει ἰδεῖν τὸν Ἰησοῦν τίς ἐστιν; v.3), and the nature of his mission "to bring good news to the poor" (4:18–19). An extended conversation between the two men, perhaps over a meal, therefore likely preceded the announcement.[50] His promise to make fourfold restitution in the event of an unintentional accusation may stem from the townspeople's criticism of him (v.7). Although Zacchaeus does not admit to having brought false charges, he acknowledges that oversights and errors are indeed part of the tax-gathering business and promises to right all wrongs if a legitimate complaint is registered against him.

More: A Story of Vindication or Conversion?," *Biblica* 72 [1991], 250; Marshall, *The Gospel of Luke*, 697; Johnson, *The Gospel of Luke*, 285; Green, *The Gospel of Luke*, 670).

[49] Both of the definitions provided in *BDAG* for the verb συκοφαντέω, "to put pressure on someone for personal gain" and "to secure someth. through intimidation" (955), suggest willful premeditation and therefore do not seem to suit the context here. As Dennis Hamm has said, "'inadvertent extortion' is an oxymoron" ("Zacchaeus Revisited Once More: A Story of Vindication or Conversion?," 249.) The verb, however, may also mean "to accuse falsely" (*LS* [Abridged], 661; A. J. Kerr, "Zacchaeus's Decision to Make Fourfold Restitution," *ET* 98 [1986], 68–70), which one may do mistakenly or unintentionally, and is reflected in the translation above. Zacchaeus does not appear to be confessing guilt but acknowledging that, in spite of his efforts to be fair, errors are always possible.

[50] Pilgrim observes a gap here in Luke's discourse as well: "Without any statement about Jesus' conversation at the table with Zacchaeus we hear only the result of Zacchaeus'[s] encounter with Jesus" (*Good News to the Poor*, 132).

A majority of commentators argue that Zacchaeus either defends his customary practice of giving half of what he owns to the poor[51] or vows to do so in the immediate future.[52] Therefore, whether δίδωμι and ἀποδίδωμι are read as customary or future present tense verbs (a longstanding *crux interpretum* still vigorously debated in the literature on this episode), Zacchaeus does not divest but gives generously to those in need while retaining some of his wealth.[53] It may be argued, however, that Zacchaeus does in fact give away all he owns, just as Jesus' closest traveling companions have done, based on the way in which the tax collector has structured his vow.[54] UBS[4], N.-A.[27], and Westcott-Hort, for good reason, have elected to place the personal pronoun μου directly after the noun ἡμίσιά ("half"). Indeed, two of our earliest and most important Greek uncial manuscripts place the pronoun here (B ℵ).[55] Because personal pronouns, when functioning as possessive genitives,

---

[51] See, e.g., A. T. Robertson, *A Grammar of the Greek New Testament in the Light of Historical Research* (New York: C. H. Doran, 1914), 869–70; Ravens, "Zacchaeus: The Final Part of a Lucan Triptych?," 23–24, 28; Alan C. Mitchell, "The Use of συκοφαντεῖν in Luke 19,8: Further Evidence for Zacchaeus's Defense," *Biblica* 72 (1991), 547; Johnson, *The Gospel of Luke*, 285–86; Green, *The Gospel of Luke*, 671–72; Fitzmyer, *The Gospel According to Luke X–XXIV*, 1221, 1223. There are, in this reader's view, two primary difficulties with this option: 1) if Zacchaeus was in the habit of giving away one-half of all he owned, he would scarcely still qualify as "rich" (v.2); and 2) Zacchaeus would align himself with the Pharisee in Jesus' most recent parable (18:9–14) who similarly defended his customary behavior yet, unlike the tax collector nearby who offered no defense, was not justified before God (see Hamm, "Luke 19:8 Once Again: Does Zacchaeus Defend or Resolve?," esp. 433–35).

[52] See, e.g., Dennis Hamm, "Luke 19:8 Once Again: Does Zacchaeus Defend or Resolve?," 431–437; Hamm, "Zacchaeus Revisited Once More: A Story of Vindication or Conversion?," 249–252; Robert F. O'Toole, "The Literary Form of Luke 19:1–10," *JBL* 110 (1991), 115; Tannehill, "The Story of Zacchaeus as Rhetoric: Luke 19:1–10," 203; Parsons, "'Short in Stature': Luke's Physical Description of Zacchaeus," 57; Marshall, *The Gospel of Luke*, 697–98.

[53] See, e.g., Phillips, *Reading Issues of Wealth and Poverty in Luke-Acts*, 172; Pilgrim, *Good News to the Poor*, 133.

[54] Robert Tannehill argues convincingly for this position, though he offers a rationale different from the one that will be presented below: "Zacchaeus has two responsibilities if he is to free himself from a life of injustice and callous greed, and his property is simply divided in half to meet those two responsibilities. There is no reference to anything being left over. Hence it is a mistake to assume that the story is trying to present a realistic compromise that permits the rich to retain part of their goods for their own use. Zacchaeus is an example of radical repentance, not of practical wisdom, and it is assumed that his response will leave him pretty much in the same financial state required of the rich ruler" (*The Narrative Unity of Luke-Acts*, 1:124). Cf. Tannehill, "The Story of Zacchaeus as Rhetoric: Luke 19:1–10," 203.

[55] Other manuscripts that retain this location for the personal pronoun include L Θ f^1 579 1071.

almost always directly follow their antecedents (e.g., ἐν τῷ οἴκῳ σου; v.5), it would not be unreasonable to suggest that μου modifies ἡμίσιά rather than the subsequent substantive participle τῶν ὑπαρχόντων ("possessions"). Zacchaeus, then, would be proposing to give away *his half* of the possessions (and therefore all he owns) rather than half of his possessions. Of course, if Zacchaeus vows to give up his half of the possessions rather than half of everything he owns, readers are then faced with the difficulty of identifying to whom the other half belongs.[56] Neither Zacchaeus nor the narrator provides any clues, but readers have already met one man from Jesus' parables who allocated his entire estate to his sons before his death (15:12) as well as several female disciples who helped fund Jesus' itinerant ministry "from their possessions" (8:3). Because both male children and women can, at least within the thought-world of this Gospel, own property or "possessions" independently of a paterfamilias, it would therefore not be unreasonable to suggest that either his son(s) or his spouse (or both!) owns the other half.[57]

One of the striking features of Zacchaeus's vow is that "the poor" stand in the emphatic position: *πτωχοῖς* δίδωμι. Even though these

---

[56] Several scribes, it appears, found the juxtaposition of μου with ἡμίσιά (as well as its implication for the translator) strange and therefore relocated it behind ὑπαρχόντων, a reading now preserved in the majority of Greek manuscripts (D A W Q U K M Δ Γ Ψ Π Λ 157 565 700 118 *f*[13] *Byz* among others). It is this conundrum—identifying the person(s) to whom the other half belongs—that initially may have motivated the pronoun's relocation. For confirmation of the various locations of μου, see Reuben Joseph Swanson's (ed.) volume *New Testament Greek Manuscripts: Variant Readings Arranged in Horizontal Lines Against Codex Vaticanus. Luke* (Sheffield: Sheffield Academic Press, 1995), 321. The variants cannot be found in the apparatuses of either N.-A.[27] or UBS[4].

[57] Those who argue that Zacchaeus relinquishes only half of his possessions face a formidable difficulty of their own, one which may prove even more troublesome. Throughout the Travel Narrative, Jesus consistently asks any who wish to become his disciples to sell all they own (e.g., 12:33; 14:33; 18:22). Jesus, we soon learn, informs Zacchaeus that his vow has merited him "salvation" (σωτηρία; v.9). If Zacchaeus has, in fact, only committed half of his possessions to the poor and not everything he owns, then Jesus suddenly and inexplicably relaxes the rigorous requirements demanded time and again throughout the Travel Narrative, most recently of the wealthy ruler in 18:22 (see, e.g., Seccombe's observation: "The surprising thing is that no attempt is made to match the sacrifice demanded of the ruler.... Presumably Zacchaeus remains materially in a comparable situation to where he began, though he has expressed his love and joy in a concrete manner" [*Possessions and the Poor in Luke-Acts*, 132]). Luke's story of Jesus, however, is presented in such a way as to fortify or enhance the protagonist's ethos for its readers, but an abrupt, unexplained modification of discipleship requirements would surely diminish it. The difficulty above of identifying who owns the other half of the possessions in Zacchaeus's household is, for this reader, less problematic in the long run than accounting for the unexpected and unexplained change in discipleship requirements.

words are transposed in several Greek manuscripts (including those in the Majority text tradition),[58] UBS[4], N.-A.[27], and Westcott-Hort all have elected to include the above word ordering in their texts.[59] The ordering is indeed significant, for it suggests that Zacchaeus's forthcoming divestiture is motivated not by a desire, for instance, to detach himself from material possessions but to make a significant contribution toward Jesus' mission to improve conditions for the poor (4:18–19). After conversing with Jesus at some length in his home, Zacchaeus divests because he has been persuaded by this itinerant Jewish teacher's unique reading of the Law and Prophets and embraced his mission of bringing good news to the poor, which in part involves a more equitable, just distribution of God's resources.

While Zacchaeus's promise to restore fourfold in the event of error or oversight is often taken both as evidence of his culpability and as confirmation of the crowd's negative perception of him (ἁμαρτωλῷ ἀνδρί; v.7),[60] neither Jesus nor the narrator has suggested that he has committed any misdeed related to his occupation as "chief tax collector" (v.2).[61] As mentioned above, in this Gospel crowds or townspeople are hardly reliable guides in assessing characters or events and should not be trusted here without corroboration from a more reliable source. Moreover, Zacchaeus carefully crafts his promise so as neither to admit guilt nor to acquiesce to the crowd's assessment of him. The promise is a simple conditional sentence in which the protasis, at least for the sake of argument, is assumed to be true. With such constructions, however, the speaker him/herself need not believe in the truth of the protasis; in fact, in many cases in the NT the speaker simply rearticulates what *others* assume to be so.[62] Here, it appears that Zacchaeus is restating why the townspeople believe him to be a "sinner" (v.7) rather than openly acknowledging his culpability. If he really were confessing misdeeds, there would be no need for him to preface the latter part of the announcement with the particle εἴ; he could, for instance, begin

---

[58] See also A K M U W Γ Δ Λ Π 118 f^{13} 2 28 157 565 700 1071. Not surprisingly, this particular ordering is found in Textus Receptus.

[59] This order is preserved in B ℵ D L Q Θ Ψ f^{1} 33 892 among others.

[60] See, e.g., Phillips, *Reading Issues of Wealth and Poverty in Luke-Acts*, 172; Seccombe, *Possessions and the Poor in Luke-Acts*, 130; Parsons, "'Short in Stature': Luke's Physical Description of Zacchaeus," 57; Marshall, *The Gospel of Luke*, 698; O'Hanlon, "The Story of Zacchaeus and the Lukan Ethic," 19.

[61] See, e.g., Ravens, "Zacchaeus: The Final Part of a Lucan Triptych?," 23–25, 32.

[62] See *BDF* 371.1; 372.1. See also *BDAG*, 277.

with a simple declaratory statement ("I brought false charges") or a causal construction ("Because I brought false charges") in order to avoid confusion.[63] It is not Zacchaeus's conduct as "chief tax collector" in Jericho with which Jesus is concerned but rather his "wealth" (πλούσιος; v.2), for which Zacchaeus swiftly and amply repents through divestiture. Zacchaeus, then, acknowledges the townspeople's criticism of him without actually admitting to intentional, wrongful action, yet he promises Jesus that if anyone does register a legitimate complaint he will be sure to provide adequate compensation.[64]

Jesus responds immediately and enthusiastically to Zacchaeus's announcement: "Today, salvation has taken place in this house (τῷ οἴκῳ τούτῳ)" (v.9). In addition to reading τῷ οἴκῳ τούτῳ as a local dative ("in this house"),[65] readers may also overhear "by means of this house" (a dative of means) or "to/for this house" (a dative of advantage). If the phrase is read as a dative of means, then Jesus is informing Zacchaeus that his vow to divest and distribute his wealth will bring "salvation" to many in and around Jericho who are poor and oppressed (4:18–19). In other words, by means of the tax collector's forthcoming act, valuable resources once owned and managed exclusively by one man will now be distributed among members of the community. (The blind beggar who just received his sight [18:35–43] may now be able to acquire adequate food and shelter!) If the phrase is taken as a dative of advantage, then the focus shifts to Zacchaeus's reward. Having said "goodbye to all of his possessions," he has become Jesus' disciple (14:33), successfully passed through the eye of a needle into God's kingdom (18:24–25), and acquired "an inexhaustible treasure in heaven" (12:33). None of these

[63] Contrast, e.g., Marshall's position on the simple conditional sentence: "The conditional clause is to be translated 'From whomsoever I have wrongfully exacted anything', and thus does not put the fact of extortion in doubt, but rather its extent" (*The Gospel of Luke*, 698).

[64] While nowhere in the Law or Prophets are persons required to restore "four times as much" in the event of a demonstrated false accusation or even extortion, in Exodus fourfold restitution is required from someone who steals a sheep (22:1). According to Lev 6:5 (cf. Num 5:6–7), any stolen property must be restored in its entirety plus "one-fifth" (see Fitzmyer, *The Gospel According to Luke X–XXIV*, 1225; Johnson, *The Gospel of Luke*, 286; Marshall, *The Gospel of Luke*, 698). Because there is no precise precedent in the Hebrew Bible for the fourfold restitution proposed by Zacchaeus, Kerr ("Zacchaeus's Decision to Make Fourfold Restitution," 70) and Fitzmyer (*The Gospel According to Luke X–XXIV*, 1225) suggest that it may have been required by Roman law.

[65] A few manuscripts make this reading explicit: ἐν τῷ οἴκῳ τούτῳ (D A sy$^{s.c}$ sa^{mss} bo^{pt}).

three possibilities for the phrase τῷ οἴκῳ τούτῳ needs to be excluded by the reader. Indeed, all three fit the context well.

Having addressed Zacchaeus directly (εἶπεν δὲ πρὸς αὐτὸν),[66] Jesus now turns to other guests, onlookers, or passersby (καθότι)[67] and offers an assessment of Zacchaeus's new status: "Now (καὶ),[68] *he* is a son of Abraham!" (v.9). Instead of reintegrating Zacchaeus back into the Jewish community, as many have argued,[69] Jesus' comment may only isolate him further. Not only does Jesus imply that many if not all of those nearby are *not* Abraham's children, his chosen exemplar of the patriarch's true progeny is a "sinner" *par excellence* (v.7) who, by vowing to divest and distribute his wealth, has also just aligned himself with a highly sectarian stance toward private property and reading of the Law and Prophets. Thus, while passing through the needle's eye into God's kingdom, Zacchaeus's open profession to sectarian ideals coupled with Jesus' incendiary redefinition of Abraham's true offspring will likely serve to distance the tax collector even further from his fellow citizens in Jericho. Like Jesus' disciples, now he too can expect to exist on the periphery of society and endure criticism and insult (e.g., 6:22; 12:11, 51–53).

Following Jesus' assessment of Zacchaeus's new status as a true "son of Abraham," the narrator intrudes briefly to offer a concluding generalization on the protagonist's role in implementing God's plan of salvation: "For, the Son of Humanity came to seek and to save

[66] In order to resolve the difficulty in v.9 presented by Jesus' rather sudden shift in addressees (from Zacchaeus to guests or onlookers), a few commentators have suggested rendering πρὸς αὐτὸν as "concerning/about him" (see, e.g., O'Hanlon, "The Story of Zacchaeus and the Lukan Ethic," 17; Marshall, *The Gospel of Luke*, 698). In this case, Jesus would be offering a single statement to all. Such a rendering, however, is not consistent with how the phrase is ordinarily used in this Gospel and therefore has not been employed here.

[67] While καθότι is typically translated "for/since" (see Luke 1:7), *BDAG* suggests that it may also serve as a marker of direct discourse (493), which is how it is understood here. In this case, it would function to distinguish Jesus' statement to Zacchaeus, introduced by ὅτι, from his subsequent declaration to guests or onlookers.

[68] While καὶ is usually rendered by translators as "even/also" here, *BDAG* suggests that the word may introduce "a fact as surprising or unexpected or noteworthy" (495), a meaning that I have tried to express with "Now."

[69] Several commentators argue that this is precisely the function of Jesus' response. See, e.g., Pilgrim, *Good News to the Poor*, 132; David E. Orton, "We Felt Like Grasshoppers: The Little Ones in Biblical Interpretation," *Biblical Interpretation* 11 (2003), 496; Ravens, "Zacchaeus: The Final Part of a Lucan Triptych?," 27, 31; Tannehill, "The Story of Zacchaeus as Rhetoric: Luke 19:1–10," 206–7, 209–10; Green, *The Gospel of Luke*, 672.

the lost."[70] Although it initially appeared as if Zacchaeus was seeking out Jesus (vv.3–4), readers can now confirm that Jesus was actually searching for Zacchaeus (vv.5, 10).[71] Because part of Jesus' vision for God's kingdom involves a more equitable distribution of resources, "it is necessary" (δεῖ; v.5) that he speak to the region's wealthy elite about his mission and their obligation as prescribed in the Law and Prophets to their fellow human beings. Bringing "good news to the poor" will, in part, depend upon conscientizing the wealthy to the daily hardships faced by the majority and to how their stockpiling of resources deprives so many of even the most basic provisions. Zacchaeus was indeed "lost," not because of his chosen occupation but because he claimed far more than his share of goods and capital. By divesting and distributing to the poor, Zacchaeus brings "salvation" to many in the region (v.9) while acquiring for himself "an inexhaustible treasure in heaven" (12:33).[72]

3. *Summary*

One of the region's "chief tax collectors," propelled by a desire "to see who Jesus is" (v.3), rushes ahead of a throng gathered in Jericho and ascends a sycamore tree in hope of catching a glimpse of the itinerant teacher as he passes through town. Although Zacchaeus is the one who takes the initiative in positioning himself advantageously along the road, Jesus actually initiates the encounter and commands him to come down from the tree (vv.4–5). When Jesus informs him that he "must" stay at his house "today," Zacchaeus welcomes Jesus joyfully, and the two men depart, though not without objection from the townspeople (vv.5–7). At some point during Jesus' visit, probably after a lengthy conversation during which Zacchaeus became acquainted with his reading of the Law and Prophets and his vision for God's kingdom, the tax collector announces that he will divest and distribute *all* that he has to the poor (v. 8), thus formally acknowledging his assent to Jesus' hermeneutical emphases as well as his commitment to furthering Jesus' mission. In response to the crowd's "grumbling" (v.7), Zacchaeus also promises to

---

[70] Alternatively, this statement may be attributed to Jesus.

[71] O'Toole, "The Literary Form of Luke 19:1–10," 111, 116.

[72] This final statement is based on the polyvalent reading of τῷ οἴκῳ τούτῳ (v.9) offered above.

provide abundant recompense *if* someone should register a legitimate complaint against him (v.8). The tax collector's announcement is received enthusiastically by Jesus, who informs him that by means of his forthcoming act he will bring "salvation" to many who are poor and oppressed while acquiring for himself "an inexhaustible treasure in heaven," a reward offered to any who renounce all for the sake of the kingdom (12:33). Finally, turning to guests or nearby onlookers, Jesus proclaims that Zacchaeus, though despised by many because of his occupation and his ties to the Empire, is actually numbered among Abraham's true progeny (v.9). Already disliked, Jesus' inflammatory redefinition of the patriarch's true children coupled with Zacchaeus's adoption of sectarian ideals will serve to isolate the tax collector only further.

At the level of story, readers inferred that some rich persons already had divested and distributed to the poor (18:24), but Zacchaeus is the first character *in Luke's discourse* to actually do so. Having repented of his "wealth" (19:2) through divestiture and distribution (19:8), he furthers Jesus' mission for a more equitable distribution of resources while passing through the needle's eye into God's kingdom (18:25). In spite of Jesus' negative portrayal of the rich in the prior parables and his initially cold, disengaged response to the ruler's inquiry, readers are able to confirm that the wealthy, with God's assistance (18:27; cf. 19:5, 10), may indeed participate in the kingdom, but only if they first cease to be rich. In fact, for Jesus "it is necessary" (v.5) that some of the region's powerbrokers and managers of capital and goods respond positively to his message and take the lead in redistributing resources.

The critique of wealth advanced in the final two parables (16:1–13; 16:19–31) and implied in Jesus' encounter with the rich ruler (18:18–23) is confirmed here. Although consumption patterns are not directly addressed, by eliminating wealth, the *material* source of overconsumption is removed as well. Apparently, Jesus does not have the ability to slay the *yetzer ha ra* ("the evil inclination");[73] it will remain.[74] Without access to excess, however, individuals may wish to indulge but no longer

[73] Cf. Ezra's "evil heart" (4 Ezra 3:21–27) and Paul's "other law," which "wages war against the law of [our] mind" (Rom 7:23).

[74] Indeed, according to Jesus, "no one (including him!) is good except one, God" (18:19).

have the option of spending extravagantly and irresponsibly on their own desires.[75] In addition to rendering the *yetzer ha ra* impotent in its quest to overindulge and luxuriate, the demise of mammon releases the land's resources from the firm grip of a few and enables all to find what they need (11:3; 12:30).

[75] Today, of course, this is no longer true in many places of the world. Generous lines of credit offer immediate access to all sorts of goods and services. In the ancient world, however, one without a surplus would have to resort to selling belongings thievery, or to pledging oneself as an indentured servant or slave.

CHAPTER FIVE

CONCLUSION

Introduction

Before analyzing four of Jesus' parables featuring protagonists with access to wealth and his two encounters with rich men while still "on the way" to Jerusalem, several preliminary conclusions and assumptions were identified. First, Jesus' inaugural address at the synagogue in Nazareth, which outlines the basic contours and purpose of his ministry (4:16–21), would serve as a programmatic text through which his later parables and interactions with others would be refracted. Consequently, bringing "good news to the poor" would remain the primary impetus behind his teaching on consumption and wealth and his conversations with the elite rather than, for instance, opening avenues to salvation for the rich or training possessors in *Gottvertrauen*. Second, it was determined that interpreting Luke's parables of Jesus would be a reader-oriented enterprise requiring creativity and hard work. Although it is often assumed that these parables of Jesus are generally more accessible than those in Matthew or Mark, little evidence was found to support this thesis. As with all of Jesus' parables, those in Luke also overflow with hermeneutical possibility and often elude, frustrate, and tease. Full of gaps and ellipses, replete with moments of undecidability, hopelessly polyvalent, they are *scriptible* narratives that must be written, not merely read. Third, while an effort would be made to listen attentively to the unique voice of this Gospel by accessing a literary, cultural, and historical repertoire available to persons of the first century Mediterranean world, all readings would be presented as constructions *produced* by a situated, interested, and perspectival flesh-and-blood reader.[1] The final product, while processed, structured, and described with the help of terminology and conceptual tools derived from narratology and narrative

[1] For this dual emphasis on respecting the unique voice of an *other* while simultaneously acknowledging the profound role a reader plays in constructing this voice, I am indebted to Fernando Segovia (*Decolonizing Biblical Studies*, esp. 34–52, 87–132). While this is not a direct quotation, I am also borrowing terminology he employs throughout his book.

criticism, would remain but one conceivable performance alongside an infinite number of possibilities—fragile and deconstructable, hovering perilously above a "seething flux" of alternate hermeneutical choices,[2] polyvalent words and phrases, and alien associations that threaten to unsettle and even overturn. Both meaning and response would originate with the reader and not lie concealed "in" the text, as if awaiting excavation and routine transfer from one idiom to another. Finally, in view of the central role to be played by the reader, a reader-position was delineated. A citizen of the United States writing at the beginning of the twenty-first century, this reader is particularly attentive to two defining features of his own social and historical context: rampant overconsumption and unprecedented personal wealth. This reader, moreover, deeply troubled by the acute concentration of wealth in the hands of a few and aware that current consumption patterns are depleting nonrenewable resources at alarming rates as well as having disastrous consequences on our planet's fragile ecosystems, enlisted the Gospel of Luke as a conversation partner with the hope that it would prove to be an insightful and challenging interlocutor, perhaps offering a vision for society that is more just and humane.

A. Retracing our Steps: A Brief Synopsis of the Journey

In Jesus' first parable (12:15–21), a wealthy landowner stumbles into an exceptionally bountiful harvest and proposes to fashion a life for himself defined by rest and celebration. After constructing larger storage facilities to accommodate his surplus and beginning to overconsume and luxuriate, God visits him one evening and announces that he will soon die and therefore no longer be able to enjoy all of "the good things" (v.18) he accumulated. Already wealthy, his unanticipated windfall awakens not a philanthropic urge but a rapacious desire to stockpile even more (vv.15, 21) as well as to spend extravagantly and indefinitely on satisfying his own desires (v.19). Wealth per se may not receive an explicit critique either in the divine pronouncement (v.20), Jesus' prefatory apostrophe (v.15), or the parable's concluding application (v.21), but readers are introduced to a pattern of behavior that will emerge in each of the

[2] See Moore, *Literary Criticism and the Gospels*, 136.

subsequent parables: persons with access to excess elect to spend on themselves rather than to share or distribute it to others.

In the second parable (15:11–32), a father's younger son demands his share of the inheritance and journeys to a distant land, where he quickly exhausts all of his resources pursuing a life of personal gratification. Penniless, he decides to return home with the hope that his father will at least grant him a job on the estate as a laborer. He carefully crafts a "confession" in advance, but when he realizes how overjoyed his father is to see him, he shrewdly omits the final request for installation as a laborer, wagering that his father's love for him will render such menial service unnecessary. Although the son offered no clear indication that he was remorseful or had altered his spending habits, the father immediately forgives him, (re)invests him with the authority and privileges appropriate to his status as "son," and throws a lavish, costly party during which the estate's only grain-fed calf is killed. The father's remark in v.24 invites us to align this parable with the previous two in 15:4–10 and rejoice with this family in having recovered a lost son, which would require a momentary suspension of the negative evaluation of wealth first introduced in the infancy narrative (1:53) and in Jesus' early preaching (6:24). On the one hand, then, the parable threatens to undermine any emerging criticisms of wealth. During the festivities, however, the intradiegetic narrator reintroduces the elder brother, who, readers learn, is reluctant to receive his brother with open arms or to join in the extravagant feast prepared by his father. It is his anger with which readers attentive to consumption and wealth sympathize and his focalization of events that provide a welcome outlet for readers' mounting frustration with other characters who fail to take waste seriously. Without his voice and his justifiable anger, overconsumption and waste go unchallenged. In view of Jesus' mission as outlined in 4:18–19, he must speak, for the parable simply cannot end with a wealthy family at play, perfectly content and feasting sumptuously. So, while the negative estimation of wealth threatens to dissolve with the invitation to rejoice with this family (see vv.24, 32), the elder son's voice both reconfirms and reinforces the critique of overconsumption that emerged in 12:15–21.

In the third parable (16:1–13), a steward is fired for exacting exorbitant commissions from his master's debtors to fund a lifestyle marked by overconsumption and waste. Having squandered everything on himself, he faces the prospect of leaving the estate with nothing and no one willing to support him until he is able to find employment. So, in order to secure basic provisions upon his release, he cancels all of his commissions (therefore leaving his master's profits intact) with the hope that at least one of the debtors will reciprocate with an offer of food and lodging. In his commentary, Jesus establishes an *a minori ad maius* argument for his disciples: If an unjust steward who overcharged and overconsumed can forego all he has and trust that he will receive what he needs, how much more so you—you who are neither unjust nor constrained by external forces to renounce everything? Although many may view wealth as a mark of distinction and honor, Jesus urges his disciples to view it as but "the smallest thing" and "alien" or "unsuitable" for those who are "on the way" (vv.10–12). Not only does wealth tend to arouse overspending, but when resources are concentrated in the hands of a few, the majority must struggle (and many will fail) to acquire even bare necessities.[3] Personal wealth, the mere presence of which testifies to an unequal and unjust distribution of land and resources, is totally incompatible with service to God (v.13) and has no place in Jesus' vision of the kingdom. Thus, it is with Jesus' comments on this parable that readers find their first clear, uncompromising critique of wealth itself.

In the final parable (16:19–31), Jesus juxtaposes the excesses and opulence of an anonymous rich man with the chronic hunger and pain of a beggar named Lazarus. A mere stone's throw from the banquet hall where the rich man and his guests gather to celebrate and feast sumptuously, Lazarus lives in dire poverty, plagued by frequent visitations from unclean street dogs, until he is carried away by angels to Abraham's bosom. Not surprisingly, the rich man, who had access to the finest foods and medical care, outlives the poor man, but he too dies, whereupon he finds himself subject to flame and torment opposite Abraham and Lazarus in one of Hades' chambers. There, Abraham informs him that his reception and enjoyment of "good things" on earth accounts for his present locale across the great chasm (v.25). How he acquired and sustained his wealth or whether he regularly tithed, gave alms, or offered the appropriate sacrifices appear to have had no bearing whatsoever on his postmortem fate. Indeed, even if the rich man had given alms to Lazarus, he still would have possessed and enjoyed "good things," which, according to Abraham, would still merit suffering

[3] Assumed is the notion of a "limited good society" in which land and resources are in finite and short supply.

in flame and torment. Presumably, the only means by which the rich man could have gained entry to the opposing chamber would have been to dispense of his wealth so as to no longer qualify as "rich" (v.19). In addition to offering readers their first vivid portrayal of daily opulence and habitual overconsumption,[4] this parable codifies the breakdown of the redistributive systems of almsgiving and beneficence in meeting the very pressing needs of society's most vulnerable. According to the intradiegetic narrator, it fails in part because persons with access to excess too often elect to spend it on themselves.[5] Moreover, both almsgiving and beneficence offer none of the lasting structural changes that might truly be received as "good news" by the poor. Under such systems, the rich need not alter their consumption habits in the least and retain their wealth as well as all the power and privileges that come with it. The poor, meanwhile, though receiving occasional, temporary relief, remain poor and struggle to subsist. Once again, readers find that personal wealth, however it is obtained or managed, is incompatible with Jesus' vision of the kingdom. Its elimination would mean the dissolution of the *material* source of overconsumption as well as greater access to land and resources for all.

A "ruler" initiates the first of Jesus' two encounters with wealthy men while "on the way" to Jerusalem with an inquiry: "Good teacher, what must I do to inherit eternal life?"(18:18). Perturbed by this man's attempt to set him apart from the crowd with a flattering appellation and possibly by his association with Judea's wealthy, ruling elite, Jesus refuses to attend seriously to the question and nonchalantly refers him to the ten commandments. Understandably dissatisfied and eager for a truly original response, the ruler affirms that he has kept them all since his youth. Surprisingly and without any explanation for his sudden change of heart, Jesus elects to give thoughtful consideration to the inquiry and proceeds to inform him that there is yet one more thing he must do in order to acquire "treasure in heaven": sell absolutely everything he owns and redistribute to the poor (v.22). While the outcome of their encounter is not narrated, the ruler's sadness suggests that he has accepted Jesus' injunction as a valid requirement for obtaining eternal life and even begun considering its cost. Significantly, the "one

[4] In the preceding parables, overconsumption was either inferred (12:15–21; 16:1–13) or mentioned only briefly without an accompanying description of how resources were spent (15:11–32).

[5] This pattern of behavior has now been observed in all four of Jesus' parables.

thing that remains" (v.22) is not presented as a unique, exceptional requirement demanded only of this man but one that must be met by *any* who are persuaded by Jesus' reading of the Law and Prophets, share his vision for God's kingdom, and wish to join him "on the way." Moreover, the purpose of Jesus' charge to divest and distribute is neither to teach dependence upon God nor to redirect attention away from the material to the spiritual realm but to foster a more equitable distribution of essential resources for the benefit of the poor (v.22; cf. 4:18–19). Once again, readers find that personal wealth has no place in Jesus' vision of the kingdom. If the wealthy wish to participate, they first must cease to be rich.

Shortly thereafter, Jesus arrives in Jericho, where he spots one of the region's "chief tax collectors" in a sycamore tree, commands him to come down, and informs him that he "must stay" at his house "today" (v.5). Zacchaeus joyfully welcomes the itinerant teacher into his home, where, after learning something about Jesus and his mission (perhaps over a meal), he announces that he will give *everything* he owns to the poor and promises to right all wrongs *if* a legitimate complaint is registered against him (v.8). Jesus receives the tax collector's words with enthusiasm. In addition to identifying the benefits of his forthcoming act both for the district's poor and for Zacchaeus, he publicly christens him a true "son of Abraham" (v.9). While Zacchaeus successfully passes through the needle's eye into God's kingdom by repenting of his wealth (18:24–25),[6] readers anticipate that he will find himself even further isolated from his fellow citizens as a consequence of his open profession to sectarian ideals and Jesus' public designation of the despised tax collector as a preeminent representative of the Jewish patriarch's true progeny. Although Jesus was initially reticent to converse with the rich ruler, in this episode he actively seeks out a member of Judea's wealthy elite and introduces him to his vision for God's kingdom. For Jesus, in fact, "it is necessary" (v.5) that at least a few of the region's powerbrokers and managers of goods and capital respond favorably to his message and assume the initiative in redistributing land and resources and furthering his ministry on behalf of the poor. As in the prior encounter, readers are able to confirm that personal wealth has no place in the kingdom. While overconsumption may not be addressed directly, by eliminating wealth, its *material* source is removed as well.

[6] Zacchaeus is the first rich person in Luke's discourse to do so.

B. Implications

In the literature on wealth and possessions in the Gospel of Luke, it is generally agreed that readers are not encouraged to renounce everything, as Jesus and his closest traveling companions do, but to give generously without expecting anything in return. Typically, the renunciation traditions either are assigned to a bygone, ideal era or come into play only during times of duress or persecution, when Christians may be required to leave behind family and possessions for the sake of the kingdom. For many critics, then, Luke's almsgiving traditions assume center-stage, and John the Baptist's exhortations to generosity and contentment (3:10–14) as well as Zacchaeus's vow to relinquish half of his belongings (19:8) are often called upon to epitomize the Gospel's overall perspective on wealth and possessions.[7]

It is, however, problematic to assign an overall perspective on wealth and possessions to the Gospel, for it involves conflating several voices or selecting only one or two characters to represent its diverse views. As Luke Johnson has said so well, "Luke consistently speaks about possessions…[but] does not speak about possessions consistently."[8] Indeed, while John preaches generosity and contentment (3:10–14), Jesus, while "on the way" to Jerusalem, asks any who would come after him to renounce everything (e.g., 12:33; 14:33; 18:22). On one occasion in the Travel Narrative, even Jesus' and God's perspectives differ. In 12:13–21, God (as constructed by Jesus) views the wealthy landowner's plan as foolish because it fails to account for life's unpredictability and transience, but Jesus highlights the broader social ramifications of this plan by implicitly ascribing πλεονεξία—an insatiable desire for more that often proceeds without out regard for others' wellbeing and at their expense—to him (v.15). In effect, only Jesus appears concerned with how the landowner's proposal to accumulate and overconsume will adversely affect others in the community. I would therefore argue that the various positions professed by each character or set of characters at separate stages in the story should be identified and preserved rather than conflated so as to squeeze a single perspective out of the narrative. Consequently, the uncompromising, sectarian position that I have ascribed to Jesus in the Travel Narrative cannot be assigned to

[7] For a detailed review of this literature, see Chapter 1, Section A.

[8] *The Literary Function of Possessions in Luke-Acts*, 13.

the Gospel as a whole. This reading has focused upon one character's understanding of wealth and possessions and was limited, in large part, to only one section of the narrative (9:51–19:27). Further research would be required in order to place this construction in conversation with wealth and possessions discourse elsewhere in the Gospel and perspectives espoused by other characters.

As stated in Chapter 1, the proposed construction of Jesus' four parables and two subsequent encounters with wealthy men from Luke's Travel Narrative is offered as but one reading of the Gospel's wealth and possessions traditions among many others. I do not intend to undermine the majority; I only hope to have shown that a more subversive reading of these traditions is both plausible and defensible. One need not, for instance, dismiss the Gospel as a benignly accommodationist "friend" of the Empire[9] and turn instead to one of the many contemporary portraits of the historical Jesus in search of a strong critique of wealth and consumption patterns. Such a critique, I have argued, may be found in Luke's *discourse* as well. But only readers will be able to judge whether this interpretation reflects a careful, attentive, and respectful "hearing"—one that has not "overridden or overwhelmed" the Gospel's distinct voice and perspectives.[10] Without doubt, in Luke ambiguity, polyvalence, gaps, and ellipses (super)abound, and each individual reader—situated, interested, and perspectival—will "perform" the text differently; yet, at the same time, each reading should demonstrate genuine, thoughtful engagement with a unique *other*.[11] It is my hope that this interpretation does so.

With good reason, some may ask: "Is the sectarian position on wealth attributed to Jesus a plausible response within the historical milieu assumed by the narrative? If so, is Jesus' call for the complete elimination of personal wealth really warranted or necessary?" Luke's story of Jesus is set against the backdrop of a highly stratified, advanced

[9] See, e.g., Paul W. Walasky, *"And So We Came to Rome": The Political Perspective of St. Luke* (New York: Cambridge University Press, 1983); Vernon Robbins, "Luke-Acts: A Mixed Population Seeks A Home in the Roman Empire, in *Images of Empire* (ed. L. Alexander; JSOTSS 122; Sheffield: Sheffield Academic Press, 1991): 202–221; Hans Conzelmann, "Luke's Place in the Development of Early Christianity," in *Studies in Luke-Acts* (ed. Leander Keck and J. Louis Martyn; Philadelphia: Fortress Press, 1980), 301–3.

[10] See Segovia, *Decolonizing Biblical Studies*, 103–5, 119–20.

[11] Ibid., 41–43, 97–98, 103–5.

agrarian society in which a very small percentage of the population[12] owned and managed most all of the land and capital.[13] The majority, consisting of small landowners, tenant farmers, and laborers, engaged in subsistence-level farming and, as a rule, were barely able to fulfill basic needs.[14] Both capital and goods were extracted by elites from the primary producers and redistributed "upwards"[15] for purposes "other than meeting the material needs of the cultivators," such as adorning "urban edifices and fostering urban culture."[16] The ruling elite, often portrayed as "corrupt and extortionate,"[17] "kept peasants and villages under a constant barrage of demands and obligations" to prevent them from accumulating any surplus,[18] which placed many families at great risk during political or environmental crises. Because taxes[19] and interest on loans were high, many peasants entered "a hopeless spiral

[12] Composed of senators, equestrians, and decurions, the Empire's imperial and civic elite accounted for less than ten percent of the total population (see Philip A. Harland, "Connections with Elites in the World of the Early Christians," in *Handbook of Early Christianity: Social Science Approaches*, [ed. Anthony J. Blasi, Jean Duhaime, and Paul-Andre Turcotte; New York: Altamira Press, 2002], 387–88; cf. Dimitris J. Kyrtatas, "Modes and Relations of Production," in *Handbook of Early Christianity: Social Science Approaches*, 536. William Herzog suggests that the majority of this top tier [5%–7%] should be classified as "retainers," those who draft laws and regulations that support rulers' interests as well as ensure their compliance, impose and collect taxes, and justify existing social and economic arrangements [*Parables as Subversive Speech*, 58, 61]).

[13] K. C. Hanson and Dennis E. Oakman, "The Denarius Stops Here: Political Economy in Roman Palestine," in *Palestine in the Time of Jesus: Social Structures and Social Conflicts* (ed. K. C. Hanson and Douglas E. Oakman; Minneapolis: Fortress Press, 1998), 112; Herzog, *Parables as Subversive Speech*, 63–64; Harland, "The Economy of First-Century Palestine: State of the Scholarly Discussion," in *Handbook of Early Christianity: Social Science Approaches*, 515.

[14] Gildas Hamel, *Poverty and Charity in Roman Palestine, First Three Centuries C.E.* (Near Eastern Studies 23; University of California Press, 1989), 142; cf. Dennis E. Oakman, *Jesus and the Economic Questions of His Day* (Lewiston, N.Y.: The Edwin Mellen Press, 1986), 72.

[15] Hanson and Oakman, "The Denarius Stops Here: Political Economy in Roman Palestine," 116, 128; Herzog, *Parables as Subversive Speech*, 58, 64; Harland, "The Economy of First-Century Palestine: State of the Scholarly Discussion," 515.

[16] Oakman, *Jesus and the Economic Questions of His Day*, 78, 211.

[17] See Jack Pastor, *Land and Economy in Ancient Palestine* (London: Routledge, 1997), 140–41.

[18] Hanson and Oakman, "The Denarius Stops Here: Political Economy in Roman Palestine," 120.

[19] For the many types of direct and indirect taxes imposed by civic and religious elites, see Hamel, *Poverty and Charity in Roman Palestine*, 144–49; Pastor, *Land and Economy in Ancient Palestine*, 138–39; Oakman, *Jesus and the Economic Questions of His Day*, 66–67. Estimates of the total tax burden assumed by the primary producers generally range between 25%–40%.

of debt that led to the loss of the family plot."[20] Consequently, first century Palestine witnessed a rise in tenancy[21] as well as an increasing concentration of landholdings in the hands of the wealthy.[22] In effect, under the extractive economy of early Roman Palestine, the rich were growing much richer while the majority labored tirelessly simply to make ends meet, often unsuccessfully. It is, as Dennis Oakman says, within "such a conflicted agrarian situation that Jesus of Nazareth proclaimed the beginning of the reign of God."[23]

Given Roman Palestine's harsh economic realities, Jesus' origin among and close association with the plebeian majority (e.g., 1:48; 2:7, 24), as well as his commitment to improving conditions for the region's poor (4:18–19), the foregoing construction of his position on wealth and consumption is neither implausible nor entirely unexpected. Admittedly, his call for the elimination of personal wealth coupled with an equitable distribution of resources for the benefit of the poor is out of step with mainstream voices. However, the situation for Palestine's primary producers and its poor during the first century—extraordinarily high taxes, rent, and interest rates as well as increasing indebtedness and loss of family land—was worsening rapidly, and dire circumstances often elicit radical proposals. For Jesus, patching the current redistributive systems of almsgiving and beneficence, which were maintained and legitimated by the religious and civic elite, was no longer a viable option. Under such systems, not only are the rich able to retain control of goods and capital, they also need not alter their consumption habits in the least. In effect, beyond periodic, temporary relief of acute suffering and deprivation, nothing changes. Offering none of the lasting, structural

---

[20] Oakman, *Jesus and the Economic Questions of His Day*, 80.

[21] Hamel, *Poverty and Charity in Roman Palestine*, 160; Oakman, *Jesus and the Economic Questions of His Day*, 77–78.

[22] Harland, "The Economy of First-Century Palestine: State of the Scholarly Discussion," 520; Hamel, *Poverty and Charity in Roman Palestine*, 159; Oakman, *Jesus and the Economic Questions of His Day*, 75.

[23] *Jesus and the Economic Questions of His Day*, 80. The preceding portrait does not necessarily reflect the Gospel's construction of the early Roman Period but is rather based on recent studies of ancient, advanced agrarian societies generally and on assessments of numerous documents from the first and second centuries CE. It reflects a broader social and economic landscape reconstructed by contemporary scholars and therefore moves far beyond the story-world implied by the text. A literary analysis, however, need not restrict itself to a narrative's story-world; it may draw upon recent developments in a variety of fields in order to augment or "fill out" readers' understanding of the setting, as long as such a move is acknowledged (see Powell, *What is Narrative Criticism?*, esp. 74–75; cf. Rhoads, "Narrative Criticism: Practices and Prospects," 264–85).

modifications that could truly be received by the poor as "good news," these systems were failing to meet the pressing needs of society's most vulnerable. Jesus' call for the dissolution of personal wealth carries the added benefit of curbing overconsumption. Since the *yetzer ha ra*, an enduring fact of human existence,[24] arouses self-interested overspending and waste,[25] for Jesus one of the most effective ways to reduce overconsumption is simply to eliminate its material source.

C. A Rejoinder[26]

Outside of the commune, kibbutz, convent, or monastery, a literal, broad-based application of Jesus' mandate to divest and redistribute is neither feasible nor even desirable. Yet, for this reader, Jesus' words are far from obsolete or irrelevant.[27] First, his perspective on wealth and consumption, forged among and for the benefit of a disenfranchised plebeian majority under the early Roman Empire, endures today as an invaluable, representative protestation "from below" to an unjust, extractive economy. Few such voices remain from the first century, and, if only for this reason, it is to be taken seriously. Second, a central feature of the Gospel's setting is still operative at the dawn of the twenty-first century under the current global markets: massive inequity between rich and poor. As in early Roman Palestine, a relatively small minority of the world's population owns and manages most of the capital and consumes a disproportionate share of the earth's resources. Admittedly, today's elite, concentrated predominantly in the global North (North

[24] A seminal part of Jesus' anthropology appears to include an "evil inclination" or an "evil heart" (4 Ezra 3:20–27). Not only does he emphatically state that "no one is good" (18:19), but he even refers to his disciples as "evil" (πονηροὶ; 11:13)—a label he gives them *after* they have left everything to follow him.

[25] In each of Jesus' four parables, excess aroused self-serving desires rather than a philanthropic urge.

[26] This response is offered from the perspective of a twenty-first century U.S. citizen who has foregrounded two defining features of his own social and historical context: rampant overconsumption and unprecedented personal wealth. This reader, I might add, while encouraged by his own religious community to prioritize engagement with the writings of the First and Second Testaments in reflecting upon and formulating a response to our present situation, views the Gospel not as an authority but as an interlocutor or conversation partner with whom one might very well disagree.

[27] Throughout this final section, I often refer to "Jesus' words," "Jesus' perspective," or "Jesus' vision for God's kingdom" without qualifiers. However, I am speaking not about the historical figure as such but about the particular portrait of the Gospel's central character and his teaching that was constructed in Chapters 2–4.

America, Europe, Japan, and South Korea),[28] constitutes a larger portion of the population than during the early Roman period, but the present gap between rich and poor is equally, if not more, stark and troubling. The recent shift from managed to remarketized capitalism, characterized by intense competition as well as increasing privatization and deregulation,[29] in the latter part of the twentieth century has vastly heightened wealth inequality around the world, and many who have been denied access to advances under industrialization and, more recently, globalization may readily identify with Jesus' critique.[30]

---

[28] Ankie Hoogvelt offers a helpful description of today's "global business élite and their supporting political classes in the nation-states" under globalization: "In the core circle we find the élites of all continents and nations, albeit in different proportions in relation to their respective geographic hinterlands. We may count in this core some 20 per cent of the world population who are 'bankable'. They are encircled by a larger, fluid, social layer of between 20 per cent and 30 per cent of the world population (workers and their families), who labour in insecure forms of employment, thrown into cut-throat competition in the global market.... The third, and largest, concentric circle comprises those who are already effectively excluded from the global system. Performing neither a productive function, nor presenting a potential consumer market in the present stage of high-tech, information-driven capitalism, there is, for the moment, neither theory, world-view nor moral injunction, let alone a programme of action, to include them in universal progress" (*Globalization and the Postcolonial World: The New Political Economy of Development*, 2nd ed. [Baltimore: The Johns Hopkins University Press, 2001], 143, 258–59).

[29] In the wake of socialism's and communism's demise during the latter half of the twentieth century, remarketized capitalism has emerged as the new orthodoxy. Few, in fact, seem to be willing to imagine future economic relations outside of capitalism's most recent permutation. Consider, for instance, James Fulcher's concluding remarks in *Capitalism: A Very Short Introduction*: "The search for an alternative *to* capitalism is fruitless in a world where capitalism has become utterly dominant, and no final crisis is in sight or, short of some ecological catastrophe, even really conceivable. The socialist alternative has lost its credibility, while contemporary anti-capitalist movements seem to lead nowhere, because of their failure to provide a credible and constructive alternative that is compatible with existing patterns of production and consumption. Those who wish to reform the world should focus on the potential for change *within* capitalism" ([New York: Oxford University Press, 2004], 127). Cf. Joshua Muravchik's remarks in *Heaven on Earth: The Rise and Fall of Socialism*: "Today, it is all but universally acknowledged that the wealth that sustains the public sector is created in the private sector. This means that any attempt to expand the public sector beyond a certain point will backfire.... Thus, it is within the context of predominantly capitalist economies that democratic societies will continue to debate about and experiment with relatively minor variations in taxes and services" ([San Francisco: Encounter Books, 2002], 319).

[30] Consider, for instance, Manfred B. Steger's brief statistical overview of this widening gap: "Data published in the 1999 and 2000 editions of the *UN Human Development Report* show that, before the onset of globalization in 1973, the income ratio between the richest and poorest countries was at about 44 to 1. Twenty-five years later it had climbed to 74 to 1. In the period since the end of the Cold War, the number of persons subsisting below the international poverty line rose from 1.2 billion in 1987 to 1.5 billion today. If current trends persist, their numbers will reach 1.9 billion by 2015. This means that, at

Jesus' call for the elimination of wealth coupled with his emphasis on consuming only what one needs (e.g. 11:3; 12:30) is fundamentally incompatible with capitalism as currently practiced. Not only is the present system dependent upon relatively high, consistent levels of consumption in order to sustain itself,[31] but it prioritizes rapid wealth generation and accumulation *above all else*.[32] As long as wealth is being created, stalwart defenders of capitalism are generally unconcerned with its uneven distribution since it is believed that technological innovations and the higher standards of living enjoyed by the elite will "trickle down" to the majority *eventually*. They may be correct, but at present we are eons away from narrowing the gap between rich and poor. It is, in fact, only increasing, and most of the world's capital "still flows between North America, Europe, and Japan."[33] Critics legitimately ask:

---

the dawn of the 21st century, the bottom 25% of humankind live on less than $140 a year. Meanwhile, the world's 200 richest people have doubled their net worth to more than $1 trillion between 1994 and 1998. The assets of the world's top *three* billionaires are more than the combined GNP of all the least developed countries and their 600 million people" (*Globalization: A Very Short Introduction* [New York: Oxford University Press, 2003], 105). Cf. A. Hoogvelt's statement: "In a world so steeped in social inequality that just three super-billionaires have an amount of wealth exceeding the combined income of all the least developed nations and their 600 million population, and the net worth of another 200 equates to the income of 41 percent of world population, measures of global wealth are simply offensive" (*Globalization and the Postcolonial World*, 91). This same trend may be observed in the global North as well, particularly in the U.S.: "The financial wealth of the top 1% of American households exceeds the combined wealth of the bottom 95% of households, reflecting a significant increase in the last 20 years" (Steger, *Globalization: A Very Short Introduction*, 107).

[31] Because overproduction is a constant threat in a capitalist economy, corporations must continually update and repackage their products, identify and exploit new markets, and persuade or remind consumers that their goods and/or services are necessary or at least desirable. The booming credit industry in many industrial countries (including, and particularly, the United States) has temporarily thwarted a crisis of overproduction, but what happens when the bulk of consumers can no longer afford the latest technological improvements and choose rather to make do with what they have? Rigorous conservation and today's capitalism cannot coexist. If everyone were to practice conservation, the global markets would collapse.

[32] Because maximizing dividends for shareholders often takes precedence over the means by which profits are created or even the quality of the final product or service, some have dubbed remarketized capitalism's primary objective "amoral accumulation" (Fulcher, *Capitalism: A Very Short Introduction*, 124).

[33] Ibid., 97. Fulcher continues: "[I]n 1998 the emerging markets accounted for only 7% of the world's capital, even though their countries contained around 85% of the world's population.... In the year 2000, the whole of Africa (excluding South Africa) received less than 1% of total world foreign direct investment, a sum equivalent to the amount received by one European country with a population of only 5 million—Finland" (Ibid.).

How long shall we wait? How many generations of human lives must be sacrificed first?

While both Jesus and proponents of today's capitalism may share the assumption that human beings are profoundly self-interested, it is unlikely that he would trust our concupiscence to work for the common good, as Adam Smith theorized. As noted above, in his four parables from the Travel Narrative, each of the protagonists with access to wealth elected to spend on himself rather than to share or redistribute. Thus, according to Jesus' anthropology, even when wealth is generated and the "forces of production" have advanced sufficiently, capitalism's primary beneficiaries would likely stockpile profits (e.g., 12:18) and use them for personal gratification (e.g., 12:19; 15:13; 16:1, 19) rather than reinvest or redistribute them for the benefit of all.[34] In effect, because wealth too often awakens hedonistic overconsumption rather than selfless generosity, it is unlikely to find its way out of the hands of the elite to the communities and persons who need it most. Capitalism may succeed in generating wealth (this it has done), but without proper redistributive measures in place or a system of checks and balances that both discourages unlimited accumulation and fosters local ownership, production, and development, very little will actually "trickle down."

Jesus' teaching, therefore, offers a challenge to current global economic structures, but is also encourages readers to explore new social and economic relationships that are more just and humane. Socialism or communism (one of socialism's many possible manifestations) are not necessarily the only alternatives to present economic arrangements,[35] yet

[34] Jesus' perception of the elite is thus far different from Karl Marx's idealized portrait of the capitalist, who is not "a pleasure-seeker who dissipates his profits in riotous self-indulgence" but "much more the disciplined, self-denying captain of industry who plows his profits back into the business, turning each increment of profit into a new element of capital with which more profit is in turn realized" (*The Communist Manifesto with selections from* The Eighteenth Brumaire of Louis Bonaparte *and* Capital [ed. Samuel H. Beer; New York: Appleton-Century-Crofts, 1955], xvii–xviii).

[35] Joshua Muravchik, in *Heaven on Earth*, chronicles the rise and fall of socialism's many forms during the previous century. While many anticipated that its coercive, authoritarian manifestations would eventually collapse, even democratic socialism failed to secure a strong foothold for any significant length of time. Rather, "democratic socialism," writes Muravchik, "turned out to be a contradiction in terms, for where socialists proceeded democratically, they found themselves on a trajectory that took them further and further from socialism" and "more accepting of markets, private enterprise and economic inequality" (319, 344). Muravchik believes that "[o]nly once did democratic socialists manage to create socialism. That was the kibbutz. After they had experienced

an aggressive, reformist agenda of some sort that strives to dismantle the "oppressive structure of global apartheid that divides the world into a privileged North and a disadvantaged South"[36] is certainly in order (and desperately needed!), for, as many now acknowledge, "mitigating poverty is now a standard against which the new global economy will be judged."[37] Traditional redistributive systems of almsgiving and beneficence, which require very little of the elite, have proven inadequate, even impotent, in remedying wealth inequality, and much more radical measures must be taken. Steps toward greater equity would minimally involve: 1) a significant reduction in consumption levels[38] coupled with a commitment to developing environmentally friendly and renewable energy sources; 2) crafting regulations that would discourage transnationals from extracting wealth from developing economies and penalize them for abusing labor forces to maximize profit margins; 3) creating incentives for companies to focus research and development on improving the quality of life for all rather than on revamping existing technologies for consumption in the global North; 4) "blanket forgiveness of all Third World Debt" (cf. the Jubilee traditions in Lev 25); and 5)

---

it, they chose democratically to abolish it" (344). He is therefore led to conclude: "After so much hope and struggle, and so many lives sacrificed around the world, socialism's epitaph turned out to be: If you build it, they will leave" (6).

[36] Steger, *Globalization: A Very Short Introduction*, 135.

[37] Daniel Yergin and Joseph Stanislaw, *The Commanding Heights: The Battle for the World Economy* (New York: Simon & Schuster, 2002), 409. The authors discuss five criteria by which future generations will assess today's global economy (408–15).

[38] Today, even relatively conservative commentators and columnists are advocating for a reduction in consumption levels, particularly with regard to the energy sector. Admittedly, rationales for such reductions rarely foreground concern for the poor but focus rather on how our insatiable appetite for fossil fuels (especially petroleum) helps fund repressive, authoritarian regimes and terrorist organizations in the Middle East while perpetuating U.S. energy dependence. Only occasionally are concerns raised over deleterious consequences for the environment. Consider, for instance, Thomas L. Friedman's proposal for a steep gasoline tax, which he believes is the most effective way to curb our consumption of petroleum and spur research and development on renewable, environmentally friendly energy sources: "The one thing we can do now . . . is to create a tax that fixes the pump price at $3.50 to $4 a gallon—no matter where the OPEC price goes. Because if consumers know that the price of oil is *never* coming down, they will change their behavior. And when consumers change their behavior in a big way, G.M., Ford and DaimlerChrysler will change their cars in a big way, and it is cars and trucks that consume the vast majority of the world's oil. . . . A permanent gasoline tax will also make solar, wind and biofuels so competitive with oil that it will drive their innovations as well" ("The New 'Sputnik' Challenges: They All Run on Oil," *The New York Times* [January 20, 2006], A19; see also Friedman, "State of the union ought to be energy independence," *The Tennessean* [January 30, 2006], 7A).

"[e]stablishment of a new world development institution financed largely by the global North through such measures as a financial transaction tax and administered largely by the global South."[39] Of course, policy changes such as these, if they are to endure, must be sustained by a shift in basic values and priorities: concern for the dignity and well-being of *all* members of the human family must displace unlimited accumulation, consumerism, and the vigorous pursuit of leisure and personal pleasure. In effect, change will occur only if the global markets' primary beneficiaries are willing to make significant sacrifices—pare back desires, modify consumption habits, discourage unlimited accumulation, penalize the powerful *and* be willing to accept the consequences. Indeed, while Jesus' and his followers' ascetic, property less existence is in part a symbolic gesture visibly expressing their conviction that God owns the land (including all resources derived from it—food, water, building materials, fuel) and human beings are but "aliens and tenants" (Lev 25:23), it also suggests that any meaningful, enduring change in current economic relations—one that can truly be received by the poor as "good news"—will come only at great personal cost.

Jesus' vision for God's kingdom in Luke is not unlike Micah's[40] vision for the restoration of the Davidic kingdom (4:1–4), in which "each person shall sit under her vine and under her fig tree" (v.4; cf. Zech 3:10).[41] Certain resources may be privately owned, according to Judah's prophet, but these resources are to be distributed equitably, and persons are to take and consume only what they need. In effect, like Jesus, Micah also envisions the dissolution of personal wealth, a redistribution of land and resources, and a reduction in consumption

---

[39] These final two steps are part of Manfred Steger's "Global New Deal," which represents a "universalist protectionism" committed to improving equity between the global North and South. He includes several others, such as "[a]bolition of offshore financial centres that offer tax havens for wealthy individuals and corporations" and "[g]reater transparency and accountability provided to citizens by national governments and international institutions" (*Globalization: A Very Short Introduction*, 135). Ankie Hoogvelt advocates implementing a wide array of hypothecated taxes, which would encourage local production while slowing many transnationals' quest for global dominance (*Globalization and the Postcolonial World*, 266).

[40] Like Jesus, Micah, from the small village of Moresheth-gath in the Judean foothills, also appears to have come from the lower classes.

[41] Both "vine" (גפן) and "fig tree" (תאנה) are singular nouns, which is obscured by the *NRSV*'s rendering: "...but they shall sit under their own vines and under their own fig trees."

levels. Unfortunately, we are a long way from realizing either prophet's vision, for today only a few enjoy respite in the shade under magnificent cedars while so many huddle perilously under a fragile bean plant out in the blazing sun, one hungry worm away from disease, starvation, or death (Jonah 4:6–8).

BIBLIOGRAPHY

Abraham, M. V. "Good News to the Poor in Luke's Gospel." *Bangalore Theological Forum* 19 (1987): 1–13.

Aland, Barbara, Kurt Aland, Eberhard Nestle, and Erwin Nestle, eds. *Nestle-Aland Novum Testamentum Graece.* 27th ed. Stuttgart: Deutsche Bibelgesellschaft, 1993.

Aland, Barabara, Kurt Aland, Johannes Karavidopoulos, Carlo M. Martini, and Bruce M. Metzger, eds. *The Greek New Testament.* 4th rev. ed. Stuttgart: Deutsche Bibelgesellschaft, 1993.

Aletti, Jean-Noël. "Jésus a Nazareth (Lc 4, 16–30): Prophétie, Écriture et Typologie." Pages 431–51 in *À Cause de L'Évangile: Études sur les Synoptiques et les Actes offertes au P Jacques Dupont, OSB à l'occasion de son 70e anniversaire.* Lectio Divina 123. Paris: Éditions du Cerf, 1985.

Allen, Graham. *Intertextuality.* The New Critical Idiom. New York: Routledge, 2000.

——. *Roland Barthes.* Routledge Critical Thinkers Series. New York: Routledge, 2003.

Alter, Robert. *The Pleasures of Reading in an Ideological Age.* New York: Simon and Schuster, 1989.

Amjad-Ali, C. M. "No Name for the Rich: The Parable of Lazarus." 32 (1990): 22–27.

Anonyme. "La Parabole du Père et des ses deux Fils: Luc 15/11–32." *ETR* 55 (1980): 77–85.

Aus, Roger D. "Luke 15:11–32 and R. Eliezer Hyrcanus's Rise to Fame." *JBL* 104 (1985): 443–69.

Bailey, Kenneth E., *Finding the Lost: Cultural Keys to Luke 15.* St. Louis: Concordia Publishing House, 1992.

——. *Poet and Peasant and Through Peasant Eyes. A Literary-Cultural Approach to the Parables in Luke.* Grand Rapids: Eerdmans, 1983.

——. *Through Peasant Eyes: More Lucan Parables, Their Culture and Style.* Grand Rapids: Eerdmans, 1980.

Bakhtin, Mikhail. "The Problem of the Text in Linguistics, Philology, and the Human Sciences: An Experiment in Philosophical Analysis." Pages 103–31 in *Speech Genres and Other Late Essays.* Translated by Vern W. McGee. Austin, TX: University of Texas Press, 1986.

——. "Heteroglossia in the Novel." Pages 195–224 in *Bakhtinian Thought: An Introductory Reader.* Edited by Simon Dentith. New York: Routledge, 1995.

Bal, Mieke. *Narratology: Introduction to the Theory of Narrative.* 2d ed. Toronto: University of Toronto Press, 1999.

Balembo, Buetubela. "Lecture Africaine de la Bible: Essai sur l'exégèse symbolique de Lc 15, 1–32." Pages 231–39 in *Théologie Africaine: Bilan et Perspectives. Actes de la Dix-septième Semaine Théologique de Kinshasa 2–8 avril 1989.* Kinshasa: Facultés Catholiques de Kinshasa, 1989.

Barthes, Roland. *Image, Music, Text.* Translated by Stephen Heath. New York: Hill and Wang, 1977.

——. *S/Z.* Translated by Richard Miller. New York: Hill and Wang, 1974.

Bauckham, Richard J. "The Rich Man and Lazarus: The Parable and the Parallels." *NTS* 37 (1991): 225–46.

Beal, Timothy K., "Ideology and Intertextuality: Surplus of Meaning and Controlling the Means of Production." Pages 27–39 in *Reading Between Texts: Intertextuality and the Hebrew Bible.* Edited by Danna N. Fewell. Literary Currents in Biblical Interpretation. Louisville: Westminster/John Knox Press, 1992.

Beavis, Mary Ann. "Ancient Slavery as an Interpretive Context for the New Testament Servant Parables with Special Reference to the Unjust Steward (Luke 16:1–8)." *JBL* 111 (1992): 37–54.

——. "The Foolish Landowner (Luke 12:16b–20." Pages 55–68 in *Jesus and his Parables: Interpreting the Parables of Jesus Today*. Edited by V. George Shillington. Edinburgh: T & T Clark, 1997.

——. "The Power of Jesus' Parables: Were They Polemical or Irenic?" *JSNT* 82 (2001): 3–30.

Beer, Samuel H., ed. *The Communist Manifesto with selections from* The Eighteenth Brumaire of Louis Bonaparte *and* Capital. New York: Appleton-Century-Crofts, 1955.

Bennett, Andrew, ed. *Readers and Reading.* Longman Critical Readers. New York: Longman, 1995.

Betz, O. "The Kerygma of Luke." *Interpretation* 22 (1968): 131–46.

Blasi, Anthony J., Jean Duhaime, and Paul-Andre Turcotte, eds. *Handbook of Early Christianity: Social Science Approaches.* New York: Altamira Press, 2002.

Blass, F. and A. DeBrunner. *A Greek Grammar of the New Testament and Other Early Christian Literature.* Translated and edited by R. W. Funk. Chicago: The University of Chicago Press, 1961.

Blomberg, Craig L. "The Parables of Jesus: Current Trends and Needs in Research." Pages 231–54 in *Studying the Historical Jesus: Evaluation of the State of Current Research.* Edited by Bruce Chilton and Craig A. Evans. New York: E. J. Brill, 1994.

Bortolussi, Marisa, and Peter Dixon. *Psychonarratology: Foundations for the Empirical Study of Literary Response.* New York: Cambridge University Press, 2003.

Bossuyt, Philippe, and Jean Radermakers. *Jésus: Parole de la Grâce selon saint Luc 2. Lecture continue.* Institut d'Etudes Théologiques: Bruxelles, 1981.

Boucher, Madeleine I. *The Parables.* New Testament Message 7. Wilmington, DE: Michael Glazier, 1981.

Bovon, François. *A Commentary on the Gospel of Luke 1:1–9:50.* Translate by Christine M. Thomas. Hermeneia. Minneapolis: Fortress Press, 2002.

——. *L'Évangile Selon Saint Luc 15,1–19,27.* Commentaire du Nouveau Testament IIIc. Genève: Labor et Fides, 2001.

Brawley, R. L. *Centering on God: Method and Message in Luke-Acts.* Literary Currents in Biblical Interpretation. Louisville: Westminster/John Knox Press, 1990.

Burnett, Fred W. "Characterization and Reader Construction of Characters in the Gospels." *Semeia* 63 (1993): 3–28.

Byrne, Brendan J. *Reckoning with Romans: A Contemporary Reading of Paul's Gospel.* Good News Studies 18. Wilmington, DE: Michael Glazier, 1986.

——. *Romans*. Sacra Pagina 6. Collegeville, MN: The Liturgical Press, 1996.

Cadbury, Henry J. "Four Features of Lucan Style." Pages 87–102 in *Studies in Luke-Acts.* Edited by Leander Keck and J. Louis Martyn. Philadelphia: Fortress Press, 1980.

Cassidy, Richard. *Jesus, Politics, and Society: A Study of Luke's Gospel.* Maryknoll, N.Y.: Orbis Books, 1978.

Charlesworth, James H., ed. *The Old Testament Pseudepigrapha.* 2 vols. Anchor Bible Reference Library. New York: Doubleday, 1983–1985.

Chatman, Seymour. *Story and Discourse: Narrative Structure in Fiction and Film.* Ithaca: Cornell University Press, 1978.

Cloete, D. D., and D. J. Smit. "Rejoicing with God...(Luke 15:11–32)." *Journal of Theology for Southern Africa* 66 (1989): 62–73.

Conzelmann, Hans. "Luke's Place in the Development of Early Christianity." Pages 298–316 in *Studies in Luke-Acts.* Edited by Leander Keck and J. Louis Martyn. Philadelphia: Fortress Press, 1980.

——. *The Theology of St Luke.* New York: Harper, 1960. A translation of the 2d ed. of *Die Mitte der Zeit: Studien zur Theologie des Lukas.* BHT 17. Tubingen: Mohr (Siebeck), 1957.

Cortes, Juan, and Florence Gatti. "On the Meaning of Luke 16:16." *JBL* 106 (1987): 247–59.

Cox, Susan Taylor, "Perspectives on Stance in Response to Literature: A Theoretical and Historical Framework." Pages 11–22 in *Reader Stance and Literary Understanding: Exploring the Theories, Research and Practice.* Edited by Joyce Many and Carole Cox. Norwood, NJ: Ablex Publishing, 1992.

Crossan, John Dominic. "Parable." *ABD* V: 146–52.

Crossan, John Dominic, and Jonathan L. Reed. *Excavating Jesus: Beneath the Stones, Behind the Texts.* San Fransisco: HarperSanFransisco, 2001.

Culpepper, R. Alan. *Anatomy of the Fourth Gospel: A Study in Literary Design.* Philadelphia: Fortress Press, 1983.

Cuvillier, Elian. "Parabole dans la Tradition Synoptique." *ETR* 66 (1991): 24–44.

D'Sa, T. "The Salvation of the Rich in the Gospel of Luke." *Vidyajyoti* 52 (1988): 170–80.

Danker, Frederick William, ed. *A Greek-English Lexicon of the New Testament and Other Early Christian Literature.* 3d ed. Chicago: University of Chicago Press, 2000. (Based on Walter Bauer's *Griechsich-deutsches Wörterbuch zu den Schriften des Neuen Testaments und der frühchristlichen Literatur.*)

Darr, John A. "'Watch How you Listen' (Luke 8.18)." Pages 87–107 in *The New Literary Criticism and the New Testament.* Edited by Elizabeth Struthers Malbon and Edgar McKnight. JSNTSS 109. Sheffield: Sheffield Academic Press, 1994.

———. "Narrator as Character: Mapping a Reader-Oriented Approach to Narration in Luke-Acts." *Semeia* 63 (1993): 43–60.

———. *On Character Building: The Reader and the Rhetoric of Characterization in Luke-Acts.* Literary Currents in Biblical Interpretation. Louisville: Westminster/John Knox Press, 1992.

Davis, Todd F., and Kenneth Womack. *Formalist Criticism and Reader-Response Theory.* New York: Palgrave, 2002.

De Certeau, Michel. "Reading as Poaching." Pages 150–63 in *Readers and Reading.* Edited by Andrew Bennett. Longman Critical Readers. New York: Longman, 1995.

De Man, Paul. "The Resistance to Theory." Pages 196–204 in *Readers and Reading.* Edited by Andrew Bennett. Longman Critical Readers. New York: Longman, 1995.

Degenhardt, Hans Joachim. *Lukas Evangelist der Armen: Besitz und Besitzverzicht in den lukanischen Schriften.* Stuttgart: Katholisches Bibelwerk, 1965.

Delling, G. "πλεονέκτης, πλεονεκτέω, πλεονεξία." *TDNT* VI: 266–74.

Delorme, J. "Intertextualities about Mark." Pages 35–42 in *Intertextuality in Biblical Writings: Essays in Honor of Bas van Iersel.* Edited by Sipke Draisma. Kampen: Uitgeversmaatschappij J. H. Kok, 1989.

Derrett, J. Duncan M. "Fresh Light on St Luke XVI. II. Dives and Lazarus and the Preceding Sayings." *NTS* 7 (1961): 364–80.

———. "The Rich Fool: A Parable of Jesus Concerning Inheritance." *HeyJ* 18 (1977): 131–51.

———. *Law in the New Testament.* London: Darton, Longman & Todd, 1970.

Dimock, Wai-Chee. "Feminism, New Historicism and the Reader." Pages 112–31 in *Readers and Reading.* Edited by Andrew Bennett. Longman Critical Readers. New York: Longman, 1995.

Dodd, C. H. *The Parables of the Kingdom.* Rev. ed. New York: Scribner, 1961.

Donahue, John R. "Two Decades of Research on the Rich and Poor in Luke-Acts." Pages 129–44 in *Justice and the Holy: Essays in Honor of Walter Harrelson.* Edited by Douglas A. Knight and Peter J. Paris. Atlanta: Scholars Press, 1989.

———. *The Gospel in Parable: Metaphor, Narrative, and Theology in the Synoptic Gospels.* Philadelphia: Fortress Press, 1988.

Draisma, Sipke, ed. *Intertextuality in Biblical Writings: Essays in Honor of Bas van Iersel.* Kampen: Uitgeversmaatschappij J. H. Kok, 1989.

Drury, J. *The Parables in the Gospels: History and Allegory.* London: SPCK, 1985.
Dupont, J. *Les beatitudes.* III. Paris: Gabalda, 1973.
Eagleton, Terry. *Literary Theory: An Introduction.* 2d ed. Minneapolis: University of Minnesota Press, 1996.
Evans, Craig A. and Shemaryahu Talmon, eds. *The Quest for Context and Meaning: Studies in Biblical Intertextuality in Honor of James A. Sanders.* New York: Brill, 1997.
Fetterly, Judith. *The Resisting Reader: A Feminist Approach to American Fiction.* Bloomington: Indiana University Press, 1978.
Fewell, Danna N., ed. *Reading Between Texts: Intertextuality and the Hebrew Bible.* Literary Currents in Biblical Interpretation. Louisville: Westminster/John Knox Press, 1992.
Fish, Stanley E. "Interpreting the *Variorum.*" Pages 164–84 in *Reader-Response Criticism: From Formalism to Post-Structuralism.* Edited by Jane P. Tompkins. Baltimore: Johns Hopkins University Press, 1980.
——. "Literature in the Reader: Affective Stylistics." Pages 70–100 in *Reader-Response Criticism: From Formalism to Post-Structuralism.* Edited by Jane P. Tompkins. Baltimore: Johns Hopkins University Press, 1980.
——. *Is There a Text in This Class? The Authority of Interpretative Communities.* Cambridge: Harvard University Press, 1980.
Fishbane, M.. "Types of Biblical Intertextuality." Pages 39–44 in *Congress Volume: Olso 1998.* Edited by Andre Lemaire and Saebo Magne. Supplements to Vetus Testamentum 80. Boston: Brill, 2000.
Fitzmyer, Joseph A. *The Gospel According to Luke I–IX; The Gospel According to Luke X–XXIV.* AB 28; 28A. Garden City, NY: Doubleday, 1981; 1985.
——. "The Matthean Divorce Texts and Some New Palestinian Evidence." *TS* 37 (1976): 197–226.
——. *The Semitic Background of the New Testament.* Grand Rapids: Eerdmans, 1997.
Flegal, K. M., M. D. Carroll, C. L. Ogden, and C. L. Johnson. "Prevalence and Trends in Obesity among U.S. Adults, 1999–2000." *JAMA* 288 (2002): 1723–27.
Foster, G. "Peasant Society and the Image of Limited Good." *American Anthropologist* 67 (1965): 293–315.
Fowler, Robert M. "Reader-Response Criticism: Figuring Mark's Reader." Pages 50–83 in *Mark & Method: New Approaches in Biblical Studies.* Edited by Janice Capel Anderson and Stephen D. Moore. Minneapolis: Fortress Press, 1992.
——. *Let the Reader Understand: Reader-Response Criticism and the Gospel of Mark.* Minneapolis: Fortress Press, 1991.
Freedman, David Noel, ed. *Anchor Bible Dictionary.* 6 vols. New York: Doubleday, 1992.
Friedel, Lawrence M. "The Parable of the Unjust Steward: Lk. 16:1–13." *CBQ* 3 (1941): 337–48.
Friedman, Thomas L. "State of the union ought to be energy independence." *The Tennessean* (January 30, 2006): 7A.
——. "The New 'Sputnik' Challenges: They All Run on Oil." *The New York Times* (January 20, 2006): A19.
Fulcher, James. *Capitalism: A Very Short Introduction.* New York: Oxford University Press, 2004.
Gillman, John. *Possessions and the Life of Faith: A Reading of Luke-Acts.* Collegeville, MN: The Liturgical Press, 1991.
Gonzalez, Justo. *Faith and Wealth: A History of Early Christian Ideas on the Origin, Significance, and Use of Money.* San Francisco: Harper & Row, 1990.
Gourgues, Michel. *TheParaboles de Luc: D'Amont en Aval.* Sciences Bibliques 3. Montréal: Médiaspaul, 1997.
Granowski, Jan Jaynes. "Jehoiachin at the King's Table: A Reading of the Ending of the Second Book of Kings." Pages 173–88 in *Reading Between Texts: Intertextuality and the Hebrew Bible.* Edited by Danna N. Fewell. Literary Currents in Biblical Interpretation. Louisville: Westminster/John Knox Press, 1992.

Green, Joel, ed. *Hearing the New Testament: Strategies for Interpretation.* Grand Rapids: Eerdmans, 1995.
——. *The Gospel of Luke.* NICNT. Grand Rapids: Eerdmans, 1997.
Gressmann, H. "Vom reichen Mann und armen Lazarus: Eine literargeschichtliche Studie." *Abhandlungen der königlich preussischen Akademie der Wissenschaften: Philosophisch-historische Klasse* 7. Berlin: Verlag der königlich Akademie der Wissenschaft, 1918.
Griffiths, J. Gwyn. "Cross-cultural Eschatology with Dives and Lazarus." *ET* 105 (1993): 7–12.
Grobel, K. "'...Whose Name was Neves.'" *NTS* 10 (1964): 373–82.
Gunn, David. "Narrative Criticism." Pages 201–29 in *To Each its Own Meaning: An Introduction to Biblical Criticisms and Their Applications.* Edited by Stephen L. McKenzie and Stephen R. Haynes. Louisville: Westminster/John Knox Press, 1999.
Hamel, Gildas. *Poverty and Charity in Roman Palestine, First Three Centuries C.E.* Near Eastern Studies 23. University of California Press, 1989.
Hamm, Dennis. "Luke 19:8 Once Again: Does Zacchaeus Defend or Resolve?" *JBL* 107 (1988): 431–37.
——. "Zacchaeus Revisited Once More: A Story of Vindication or Conversion?" *Biblica* 72 (1991): 248–52.
Hanson, K. C. and Douglas E. Oakman, eds. *Palestine in the Time of Jesus: Social Structures and Social Conflicts.* Minneapolis: Fortress Press, 1998.
Harrill, J. Albert. "The Indentured Labor of the Prodigal Son (Luke 15:15)." *JBL* 115 (1996): 714–17.
Hauck, F. "μαμωνᾶς." *TDNT* IV: 388–90.
Hedrick, Charles. *Many Things in Parables: Jesus and his Modern Critics.* Louisville: Westminster/John Knox Press, 2004.
——. *Parables as Poetic Fictions: The Creative Voice of Jesus.* Peabody, MA: Hendrickson Publishers, 1994.
Heil, John Paul. "Reader-Response and the Narrative Context of the Parables about Growing Seed in Mark 4:1–34." *CBQ* 54 (1992): 271–86.
Hendrickx, Herman. *The Parables of Jesus.* Rev. ed. Studies in the Synoptic Gospels. San Francisco: Harper & Row, 1986.
——. *The Third Gospel for the Third World Volume Two-A: Ministry in Galilee (Luke 3:1–6:49).* Collegeville, MN: The Liturgical Press, 1997.
——. *The Third Gospel for the Third World Volume Two-B: Ministry in Galilee (Luke 7:1–9:50).* Collegeville, MN: The Liturgical Press, 1998.
Hengel, Martin. *Property and Riches in the Early Church.* Philadelphia: Fortress Press, 1974.
Herzog, William R., II *Parables as Subversive Speech: Jesus as Pedagogue of the Oppressed.* Louisville: Westminster/John Knox Press, 1994.
Hiers, Richard H. "Friends by Unrighteous Mammon: The Eschatological Proletariat (Luke 16:9)." *JAAR* 38 (1970): 30–36.
Hock, Ronald F. "Lazarus and Micyllus: Greco-Roman Backgrounds to Luke 16:19–31." *JBL* 106 (1987): 447–63.
Hoogvelt, Ankie. *Globalization and the Postcolonial World: The New Political Economy of Development.* 2d ed. Baltimore: The Johns Hopkins University Press, 2001.
Hughes, Frank W. "The Parable of the Rich Man and Lazarus (Luke 16:19–31) and Graeco-Roman Rhetoric." Pages 29–41 in *Rhetoric and the New Testament: Essays from the Heidelberg Conference.* Edited by Stanley E. Porter and Thomas H. Olbricht. Sheffield: Sheffield Academic Press, 1993.
Hultgren, Arland J. *The Parables of Jesus: A Commentary.* Grand Rapids: Eerdmanns, 2000.
Ireland, Dennis J. *Stewardship and the Kingdom of God: An Historical, Exegetical, and Contextual Study of the Parable of the Unjust Steward in Luke 16:1–13.* Supplements to Novum Testamentum 70. New York: E. J. Brill, 1992.

Iser, Wolfgang. "The Reading Process: A Phenomenological Approach." Pages 50–69 in *Reader-Response Criticism: From Formalism to Post-Structuralism.* Edited by Jane P. Tompkins. Baltimore: Johns Hopkins University Press, 1980.

——. *Prospecting: From Reader-Response to Literary Anthropology.* Baltimore: The Johns Hopkins University Press, 1989.

——. *The Act of Reading: A Theory of Aesthetic Response.* Baltimore: Johns Hopkins University Press, 1978.

Jauss, Hans Robert. "The Identity of the Poetic Text in the Changing Horizon of Understanding." Pages 7–28 in *Reception Study: From Literary Theory to Cultural Studies.* Edited by James L. Machor and Philip Goldstein. New York: Routledge, 2001.

——. *Toward an Aesthetic of Reception.* Translated by Timothy Bahti. Brighton: Harvester Press, 1982.

Jeremias, Joachim. *The Parables of Jesus.* 2d rev. ed. New York: Scribner, 1972.

——. *Rediscovering the Parables.* New York: Charles Scribner's Sons, 1966.

Johnson, Luke Timothy. *The Gospel According to Luke.* Sacra Pagina 3. Collegeville, MN: The Liturgical Press, 1991.

——. *The Literary Function of Possessions in Luke-Acts.* SBL Dissertation Series 39. Missoula, MT: Scholars Press, 1977.

Johnston, David Cay. "Richest are Leaving Even the Rich Far Behind." *The New York Times* (June 5, 2005). Online: http://www.nytimes.com/2005/06/05/national/class/HYPER-FINAL.html.

Judt, Tony. "Europe vs. America." *The New York Review of Books* 52 (February 10, 2005). Online: http://www.nybooks.com/articles/17726.

Jülicher, Adolph. *Die Gleichnisreden Jesus.* Darmstadt: Wissenschaftliche Buchgesellschaft, 1969.

Karris, Robert. "Poor and Rich: The Lukan *Sitz-im-Leben.*" Pages 112–125 in *Perspectives on Luke-Acts.* Edited by Charles H. Talbert. Perspectives in Religious Studies. Edinburgh: T. & T. Clark, 1978.

Kelber, Werner H. *The Oral and Written Gospel: The Hermeneutics of Speaking and Writing in the Synoptic Tradition, Mark, Paul, and Q.* Philadelphia: Fortress Press, 1983.

Kennedy, George A. *New Testament Interpretation through Rhetorical Criticism.* Chapel Hill: The University of North Carolina Press, 1984.

Kennickell, Arthur B. *A Rolling Tide: Changes in the Distribution of Wealth in the U.S., 1989–2001.* Annandale-on-Hudson, NY: Levy Economics Institute, 2003.

Kerr, A.J. "Zacchaeus's Decision to Make Fourfold Restitution." *ET* 98 (1986): 68–71.

Kilgallen, John J. "Luke 15 and 16: a Connection." *Biblica* 78 (1997): 369–76.

Kim, Kyoung-Jin. *Stewardship and Almsgiving in Luke's Theology.* JSNTSS 155. Sheffield: Sheffield Academic Press, 1998.

Kittel, G., and G. Friedrich, eds. *Theological Dictionary of the New Testament.* 10 vols. Grand Rapids: Eerdmans, 1964–1976.

Kitzberger, Ingrid R., ed. *The Personal Voice in Biblical Interpretation.* New York: Routledge, 1999.

Kloppenborg, John S. "The Dishonoured Master (Luke 16, 1–8a)." *Biblica* 70 (1989): 474–95.

Knight, George W. "Luke 16:19–31: The Rich Man and Lazarus." *Review and Expositor* 94 (1997): 277–284.

Kodell, J. "The Theology of Luke in Recent Study." *BTB* 1 (1971): 115–44.

Kreitzer, Larry. "Luke 16:19–31 and 1 Enoch 22" *Expository Times* 103 (1992): 139–42.

Kristof, Nicholas D. "Land of Penny Pinchers." *The New York Times* (January 5, 2005). Online: http://www.nytimes.com/2005/01/05/opinion/05kris.html.

Landry, David T. "Honor Restored: New Light on the Parable of the Prudent Steward (Luke 16:1–8a)." *JBL* 119 (2000): 287–309.

Lehitpuu, Outi. "Characterization and Persuasion: The Rich Man and the Poor Man in Luke 16:19–31." Pages 73–105 in *Characterization in the Gospels: Reconceiving Narrative Criticism.* JSNTSS 184. Edited by David M. Rhoads and Kari Syreeni. Sheffield: Sheffield Academic Press, 1999.

Leitch, Vincent B. *American Literary Criticism from the Thirties to the Eighties.* New York: Columbia University Press, 1988.

Lemaire, Andre and Saebo Magne, eds. *Congress Volume: Olso 1998.* Supplements to Vetus Testamentum 80. Boston: Brill, 2000.

Liew, Tat-siong Benny. *Politics of Parousia: Reading Mark Inter(con)textually.* Boston: Brill, 1999.

Loader, William R. G. "Jesus and the Rogue in Luke 16:1–8a: The Parable of the Unjust Steward." *Revue Biblique* 96 (1989): 518–32.

Loewe, William P. "Towards an Interpretation of Lk 19:1–10." *CBQ* 36 (1974): 321–31.

Longenecker, Richard N., ed. *The Challenge of Jesus' Parables.* Grand Rapids: Eerdmans, 2000.

Luttikhuizen, G. "Intertextual References in Readers' Response to the Apocryphon of John." Pages 117–26 in *Intertextuality in Biblical Writings: Essays in Honor of Bas van Iersel.* Edited by Sipke Draisma. Kampen: Uitgeversmaatschappij J. H. Kok, 1989.

Lygre, John G. "Of What Charges? (Luke 16:1–2)." *BTB* 32 (2002): 21–28.

Lys, Daniel. "Les Richesses Injustes (Luc 16/1–13)." *ETR* 76 (2001): 391–98.

Mack, Burton L., and Vernon K. Robbins. *Patterns of Persuasion in the Gospels.* Sonoma, CA: Polebridge Press, 1989.

Malbon, Elizabeth Struthers. "Narrative Criticism: How Does the Story Mean?" Pages 23–49 in *Mark & Method: New Approaches in Biblical Studies.* Edited by Janice Capel Anderson and Stephen D. Moore. Minneapolis: Augsburg Fortress Press, 1992.

Malherbe, Abraham J. "The Christianization of a Topos (Luke 12:13–34)." *Novum Testamentum* 38 (1996): 123–35.

Malina, B. J. *The New Testament World: Insights from Cultural Anthropology.* Louisville: Westminster/John Knox Press, 1993.

Malina, B. J., and R. L. Rohrbaugh. *Social-science Commentary on the Synoptic Gospels.* Minneapolis: Fortress Press, 1992.

Marguerat, Daniel. *How to Read Bible Stories: An Introduction to Narrative Criticism.* London: SCM Press, 1999.

Marguerat, Daniel, and Adrian Curtis, eds. *Intertextualitiés: La Bible en échos.* Le Monde de la Bible 40. Geneva: Labor et Fides, 2000.

Marion, Denis. "Paraboles of Crise: Le Riche Insensé; Le Riche et Lazarus." *Esprit et Vie* 106 (1996): 15, 226–30, 235–36.

Marshall, I. Howard. *The Gospel of Luke: A Commentary on the Greek Text.* The New International Greek Testament Commentary. Grand Rapids: Eerdmans, 1983.

May, David. "Drawn from Nature and Common Life: Social and Cultural Reading Strategies for the Parables." *Review and Expositor* 92 (1997): 199–214.

——. "Leaving and Receiving: A Social-Scientific Exegesis of Mark 10:29–31." *PRS* 17 (1990): 141–51, 154.

McKenzie, Steven L., and Stephen R. Haynes, eds. *Biblical Criticisms and Their Application: To Each its Own Meaning.* Louisville: Westminster/John Knox Press, 1999.

McKnight, Edgar V. *The Bible and the Reader: An Introduction to Literary Criticism.* Philadelphia: Fortress Press, 1985.

——. "Reader-Response Criticism." Pages 230–52 in *To Each its Own Meaning: An Introduction to Biblical Criticisms and Their Application.* Edited by Stephen L. McKenzie and Stephen R. Haynes. Louisville: Westminster/John Knox Press, 1999.

Menken, M. J. J. "The Position of ΣΠΛΑΓΧΝΙΖΕΣΘΑΙ and ΣΠΛΑΓΧΝΑ in the Gospel of Luke." *Novum Testamentum* 30 (1988): 107–14.

Merenlahti, Peter. *Poetics for the Gospels? Rethinking Narrative Criticism.* Studies of the New Testament and its World. London: T. & T. Clark, 2002.

Metzger, Bruce. *A Textual Commentary on the Greek New Testament.* 2d ed. Stuttgart: Deutsche Bibelgesellschaft, 2001.

Meynet, Roland. *L'Evangile Selon Saint Luc: Analyse Rhétorique.* Paris: Cerf, 1988.

MacDonald, Dennis R., ed. *Mimesis and Intertextuality in Antiquity and Christianity.* Harrisburg, P.A.: Trinity Press International, 2001.

Mitchell, Alan C. "The Use of συκοφαντεῖν in Luke 19, 8: Further Evidence for Zacchaeus's Defense." *Biblica* 72 (1991): 546–47.

Molina, J. P. "Luc 16/1 a 13: L'Injuste *Mamon.*" *ETR* 53 (1978): 371–75.

Moore, Stephen D. *Literary Criticism and the Gospels: The Theoretical Challenge.* New Haven: Yale University Press, 1989.

Moxnes, Halvor. *The Economy of the Kingdom. Social Conflict and Economic Relations in Luke's Gospel.* Philadelphia: Fortress Press, 1988.

Muravchik, Joshua. *Heaven on Earth: The Rise and Fall of Socialism.* San Francisco: Encounter Books, 2002.

Neyrey, Jerome, ed. *The Social World of Luke-Acts: Models for Interpretation.* Peabody, M.A.: Hendrickson, 1991.

Nickelsburg, G. W. E. "Riches, the Rich, and God's Judgement in 1 Enoch 92–105 and the Gospel according to Luke." *NTS* 25 (1979): 324–44.

——. "Revisiting the Rich and the Poor in 1 Enoch 92–105 and the Gospel According to Luke." *SBL Seminar Papers* 37 (1998): 579–605.

Nielsen, K. "Intertextuality and the Hebrew Bible." Pages 17–31 in *Congress Volume: Olso 1998.* Edited by Andre Lemaire and Saebo Magne. Supplements to Vetus Testamentum 80. Boston: Brill, 2000.

Nielsen, Samara Joy, and Barry M. Popkin. "Patterns and Trends in Food Portion Sizes." *JAMA* 289 (2003): 450–53.

Noel, D., "Parables in Context: Developing a Narrative-Critical Approach to Parables in Luke." Ph.D. diss., Southern Baptist Theological Seminary, 1986.

O'Hanlon, John. "The Story of Zacchaeus and the Lukan Ethic." *JSNT* 12 (1981): 2–26.

O'Toole, Robert F. "The Literary Form of Luke 19:1–10." *JBL* 110 (1991): 107–16.

Oakman, Douglas E. "The Countryside in Luke-Acts." Pages 151–79 in *The Social World of Luke-Acts: Models for Interpretation.* Edited by Jerome Neyrey. Peabody, M.A.: Hendrickson, 1991.

——. *Jesus and the Economic Questions of His Day.* Lewiston, N.Y.: The Edwin Mellen Press, 1986.

Oesterley, W. O. E. *The Gospel Parables in the Light of Their Jewish Background.* New York: MacMillan Company, 1938.

Okorie, A. M. "The Function of the Parables in the Narrative of Luke." *Revista Biblica* 60 (1998): 183–93.

Orton, David E. "We Felt Like Grasshoppers: The Little Ones in Biblical Interpretation." *Biblical Interpretation* 11 (2003): 488–502.

Paffenroth, Kim. *The Story of Jesus According to L.* JSNTSS 147. Sheffield: Sheffield Academic Press, 1997.

Parrott, Douglas M. "The Dishonest Steward (Luke 16:1–8a) and Luke's Special Parable Collection." *NTS* 37 (1991): 499–515.

Parsons, Mikeal C. "The Prodigal's Elder Brother: The History and Ethics of Reading Luke 15:25–32." *PRS* 23 (1996): 147–74.

——. "'Short in Stature': Luke's Physical Description of Zacchaeus." *NTS* 47 (2001): 50–57.

Pastor, Jack. *Land and Economy in Ancient Palestine.* London: Routledge, 1997.

Phillips, Thomas E. *Reading Issues of Wealth and Poverty in Luke-Acts.* Studies in the Bible and Early Christianity 48. Lewiston, N.Y.; Edwin Mellen Press, 2001.

Philonenko, Marc. "De L'intérêt des Deutérocanoniques pour L'interprétation du Nouveau Testament: L'example de *Luc* 16,9." *Revue des Sciences Religieuses* 73 (1999): 177–83.
Pickar, Charles H. "Exegetical Notes: The Unjust Steward (Lk. 16:1–9)." *CBQ* 1 (1939): 250–53.
Pilgrim, Walter. *Good News to the Poor.* Minneapolis: Augsburg, 1981.
Piper, Ronald. "Social Background and Thematic Structure in Luke 16." Pages 1637–62 in *The Four Gospels 1992. Festschrift Frans Neirynck.* Vol. 2. Edited by F. Van Segbroeck, C. M. Tuckett, G. Van Belle, and J. Verheyden. Leuven: Leuven University Press, 1992.
Porter, Stanley E. "The Parable of the Unjust Steward (Luke 16:1–13): Irony is the Key." Pages 127–53 in *The Bible in Three Dimensions.* Edited by David J. A. Clines, Stephen E. Fowl, and Stanley E. Porter. JSOTSS 87. Sheffield: JSOT Press, 1990.
Powell, Mark A. "Narrative Criticism." *ABD* IV: 201–04.
——. "Narrative Criticism." Pages 239–55 in *Hearing the New Testament: Strategies for Interpretation.* Edited by Joel Green. Grand Rapids: Eerdmans, 1995.
——. *What is Narrative Criticism?* Guides to Biblical Scholarship. Minneapolis: Fortress Press, 1990.
——. *What are They Saying About Luke?* New York: Paulist Press, 1989.
Pregeant, Russel. *Engaging the New Testament: An Interdisciplinary Approach.* Minneapolis: Fortress Press, 1997.
Prior, Michael. "The Liberation Theology of the Lucan Jesus." *Liber Annuus* 49 (1999): 79–99.
Provan, Iain. "'All these I have kept since I was a boy' (Luke 18:21): Creation, Covenant, and the Commandments of God." *Ex auditu* 17 (2001): 31–46.
Räisäsen, Heikki. "The Prodigal Gentile and his Jewish Christian Brother (Lk 15, 11–32.)" Pages 1617–36 in *The Four Gospels 1992. Festschrift Frans Neirynck.* Vol. 2. Edited by F. Van Segbroeck, C. M. Tuckett, G. Van Belle, and J. Verheyden. Leuven: Leuven University Press, 1992.
Ramsey, George M. "Plots, Gaps, Repetitions, and Ambiguity in Luke 15." *PRS* 17 (1990): 33–42.
Ravens, D. A. S. "Zacchaeus: Final Part of a Lucan Triptych?" *JSNT* 41 (1991): 19–32.
Regalado, Ferdinand O. "The Jewish Background of the Parable of the Rich Man and Lazarus." *Asia Journal of Theology* 16 (2002): 341–48.
Reid, Barbara. *Parables for Preachers: The Gospel of Luke Year C.* Collegeville, MN: The Liturgical Press, 2000.
Reinstorf, D. H. "The rich, the poor, and the law." *Hervormde Teologiese Studies* 60 (2004): 329–48.
Resseguie, James. "Reader-Response Criticism and the Synoptic Gospels." *Journal of the American Academy of Religion* 52 (1984): 307–24.
Rhoads, David M. "Narrative Criticism: Practices and Prospects." Pages 264–85 in *Characterization in the Gospels: Reconceiving Narrative Criticism.* JSNTSS 184. Edited by David M. Rhoads and Kari Syreeni. Sheffield: Sheffield Academic Press, 1999.
——. "Social Criticism: Crossing Boundaries." Pages 135–61 in *Mark & Method: New Approaches in Biblical Studies.* Edited by Janice Capel Anderson and Stephen D. Moore. Minneapolis: Fortress Press, 1992.
Rimmon-Kenan, Schlomith. *Narrative Fiction.* 2d ed. New York: Routledge, 2002.
Ringe, Sharon H. "Luke 4:16–44—A Portrait of Jesus as Herald of God's Jubliee." *Proceedings of the Eastern Great Lakes Biblical Society* 1 (1981): 73–84.
——. *Luke.* Westminster Bible Companion. Louisville: Westminster/John Knox Press, 1995.

Robbins, Vernon. "Luke-Acts: A Mixed Population Seeks A Home in the Roman Empire." Pages 202–21 in *Images of Empire*. Edited by L. Alexander. JSOTSS 122. Sheffield: Sheffield Academic Press, 1991.
Robertson, A. T. *A Grammar of the Greek New Testament in the Light of Historical Research.* New York: C. H. Doran, 1914.
Roemer, Kenneth M. *Utopian Audiences: How Readers Locate Nowhere.* Boston: University of Massachusetts Press, 2003.
Ryken, Leland. *The New Testament in Literary Criticism.* A Library of Literary Criticism. New York: F. Ungar Pub. Co., 1984.
Schmidt, T. E. *Hostility to Wealth in the Synoptic Gospels.* JSNTSS 15. Sheffield: Sheffield Academic Press, 1987.
Schmithals, Walter. "Lukas—Evangelist der Armen." *Theologia Viatorum* 12 (1973–1974): 153–67.
Schoors, Antoon. "(Mis)use of Intertextuality in Qoheleth Exegesis." Pages 45–59 in *Congress Volume: Olso 1998.* Edited by Andre Lemaire and Saebo Magne. Supplements to Vetus Testamentum 80. Boston: Brill, 2000.
Schottroff, Luise. "Das Gleichnis vom verlorenen Sohn." *ZTK* 68 (1971): 27–52.
Schottroff, Luise and Wolfgang Stegemann. *Jesus and the Hope of the Poor.* Translated by Matthew J. O'Connell. Maryknoll, N.Y.: Orbis Books, 1986.
Schweickart, Patrocino, and Elizabeth A. Flynn, eds. *Reading Sites: Social Difference and Reader Response.* New York: MLA, 2004.
Scott, Bernard Brandon. *Hear Then the Parable: A Commentary on the Parables of Jesus.* Philadelphia: Fortress Press, 1989.
Seccombe, David Peter. *Possessions and the Poor in Luke-Acts*. Studien zum Neuen Testament und Seiner Umwelt. Series B 6. Linz: A. Fuchs, 1982.
Segovia, Fernando F. *Decolonizing Biblical Studies: A View from the Margins.* Maryknoll, N.Y.: Orbis, 2000.
——, ed. *What is John?* Vol. 1. SBL Symposium Series 3. Atlanta: Scholars Press, 1996.
Sellew, Philip. "Interior Monologue as a Narrative Device in the Parables of Luke." *JBL* 111 (1992): 239–253.
Sheeley, Steven M. *Narrative Asides in Luke-Acts.* JSNTSS 72. Sheffield: Sheffield Academic Press, 1992.
Shillington, V. George. "Imaginative Participation and Parable Interpretation." Pages 45–61 in *The Bible and the Church: Essays in Honor of David Ewert.* Edited by A. J. Dueck, H. J. Giesbrecht, and V. G. Shillington. Winnipeg: Kindred Press, 1988.
——. ed. *Jesus and His Parables.* Edinburgh: T. & T. Clark, 1997.
Siker, J. "'First to the Gentiles': A Literary Analysis of Luke 4:16–30." *JBL* 111 (1992): 73–90.
Slesnick, Daniel. *Consumption and Social Welfare: Living standards and their distribution in the United States.* New York: Cambridge University Press, 2001.
Sloan, R. B. *The Favourable Year of the Lord: A Study of Jubilary Theology in the Gospel of Luke.* Austin, TX: Schola Press, 1977.
Spicq, Ceslas. "πλεονεξία." *TLNT* III: 117–19.
——. *Theological Lexicon of the New Testament.* 3 vols. Translated and edited by James D. Ernest. Peabody, Mass: Hendrickson, 1994.
Stacy, R. Wayne. "Luke 12:13–21: The Parable of the Rich Fool." *Review and Expositor* 94 (1997): 285–92.
Stagg, Frank. "Luke's Theological Use of Parables." *Review and Expositor* 94 (1994): 215–29.
Staley, Jeffery. "'With the Power of the Spirit': Plotting the Program and Parallels of Luke 4:14–37." *SBL Seminar Papers* 32 (1993): 281–302.
Steger, Manfred B. *Globalization: A Very Short Introduction.* New York: Oxford University Press, 2003.

Stein, Robert H. *An Introduction to the Parables of Jesus*. Philadelphia: Westminster Press, 1981.

Still, Judith and Michael Worton, eds. *Intertextuality: Theories and Practice*. Manchester, N.Y.: Manchester University Press, 1990.

Swanson, Reuben Joseph, ed. *New Testament Greek Manuscripts: Variant Readings Arranged in Horizontal Lines Against Codex Vaticanus: Luke*. Sheffield: Sheffield Academic Press, 1995.

Tanghe, Vincent. "Abraham, son fils et son envoye (Luc 16:19–31)." *Revue Biblique* 91 (1984): 557–77.

Tannehill, Robert C. "The Story of Zacchaeus as Rhetoric: Luke 19:1–10." *Semeia* 64 (1994): 201–21.

——. *The Narrative Unity of Luke-Acts. A Literary Interpretation. Volume 1: The Gospel According to Luke*. Foundations and Facets. Philadelphia: Fortress Press, 1986.

Tolbert, Mary Ann. "The Prodigal Son: An Essay in Literary Criticism from a Psychoanalytic Perspective." *Semeia* 9 (1977): 1–20.

——. *Perspectives on the Parables: An Approach to Multiple Interpretations*. Philadelphia: Fortress Press, 1979.

——. *Sowing the Gospel: Mark's World in Literary-Historical Perspective*. Minneapolis: Fortress Press, 1989.

Tolmie, François. *Narratology and Biblical Narratives: A Practical Guide*. San Francisco: International Scholars Publications, 1999.

Tompkins, Jane P., ed., *Reader-Response Criticism: From Formalism to Post-Structuralism*. Baltimore: Johns Hopkins University Press, 1980.

Topel, L. John. "On the Injustice of the Unjust Steward: Lk. 16:1–13." *CBQ* 37 (1975): 216–227.

Troost, Arie. "Reading for the Author's Signature: Genesis 21.1–21 and Luke 15:11–32 as Intertexts." Pages 251–72 in *A Feminist Companion to Genesis*. Edited by Athalya Brenner. The Feminist Companion to the Bible 2. Sheffield: Sheffield Academic Press, 1993.

Trudinger, Paul. "Exposing the Depth of Oppression (Luke 16:1b–8a): The Parable of the Unjust Steward." Pages 121–37 in *Jesus and His Parables*. Edited by V. George Shillington. Edinburgh: T & T Clark, 1997.

——. "Ire or Irony? The Enigmatic Character of the Parable of the Dishonest Steward (Luke 16:1–13)." *Downside Review* 116 (1998): 85–102.

Tucker, Jeffery T. *Example Stories: Perspectives on Four Parables in the Gospel of Luke*. JSNTSS 162. Sheffield: Sheffield Academic Press, 1998.

Tull, Patricia K. "Rhetorical Criticism and Intertextuality." Pages 156–80 in *To Each its Own Meaning: An Introduction to Biblical Criticisms and Their Application*. Edited by Stephen L. McKenzie and Stephen R. Haynes. Louisville: Westminster/John Knox Press, 1999.

——. "The Rhetoric of Recollection." Pages 71–78 in *Congress Volume: Olso 1998*. Edited by Andre Lemaire and Saebo Magne. Supplements to Vetus Testamentum 80. Boston: Brill, 2000.

U.S. Energy Information Administration. "Annual Energy Outlook 2005." Online: http://www.eia.doe.gov/oiaf/aeo/forecast.htm.

Urbach, E. E. *The Sages: Their Concepts and Beliefs*. Vol. 1. Translated by Israel Abrahams. Jerusalem: The Magnes Press, 1975.

VanHoozer, Kevin. "The Reader in New Testament Interpretation." Pages 301–28 in *Hearing the New Testament: Strategies for Interpretation*. Edited by Joel Green. Grand Rapids: Eerdmans, 1995.

Van Wolde, Ellen. "Trendy Intertextuality?" Pages 43–49 in *Intertextuality in Biblical Writings: Essays in Honor of Bas van Iersel*. Edited by Sipke Draisma. Kampen: Uitgeversmaatschappij J. H. Kok, 1989.

Via, Dan Otto, Jr. *The Parables: Their Literary and Existential Dimension.* Philadelphia: Fortress Press, 1967.

Voelz, James W. "Multiple Signs and Double Texts: Elements of Intertextuality." Pages 27–34 in *Intertextuality in Biblical Writings: Essays in Honor of Bas van Iersel.* Edited by Sipke Draisma. Kampen: Uitgeversmaatschappij J. H. Kok, 1989.

Vogels, Walter. "Having or Longing: A Semiotic Analysis of Luke 16:19–31." *Église et Théologie* 20 (1989): 27–46.

Walasky, Paul W. *"And So We Came to Rome": The Political Perspective of St. Luke.* New York: Cambridge University Press, 1983.

Walton, S. "Luke's View of the Roman Empire." Pages 1–41 in *Rome in the Bible and the Early Church.* Edited by Peter Oakes. Grand Rapids: Baker Academic, 2002.

Warden, Duane. "The Rich Man and Lazarus: Poverty, Wealth, and Human Worth." *SCJ* 6 (2003): 81–93.

Watts, Alan. *The Wisdom of Insecurity: A Message for an Age of Anxiety.* New York: Vintage Books, 1951.

Weber, Randall C. *Reader-Response Analysis of the Epistle of James.* San Francisco: International Scholars Publications, 1996.

Wehrli, Eugene S. "Luke 16:19–31." *Interpretation* 31 (1977): 276–80.

Wright, J. D., J. Kennedy-Stephenson, C. Y. Wang, M. A. McDowell, and C. L. Johnson. "Trends in Intake of Energy and Macronutrients, United States, 1971–2000." *Morbidity Mortality Weekly Report* 53 (2004): 80–82.

Wright, Stephen. "Parables on Poverty and Riches (Luke 12:13–21; 16:1–13; 16:19–31)." Pages 217–39 in *The Challenge of Jesus' Parables.* Edited by Richard N. Longenecker. Grand Rapids: Eerdmans, 2000.

Yergin, Daniel and Joseph Stanislaw. *The Commanding Heights: The Battle for the World Economy.* New York: Simon & Schuster, 2002.

Yoder, J. H. *The Politics of Jesus.* 2d ed. Grand Rapids: Eedrmans, 1994.

York, J. O. *The Last Shall Be First: The Rhetoric of Reversal in Luke.* JSNTSS 46. Sheffield: Sheffield Academic Press, 1991.

Young, Brad H. *The Parables: Jewish Tradition and Christian Interpretation.* Peabody, MA: Hendrickson Publishers, 1998.

——. *Jesus and His Jewish Parables: Rediscovering the Roots of Jesus' Teaching.* New York: Paulist Press, 1989.

Zumstein, Jean. "Jésus et les Paraboles." Pages 89–108 in *Les Paraboles Évangéliques: Perspectives Nouvelles.* Edited by Jean Delorme. Lectio Divina 135. Paris: Éditions du Cerf, 1989.

INDEX

Abraham, 143–154
"Abraham's bosom," 140
acceptance and rejection, 12
almsgiving
  Abraham's, 150
  Jesus' new interpretation of, 150, 170
  lack of, among parable characters, 139–140
  nature and purpose, 6–8
  preserves existing social order, 150, 155–156, 187
  rationale for, 8–10
  reconciling with divestiture, 2
  vs. dispossession, 2–6
anger, 102
Augustan ideals, 8, 8n97

Bal, Mieke, 49–50
Beavis, Mary Ann, 79n68, 80n69
Beispielerzählungen, 16
Ben Sira, 76, 88
Biblical Studies
  Intertextuality in, 51–54
  Narrative criticism in, 47–49
  Reader-response criticism in, 31–40
Bleich, David, 32, 39n181
Bortolussi, Marisa, 25n102
Brawley, Robert, 35–36

Cadbury, Henry J., 89n91
Capernaum, 29
capitalism, remarketized, 194–196
Centering on God: Method and Message in Luke-Acts (Brawley), 35–36
church, time of, 4n15
Codex Bezae, 76n56
Congress Volume: Olso 1998 (Lemaire and Magne), 52
consistency-building, in textual reading, 44–45
Conzelmann, Hans, 4n15
Crossan, John Dominic, 19n77, 24
Cuvillier, E., 17, 21
Cynic philosophers, 3
Cynicus, 3

Darr, John, 34–35
Degenhardt, Hans Joachim, 4
democratic socialism, 196n35
Dio Chrysostom, on greed, 68
Diodorus Siculus, on greed, 68
discipleship model
  dispossession and, 125–127
  in natural world, 84–85
  personal cost, 64
  prioritization of mission over family, 133n88
  prodigal son and, 90–91, 95–96
dispossession
  God or mammon choice, 129–130
  Jesus advises all who seek eternal reward, 168–169
  Jesus advises rich ruler, 164–165
  motives for, 125–128
  reconciling with almsgiving, 2
  vs. almsgiving, 2–6
divesture. *See* dispossession
divorce, 133–134, 134n89
Dixon, Peter, 25n102
Drury, J., 16

The Economy of the Kingdom (Moxnes), 11
Enoch (1), wealth in, 146–147
Epicurianism, 78
Essenes, 134
"example stories," in Luke, 16

Fish, Stanley, 32, 34, 37, 39n181, 41–43
Flynn, Elizabeth A., 39
fourfold restitution, 178n64
Fowler, Robert, 33
Friedman, Thomas L., 197n38

gasoline tax, 197n38
gates, walls, and chasms, 137, 144
Gentile behavior, 104n147
Gillman, John, 5, 8, 11, 15n63
globalization, and wealth, 193–199
Gonzales, Justo, 9n40
Good News to the Poor (Pilgrim), 7, 11, 12

Gottvertrauen, 10, 183
greed, 67–69
Gressmann, H., 145

Hades, 144n134
Heaven on Earth (Muravchik), 196n35
hedonism
  of wealthy landowner, 78, 83
Hedrick, Charles, 17, 77
Heil, J. P., 36
Holland, Norman, 32, 39n181
honor-shame code, 122
honorable/dishonorable rich, 135, 156

inheritance law, 65
inheritance law and custom, 87–89
insatiable desire, 68–69, 84, 189
interest, and loans, 119–120
interior monologue, in Lukan parables, 93–94
"Interior Monologue as a Narrative Device in the Parables of Luke" (Sellew), 15n66
"Interpreting the *Variorum*" (Fish), 41
Intertextuality
  in Biblical Studies, 51–54
  as employed in this study, 54–56
Intertextuality in Biblical Writings: Essays in Honor of Bas van Iersel (Draisma), 52, 53
Iser, Wolfgang, 32, 38n177, 41n191, 43–46
Israel, as "poor", 10
Israel, time of, 4n15

Jesus
  announcement in Nazareth, 9, 25–31, 183
  on divorce, 133–134
  encounter with the rich ruler (18:18–23), 160–170, 187–188
  encounter with Zacchaeus (19:1–10), 170–182, 188
  ministry of healing and release, 26–31
  parabolic discourse of, 18–21
  reliable character, in Luke, 19n84
  "time of Jesus," 4n15
Jesus and the Hope of the Poor (Schottroff and Stegemann), 11
John the Baptist, 1, 7–8, 8n97, 13, 189
Johnson, L. T., 12, 17
jubilary language, 30, 31, 128n75
jubilee year, 30

Karris, Robert, 5, 11
Kelber, Werner, 23
kibbutz, 196n35
Kim, Kyoung-Jin, 8
Kingdom of God, 133n86
Kitzberger, Ingrid R., 39–40
koinonia, 9n40
Konkretisation, 45–46
Kristeva, Julia, 51

Lazarus. *See* Parable of the Rich Man and Lazarus
"Literature in the Reader: Affective Stylistics" (Fish), 41, 42
Literary Criticism and the Gospels: The Theoretical Challenge (Moore), 48n254
Luke
  salvation history in, 4n15

mammon, critique of, 126–130
Mark, differences from Luke, 1, 15–16, 19n77
marriage, 133n88, 134n89
Matthew, differences from Luke, 1, 15–16
McKnight, Edgar, 32–33, 41n192
Merenlahti, Peter, 48, 49
Moore, Stephen, 36–37, 48
Moxnes, Halvor, 8, 11
Muravchik, Joshua, 196n35

Narrative criticism
  in Biblical Studies, 47–49
  as employed in present study, 49–51
Narrative Fiction (Rimmon-Kenan), 50
narrative parable, 19n77
Narratology. *See* Narrative criticism
Narratology: Introduction to the Theory of Narrative (Bal), 49, 50
narrators, of parables, 25n102
Nazareth, Jesus' announcement in, 9, 25–31

Oakman, Douglas, 6–7
On Character Building: The Reader and the Rhetoric of Characterization in Luke-Acts (Darr), 34
overconsumption and personal wealth in U.S., 57–60, 193–199

Parable of the Lost Coin (15:8–10), 85
Parable of the Lost Sheep (15:3–7), 85
Parable of the Prodigal Son (15:11–32)
  anger of elder, 101–102
  audience for, 86, 106

elder hears of younger's return, 100–101
elder's rationale, 102–104
father consoles elder, 102
father's rationale, 104–105
interpretive remarks, 22
introduction, 86–87
Jesus' teaching on wealth and possessions in 12:22–15:10, 84–86
journey and overconsumption of younger, 90–91
reading the parable, 86–106
repentance of younger, 93–96
request for inheritance by younger, 87–89
response of father, 98–100
return of younger, 96–98
suffering and need of younger, 91–92
summary, 106–108
synopsis of, 185

Parable of the Rich Man and Lazarus (16:19–31)
Abraham denies second request, 149–151
Abraham denies third request, 152–154
Abraham explains impossibility of rich man's request, 143–147
introduction of Lazarus' condition, 136–140
introduction of rich man's overconsumption, 134–136
Lazarus and rich man die, 140–141
pre-text of, 132–134
reading the parable, 134–154
rich man entreats Abraham from Hades, 141–143
rich man makes second entreaty to Abraham, 147–148
rich man makes third entreaty to Abraham, 151–152
summary, 154–157
synopsis of, 186–187

Parable of the Sower (8:4–15), 18–21

Parable of the Two Debtors (7:36–50), 16n72

Parable of the Unjust Steward (16:1–13)
interpretive remarks, 22
introduction, 109
Jesus' comments on parable, 123–131
reading the parable, 109–130
rich man confronts steward, 111–112
rich man dismisses steward, 112–113
rich man praises steward's actions, 121–123
steward accused of wastefulness, 109–111
steward considers options, 113–114
steward formulates plan, 115–116
steward reduces debtors' debts, 116–121
summary, 130–132
synopsis of, 185–186

Parable of the Wealthy Landowner (12:16–21)
accessibility of, 16n72
God's intervention, 78–82
interpretive remarks, 22
introduction, 69–71
Jesus' encounter with man from the crowd, 64–69
Jesus' teaching on wealth and possessions in 9:51–12:12, 63–64
landowner's dilemma, 71–72
landowner's rationale, 74–78
landowner's solution, 72–74
reading the parable, 69–82
summary, 82–84
synopsis of, 184–185

Parable of the Widow and the Unjust Judge (18:1–8), 15, 16n72

parabolic discourse, 18n77

parabolic discourse, in Luke
an approach to reading, 22–25
difficulties of understanding, 23–24
interior monologue, 93–94
nature of, 15–22

patronage system, 7, 8

The Personal Voice in Biblical Interpretation (Kitzberger), 39–40

Peter, 168–169

Pharisees, 132–133

Phillips, Thomas E., 4, 7, 12–13, 15n63

Pilgrim, Walter, 4, 7, 11, 12

Plutarch, on greed, 68

Poetics for the Gospels? Rethinking Narrative Criticism (Merenlahti), 48n254

The Politics of Jesus (Yoder), 30

poor, the
concern for, as motive for almsgiving, 9–10
cycle of poverty, 191–193
Jesus' interest in, 31, 183
nature of, in Luke, 25–31
redistribution to aid, 170
Zacchaeus' vow to aid, 176–177

"Poor and Rich: The Lukan *Sitz-im-Leben*" (Karris), 11

Possessions and the Life of Faith (Gillman), 11, 15n63

Possessions and the Poor in Luke-Acts (Seccombe), 12
Prior, Michael, 28n119
prostitution, 104n149
purity code, Torah's, 149n149

Reader-position, in present study, 56–57
"Reader-Response and the Narrative Context of the Parables about Growing Seed in Mark 4:1–34" (Heil), 36
Reader-response criticism
in Biblical Studies, 31–40
as employed in present study, 40–41
Fish's reading method, 41–43
Iser's phenomenology of reading, 43–46
Reading Between Texts: Intertextuality and the Hebrew Bible (Fewell), 52–53
Reading Issues of Wealth and Poverty in Luke-Acts (Phillips), 12–13, 15n63
remarriage, 134n89
renunciation *vs.* almsgiving, 2–6
repentance, nature of, 94–96, 97
Resseguie, James, 33
Rhoads, David, 48, 49
rich, the
and almsgiving, 150, 155–156, 165n19
audience/reader impressions of, 72
honorable/dishonorable rich, 135, 156
Jesus' three woes against, 70, 83n75
negative evaluation of, in Luke, 99, 106, 110
salvation of, 5–6, 10, 163, 164n16, 167–170, 181
self-preservation and, 121
rich ruler, Jesus' encounter with (18:18–23), 160–170, 187–188
Roemer, Kenneth M., 39, 39n186
Roman society
patronage system, 7, 8

salvation
dispossession *vs.* almsgiving, 3–6
as motive for almsgiving, 10–11
of the rich, 5–6, 10, 163, 164n16, 167–170, 181
Schmidt, T. E., 10
Schmithals, Walter, 4, 5
Schottroff, Luise, 3, 11
Schweickart, Patrocinio P., 39
Scott, Bernard B., 72, 75, 78, 86–87
Seccombe, David P., 5, 10, 12
Segovia, Fernando F., 45n222, 46n226, 183n1
self-interest, drives dispossession, 125–128
Sellew, Phillip, 15n66
social status, 114n20
socialism, 196n35
sons of light, 123–124
Stagg, Frank, 16n72
Stegemann, Wolfgang, 3, 11
Story and Discourse: Narrative Structures in Fiction and Film (Chatman), 50

"The Liberation Theology of the Lucan Jesus" (Prior), 28n119
The Literary Function of Possessions in Luke-Acts (Johnson), 12
Theophilus, 2, 6, 9
Tolbert, Mary Ann, 19n77
two-sons mytheme, 86–87, 90, 105

Utopian Audiences: How Readers Locate Nowhere (Roemer), 39

Vanhoozer, Kevin, 34
Vom reichen Mann und armen Lazarus: eine literargeschichtliche Studie (Gressmann), 145

Walasky, Paul W., 7–8
wealth. *See also* rich, the
in biblical narrative, 70
global disparities in, 193–199
in Parable of the Rich Man and Lazarus, 127–130
personal, in U.S., 56–60, 193–199
in Parable of the Unjust Steward, 127–130
wealth and possessions, in Luke. *See also* almsgiving; rich, the
focus on salvation of rich, 5–6
inconsistency of message, 1–2, 189
methodology of past approaches to, 11–13
will-to-power, 68–69, 84, 189

Yoder, J. H., 30
York, J. O., 5

Zacchaeus, 2, 6, 7, 8n97
Zacchaeus, Jesus' encounter with (19:1–10), 170–182, 188